Feminine Endings

Feminine Endings
Music, Gender, and Sexuality

Susan McClary

University of Minnesota Press
Minnesota
London

"Constructions of Gender in Monteverdi's Dramatic Music" first appeared in *Cambridge Opera Journal* 1, no. 3 (November 1989), reprinted by permission of Cambridge University Press; "This Is Not a Story My People Tell: Musical Time and Space According to Laurie Anderson" first appeared in *Discourse* 12, no. 1 (Fall-Winter 1989-90); "Living to Tell: Madonna's Resurrection of the Fleshly" first appeared in *Genders* 7 (Spring 1990), reprinted by permission of the University of Texas Press; an earlier version of "Getting Down Off the Beanstalk: The Presence of a Woman's Voice in Janika Vandervelde's *Genesis II*" appeared in *Minnesota Composers Forum Newsletter* (February 1987); "The Ninth Symphony of Beethoven Understood at Last as a Sexual Message" is reprinted from *Poems, Selected and New, 1950-1974*, by Adrienne Rich, by permission of the author and W. W. Norton & Company, Inc. Copyright © 1975, 1973, 1971, 1969, 1966 by W. W. Norton & Company, Inc. Copyright © 1967, 1963, 1962, 1961, 1960, 1959, 1958, 1957, 1956, 1955, 1954, 1953, 1952, 1951 by Adrienne Rich. Laurie Anderson, text and photographs from *United States*, © 1984 by Laurie Anderson. Reprinted by permission of Harper Collins Publishers.

Published by the University of Minnesota Press
2037 University Avenue Southeast, Minneapolis, MN 55455-3092
Printed in the United States of America on acid-free paper
Third printing, 1994

Library of Congress Cataloging-in-Publication Data

McClary, Susan.
Feminine endings : music, gender, and sexuality / Susan McClary.
p. cm.
Includes bibliographical references and index.
ISBN 0-8166-1898-4.
ISBN 0-8166-1899-2 (pbk.)
1. Feminism and music. 2. Sexuality in music. I. Title.
ML82.M38 1991
780'.82—dc20   90-11169
                                CIP

The University of Minnesota
is an equal-opportunity
educator and employer.

Contents

Acknowledgments

This book bears the traces of countless voices—voices distinctly or only half remembered from articles, conference papers, letters, dinner conversations, debates in the classroom. While it is impossible to recall them all, I would like to acknowledge at least a few of the individuals who influenced me most as I worked on this project. None of the essays in this collection would even have come into being without the prompting of colleagues who invited me to write on these issues for conferences or journals. I wish to thank Jane Bowers, Randall Davidson, Ruth-Ellen Joeres, Corin Kagan, Judy Lochhead, Gregory Sandow, Louise Stein, Lloyd Whitesell, and Carol Zemel for giving me the incentive to explore the various topics represented in this volume.

I have benefited greatly from critical responses to these essays from Philip Brett, Simon Frith, Arthur Groos, Joseph Kerman, David Lewin, Greil Marcus, Sherry Ortner, Edward Said, John Shepherd, Mike Steele, Rose Subotnik, Richard Taruskin, Gary Tomlinson, Janet Wolff, and Winifred Woodhull. Their encouragement and insistence that I work harder on my formulations have made this a much better book than it would have been otherwise. And I have received ideas, moral support, and an exhilarating sense of community from other feminist musicologists including Linda Austern, Tamara Bernstein, Susan Cook, Suzanne Cusick, Michele Edwards, Ellie Hisama, Jenny Kallick, Ellen Rosand, Ruth Solie, Judith Tick, and Elizabeth Wood.

My colleagues at the University of Minnesota cheered me on when the task of writing this book seemed daunting, but they also argued with me when I tried to pass off easy solutions to difficult problems. I am especially grateful to Nancy Armstrong, Michael Cherlin, Richard Leppert, George

Lipsitz, John Mowitt, Julia Robinson, Peter Robinson, Thomas Russell, Naomi Scheman, Leonard Tennenhouse, and Gary Thomas. My friends in the art world likewise have contributed heavily to the development of my ideas. Special thanks to Jeffrey Bartlett, Melisande Charles, Maria Cheng, Stephen Houtz, Maria Jette, Nicola LeFanu, Patty Lynch, Matthew Maguire, Agnes Smuda, Janika Vandervelde, and Lovice Weller for sharing with me their experiences as creative artists.

My students have provided me with my most consistent feedback. Over the years they patiently questioned and helped me to refine my ideas as they developed from informal classroom improvisations to theoretical models. I cannot begin to name them all, but among those who read drafts and offered invaluable suggestions are Christine Bezat, Ann Dunn, Barbara Engh, Lydia Hamessley, Andrew Jones, Christopher Kachian, Merilee Klemp, Lisbeth Lipari, Sowah Mensah, Kitty Millet, Thomas Nelson, Yamuna Sangarasivam, Nancy Thompson, Lawrence Zbikowski, and everyone who participated in my seminar "Feminist Theory and Music" in Fall 1989.

The motivation for this collection came from Terry Cochran, who worked closely with me during every phase of its formation. As humanities editor at the University of Minnesota Press, Terry provided me with the intellectual and institutional support necessary for the realization of this and other projects. I deeply appreciate his confidence in me, his personal generosity, and his indispensable critical insights.

Finally, I wish to thank Robert Walser. Rob's influence is discernible on every page of this volume: he listened to music with me for hours, inspired and contributed many of the ideas that appear in these essays, worked with me (elsewhere as a co-author) on how best to account theoretically for what we heard, and strengthened my prose by observing when my tone became either too strident or too passive. He read more drafts of these essays than either one of us would care to remember, and he sustained me emotionally throughout the entire process. I dedicate this book to him with my love.

Feminine Endings

Chapter 1
Introduction: A Material Girl in Bluebeard's Castle

In the grisly fairy tale of Bluebeard, the new bride, Judith, is given keys to all the chambers in her husband's castle with strict instructions that she is never to unlock the seventh door. Upon opening the first six doors, Judith discovers those aspects of Bluebeard that he wishes to claim—his wealth, strength, political dominion, love of beauty, and so on. Bluebeard offers a form of symbolic self-representation in these chambers: he reveals himself as the man he wants Judith to adore. But throughout her explorations— behind every door—she finds traces of something else, something hidden that sustains all she is actually shown, something that resonates with the old tales of horror she has heard. And in opening the final door she comes face to face with that unspoken, forbidden factor.

In some versions of the Bluebeard story, what Judith discovers behind the forbidden door are the mangled bodies of previous wives who likewise went too far in their quests for knowledge. Bruno Bettelheim assumes that she and Bluebeard's other hapless victims must have committed carnal transgressions of the magnitude of adultery in order to be deserving of such dreadful ends.[1] But it is also possible to interpret the story rather more literally: Judith and her sisters were simply not satisfied with the contradictory versions of reality given to them by a self-serving patriarch, and they aspired to discover the truth behind the façade.

The version of the story set by Bartók in his opera *Bluebeard's Castle* tends to support such a reading. Judith discovers not only Bluebeard's crimes but also his pain, his fears, his vulnerability. For this she is not executed but rather is exiled into darkness along with the other still-living wives, away from the light of his presence. The last speech is uttered by Bluebeard, whose tragedy this opera finally is. He is forever being betrayed by women who do not take him at his word, who insist on knowing the truth: the truth of his human rather than transcendental status. And he cannot live with someone who thus understands his mortality and materiality. Thus he is fated always to live alone, yet safe with his delusions of control and magnanimity—at least so long as no one tampers with that seventh door.

As a woman in musicology, I find myself thinking about Judith quite often—especially now, as I begin asking new kinds of questions about music with the aid of feminist critical theory. Like Judith, I have been granted access by my mentors to an astonishing cultural legacy: musical repertories from all of history and the entire globe, repertories of extraordinary beauty, power, and formal sophistication. It might be argued that I ought to be grateful, since there has really only been one stipulation in the bargain—namely, that I never ask what any of it means, that I content myself with structural analysis and empirical research.

Unfortunately that is a stipulation I have never been able to accept. For, to put it simply, I began my career with the desire to understand music. I suppose this must also be true of most other music professionals. Yet what I desired to understand about music has always been quite different from what I have been able to find out in the authorized accounts transmitted in classrooms, textbooks, or musicological research. I was drawn to music because it is the most compelling cultural form I know. I wanted evidence that the overwhelming responses I experience with music are not just in my own head, but rather are shared.

I entered musicology because I believed that it would be dedicated (at least in part) to explaining how music manages to create such effects. I soon discovered, however, that musicology fastidiously declares issues of musical signification to be off-limits to those engaged in legitimate scholarship. It has seized disciplinary control over the study of music and has prohibited the asking of even the most fundamental questions concerning meaning. Something terribly important is being hidden away by the profession, and I have always wanted to know why.

Just as Bartók's Judith discovers telltale traces of blood on the treasures in the first six chambers (even though Bluebeard adamantly refuses to corroborate her observations), so I have always detected in music much more than I was given license to mention. To be sure, music's beauty is often overwhelming, its formal order magisterial. But the structures graphed by theorists and the beauty celebrated by aestheticians are often stained with such things as violence, misogyny, and racism. And perhaps more disturbing still to those who would present music as autonomous and invulnerable, it also frequently betrays fear—fear of women, fear of the body.

It is finally feminism that has allowed me to understand both why the discipline wishes these to be nonissues, and also why they need to be moved to the very center of inquiries about music. Thus I see feminist criticism as the key to the forbidden door: the door that has prevented me from really being able to understand even that to which I was granted free access. To the extent that I live in a world that is shaped profoundly by musical discourses, I find it necessary to begin exploring whatever lies behind the last door, despite—but also because of—disciplinary prohibitions.

1

When feminist criticism emerged in literary studies and art history in the early 1970s, many women musicologists such as myself looked on from the sidelines with interest and considerable envy. But at the time, there were formidable obstacles preventing us from bringing those same questions to bear on music. Some of these obstacles were, of course, institutional: the discipline within which we were located was still male-dominated, and most of us were loath to jeopardize the tentative toeholds we had been granted.

Nevertheless, a few of the more courageous women began to excavate the history of women composers and musicians. And even though these projects were initially regarded with scorn, they have uncovered an enormous amount of rich material: the long-forgotten music of such extraordinary figures as Hildegard von Bingen, Barbara Strozzi, Clara Schumann, Ethel Smyth, Ruth Crawford Seeger, and many others is being made widely available for the first time.[2] Likewise the history of women performers, teachers, patrons, and civic promoters of music has been brought to light, as well as the history of the conditions that consistently have served to exclude or marginalize female participation in music.[3] As a result of this research, our understanding of music institutions and of specific people engaged in musical activities has been substantially altered.

Yet until very recently, there was virtually no public evidence (that is, in official conferences or refereed journals) of feminist music criticism. I am painfully aware that this volume—one of the first books of feminist criticism in the discipline of musicology—is being assembled at a time when cynical voices in many other fields are beginning to declare feminism to be passé. It almost seems that musicology managed miraculously to pass directly from pre- to postfeminism without ever having to change—or even examine—its ways.

Indeed, one of the few signs that the discipline has even noticed the challenges feminism has presented elsewhere is that musicology appears to be in the vanguard of antifeminist backlash. Norton's specially reprinted collections from *The New Grove Dictionary of Music* (the principal disciplinary reference tool since its publication in 1980) are entitled "Masters of Italian Opera," "Masters of the Second Viennese School," and so forth, perhaps taking their cue from the successful "Masters of the Universe" series on Saturday morning television.[4] There is also a prestigious new series of books and videos on the various periods of music history from Prentice-Hall called *Man and Music*, and still another new set of videos from Brown called *The Music of Man*.[5] It is impossible to believe that anyone who has lived through the last fifteen years can have failed to observe that terms such as "master" or "man" have been so thoroughly problematized that they are no longer in general circulation in most academic communities. If musicology has lagged behind in admitting feminist criticism to its list of legitimate areas of inquiry, it is way ahead of the game in its efforts to expunge all evidence that feminism ever existed.

Yet all is not hopeless in the field. Two conferences occurred in spring 1988—one at Carleton University in Ottawa and the other at Dartmouth—in which feminist criticism was highlighted.[6] Moreover, the program committee for the 1988 meeting of the American Musicological Society actively solicited and accepted several papers in feminist criticism, and the 1989 meeting offered the first discipline-sponsored workshop in feminist theory and music.[7] The most important consequence of these conferences is that they have enabled those of us who have been trying to develop and perform feminist criticism in isolation to become aware of others who have been grappling with similar issues and methods. Feminist critics of music, encouraged by the knowledge that a community does in fact exist, are currently organizing at least two anthologies of feminist music criticism.[8] Furthermore, several professional journals have begun to request feminist articles.

Most of the essays in this collection predate this recent surge of interest in feminist criticism, and they are virtually all marked by a sense of disciplinary solitude. They are often as concerned with questioning why there has been no feminist criticism in musicology as in exploring what one might do with such methods if one were allowed to pursue them. To that extent, these pieces bear the traces of a moment in the history of the discipline, and I have decided not to erase them. It is heartening, however, to know that it may no longer be necessary to concentrate quite so heavily on the issue of whether or not there ought to be a feminist criticism of music. That battle seems perhaps to have been won, at least in sympathetic quarters. Whether or not the mainstream of the discipline approves, feminist music criticism does exist. However, the more interesting questions remain: What would a feminist criticism of music look like? What issues would it raise, and how would it ground its arguments theoretically?

2

The roads taken by other feminist music critics have been similar to mine in some respects, very different in others. All of us are heavily indebted to the feminist theory and criticism that has taken shape in disciplines such as literary or film studies over the last twenty years. This work makes it possible for us to proceed without having to define *ex nihilo* such basic concepts as gender, sexuality, and femininity. We are able to benefit from the debates that have enlivened feminist scholarship and to arrive at our tasks with a sophisticated theoretical apparatus already at hand.

Nevertheless, it is not possible to transfer the key questions of other branches of feminist study directly to music, for music has its own constraints and capabilities that have to be identified and queried. As pioneering feminist critics of music, we have developed rather different agendas and procedures reflecting our intellectual training, our musical tastes, and the particular versions of feminist theory to which we have been exposed. At this moment, I cannot begin to give any kind of overview of the rich variety of approaches that appear to be emerging within the discipline. Therefore, I will only address my own work—the issues I have found most compelling and the circuitous methodological route that has permitted me at last to feel I can responsibly address some of the concerns of feminist criticism in music.

The questions I have pursued in my feminist work cluster into five groups. They are not always entirely separable; in fact, most of the essays in this collection engage with all five sets of questions in some way or other. Nevertheless, it seems useful to outline them at this point for the sake of setting out a provisional methodology.

1. *Musical constructions of gender and sexuality*. This is probably the most obvious aspect of feminist music criticism. In most dramatic music, there are both female and male characters, and usually (though not always) the musical utterances of characters are inflected on the basis of gender. Beginning with the rise of opera in the seventeenth century, composers worked painstakingly to develop a musical semiotics of gender: a set of conventions for constructing "masculinity" or "femininity" in music. The codes marking gender difference in music are informed by the prevalent attitudes of their time. But they also themselves participate in social formation, inasmuch as individuals learn how to be gendered beings through their interactions with

cultural discourses such as music. Moreover, music does not just passively reflect society; it also serves as a public forum within which various models of gender organization (along with many other aspects of social life) are asserted, adopted, contested, and negotiated.[9]

These codes change over time — the "meaning" of femininity was not the same in the eighteenth century as in the late nineteenth, and musical characterizations differ accordingly. To be sure, many aspects of the codes are strikingly resilient and have been transmitted in ways that are quite recognizable up to the present: for instance, musical representations of masculine bravura or feminine seductiveness in Indiana Jones movies resemble in many respects those in Cavalli's seventeenth-century operas. But if some aspects of the codes prove stable, it is not because music is a "universal language," but rather because certain social attitudes concerning gender have remained relatively constant throughout that stretch of history. Thus the musical semiotics of gender can tell us much about the actual music (why *these* particular pitches and rhythms as opposed to others). And studying music from this vantage point can also provide insights into social history itself, insofar as repertories testify eloquently to the various models of gender organization (whether hegemonic or resistant) available at any given moment.

Music is also very often concerned with the arousing and channeling of desire, with mapping patterns through the medium of sound that resemble those of sexuality. While the topic of sexuality is rarely broached in musicology, it has received considerable attention in recent literary and film theory. As a result of this investigation, much of what had been assumed as biological and immutable in human sexual experience has been radically reinterpreted as socially constructed. Stephen Heath sums up the revisionist position well when he writes:

> There is no such thing as sexuality; what we have experienced and are experiencing is the fabrication of a "sexuality," the construction of something called "sexuality" through a set of representations — images, discourses, ways of picturing and describing — that propose to confirm, that make up this sexuality to which we are then referred and held in our lives, a whole sexual fix precisely.[10]

As reasonably clear instances of "fabrications of sexuality" in music, we might consider the prelude to Wagner's *Tristan und Isolde*, Debussy's *Prélude à l'après-midi d'un faune,* or Madonna and Prince's recent duet, "This Is Not a Love Song." Even though such pieces may seem extraordinarily erotic — as though they have managed to bypass cultural mediation to resonate di-

rectly with one's own most private experiences—they are in fact constructions. Indeed, the three tunes just mentioned present very different notions
of what qualifies as "the erotic" (most listeners would tend to identify one
or two of them as representations of desire and to reject the others as incomprehensible or as rubbish). Because such pieces influence and even constitute
the ways listeners experience and define some of their own most intimate
feelings, they participate actively in the social organization of sexuality.
Thus, one of the principal tasks of feminist music criticism would be to examine the semiotics of desire, arousal, and sexual pleasure that circulate in
the public sphere through music.

2. *Gendered aspects of traditional music theory.* The images of gender or sexuality addressed above are usually rhetorically generated; that is, they are produced by more or less deliberate choices by composers, along with other
dramatic and affective strategies of particular pieces. This is not to say that
every element of every construction of, say, "femininity" must be entirely
intentional, for these codes often are taken to be "natural"—when composing music for a female character, a composer may automatically choose
traits such as softness or passivity, without really examining the premises
for such choices. But still, the fact that gender or arousal is at stake is reasonably clear.

My next two groups of issues are less obvious but are far more crucial to
the enterprise of feminist criticism, especially given that musical institutions
like to claim that music for the most part is not concerned with mundane
issues such as gender or sexuality. Most of the essays in this collection seek
to identify and analyze the ways in which music is shaped by constructions
of gender and sexuality—not only in the context of opera or programmatic
music, but also in some of the most fundamental of musical concepts and
procedures.

For instance, music theorists and analysts quite frequently betray an explicit reliance on metaphors of gender ("masculinity" vs. "femininity") and
sexuality in their formulations. The most venerable of these—because it has
its roots in traditional poetics—involves the classification of cadence-types
or endings according to gender. The 1970 edition of the *Harvard Dictionary
of Music*, for instance, includes the following entry:

> **Masculine, feminine cadence**. A cadence or ending is called
> "masculine" if the final chord of a phrase or section occurs on
> the strong beat and "feminine" if it is postponed to fall on a
> weak beat. The masculine ending must be considered the normal
> one, while the feminine is preferred in more romantic styles.[11]

This standard definition makes it clear that the designations "masculine" and "feminine" are far from arbitrary. The two are differentiated on the basis of relative strength, with the binary opposition masculine/feminine mapped onto strong/weak. Moreover, this particular definition betrays other important mappings: if the masculine version is ("must be considered") normal, then the implication is that the feminine is abnormal. This is so self-evident that the author, Willi Apel, does not think it worthy of explicit mention. Instead, he engages yet another binary: if the feminine is preferred in "more romantic styles," then the masculine must be (and, of course, *is*) identified with the more objective, more rational of musical discourses. In two brief sentences focused ostensibly upon a technical feature of musical rhythm, Apel has managed to engage some of the most prominent of Western beliefs concerning sexual difference. The "feminine" is weak, abnormal, and subjective; the "masculine" strong, normal, and objective. And this whole metaphysical apparatus is brought to bear and reinscribed in the conventional terminology used to distinguish mere cadence-types.

It might be argued that no one takes the gender implications of that music-theoretical distinction literally anymore, that these are but the reified traces of dead metaphors. But how, then, is one to explain theorist Edward T. Cone's strangely moralistic discussion of the performance "problem" of feminine cadences in Chopin?

> Even in the case of movements that seem to remain *incorrigibly feminine*, some differentiation can still be made. In the case of Chopin's Polonaise in A major, for example, a clever emphasis on one of the concealed cross-rhythms at the cadence can make the last chord sound, *if not precisely masculine*, at least like a strong tonic postponed by a suspension of the entire dominant.[12] (my emphasis)

Cone is concerned here with "butching up" a polonaise, a genre that is distinguished from other dances by what Apel labels as "feminine" endings. Now, Chopin's polonaise is a remarkably vigorous, even aggressive composition, and I would argue that it is precisely the emphatic stress on the second ("weak") beat that gives the polonaise its arrogant swagger, its quality of always being poised to plunge into the next phrase. But given that this technicality is conventionally classified as "feminine," Cone feels the need to rescue the piece from its "incorrigibly feminine" endings. He can do so only by violating Chopin's score and in effect weakening the rhythmic integrity of the composition. But at least then the cadences won't sound "feminine" (even if the resulting performance concludes with what sounds like a failure of nerve, a normalization that "corrects" the groove's idiosyncrasy).

Cone's nervousness over the "feminine" cast of this ending suggests that more must be at stake than mere "weakness." Apel defines "feminine endings" as those in which the final sonority is postponed beyond the downbeat. But we could also describe such events in terms of *excess* — a feminine ending then becomes one that refuses the hegemonic control of the barline. Such a description alters the assumed power relationship between the two types, but it begins to account for the anxiety that marks Cone's discussion of these "incorrigible" moments. For his proposed solution attempts to manipulate the music so that it *sounds* as though its "feminine" components are complying with the law of the downbeat. If gendered terminology can lead astray Edward Cone, who is unquestionably one of the finest theorists and analysts in the field, then it certainly needs to be interrogated seriously.

Nor are masculine/feminine distinctions limited to cadences. The eighteenth-century theorist Georg Andreas Sorge explained the hierarchical distinction between major and minor triads in terms he regarded as both natural and God-given — the respective powers of male and female:

> Just as in the universe there has always been created a creature more splendid and perfect than the others of God, we observe exactly this also in musical harmony. Thus we find after the major triad another, the minor triad, which is indeed not as complete as the first, but also lovely and pleasant to hear. The first can be likened to the male, the second to the female sex. And just as it was not good that the man (Adam) was alone, thus it was not good that we had no other harmony than the major triad; for how far would we come in a progression from one chord to the other? . . . And just as the womanly sex without the man would be quite bad, thus with music it would be in a bad way if we had no other harmony than that which the minor triad gives. We could not once make an authentic cadence.[13]

Because it might be objected that Sorge is a figure too far in the past to be relevant to anything today, I offer here a later mapping of major/minor onto masculine/feminine in Arnold Schoenberg's *Theory of Harmony*: "The dualism presented by major and minor has the power of a symbol suggesting high forms of order: it reminds us of male and female and delimits the spheres of expression according to attraction and repulsion. . . . The will of nature is supposedly fulfilled in them."[14] This passage occurs in a context in which Schoenberg has just defined the major mode as "natural," minor as "unnatural," and his mapping of masculine/feminine onto modes follows the same logic as Apel's, Cone's, or Sorge's. Yet even though he bears witness to this received wisdom, it is important to note that Schoenberg (unlike most others) also calls it into question and strives to resist it. For *Theory of Harmony* is in large measure an attempt at imagining a musical language that could eschew binarisms, whether they be major/minor, consonance/dissonance, or masculine/feminine. After the passage just quoted, he goes on to express his longing for a musical discourse that is, like the angels, "asexual"—a discourse no longer driven by the attraction and repulsion between major and minor. His success at locating the metaphysical categories (such as gender) that structure musical thought and his struggle to transcend them make his an exceptionally brave, if tortured, intellectual agenda.[15]

Sometimes sexual metaphors are used to structure musical concepts without reference to gender distinctions. For instance, the theoretical writings of Heinrich Schenker often draw explicitly on analogies to sexuality. Throughout *Harmony*, he describes musical logic—whether motivic or harmonic—as the product of "procreative urges":

> Obviously, every tone is possessed of the same inherent urge to procreate infinite generations of overtones. Also this urge has its analogy in animal life; in fact, it appears to be in no way inferior to the procreative urge of a living being. This fact again reveals to us the biological aspect of music, as we have emphasized it already in our consideration of the procreative urge of the motif.[16]

One explanation for such a passage is that Schenker simply found this particular verbal trope of sexuality handy for describing the dynamic quality of pure, abstract tonal music. Yet the nineteenth-century repertory he is accounting for was itself generated in accordance with a crucial set of biological, "organic" metaphors.[17] Schenker's tropes spring from and participate in the same cultural milieu that gave rise to the music he analyzes. They merely testify in words to the processes that likewise underwrite the musical imagery.[18]

3. *Gender and sexuality in musical narrative.* Not only do gender and sexuality inform our "abstract" theories, but music itself often relies heavily upon the metaphorical simulation of sexual activity for its effects. I will argue throughout this volume that tonality itself—with its process of instilling expectations and subsequently withholding promised fulfillment until climax—is the principal musical means during the period from 1600 to 1900 for arousing and channeling desire. Even without texts or programs, tonal compositions ranging from Bach organ fugues to Brahms symphonies whip

up torrents of libidinal energy that are variously thwarted or permitted to gush. The principal theorist to acknowledge and examine this aspect of tonality systematically is Schenker: the purpose of his quasi-mathematical diagrams (in addition to his explicitly sexualized tropes) is to chart simultaneously the principal background mechanisms through which tonal compositions arouse desire and the surface strategies that postpone gratification. Through rigorous theoretical language and graphing techniques, he plots out the mechanisms whereby certain simulations of sexual desire and release are constituted within the musical medium.

His mystical statements of intention to the contrary, Schenker's graphs can be read as demonstrating in fully material terms that the excitement achieved in these pieces is *constructed* (is not, in other words, the tracing of the German *Geist* or Schopenhauer's Will). And any medium—whether music or fiction—that regularly achieves such powerful effects needs to be studied carefully, not only technically (as in Schenker), but also ideologically. What are the assumptions that fuel these mechanisms so often called by the neutral name of "tension and release" (or by Schoenberg's explicitly sexualized "attraction and repulsion")? Whose models of subjectivity are they, given that they are not universal? To what ends are they employed in compositions? What is it, in other words, that the listener is being invited to desire and why?

Similarly, the various narrative paradigms that crystallized during the history of tonality contain many features that are in effect gendered. This is especially clear in the case of sonata-allegro procedure, for which there even used to be the custom of calling the opening theme "masculine" and the subsidiary theme "feminine." To be sure, this custom extends back only as far as the mid-nineteenth century. Theorist A. B. Marx seems to have been the first to use this terminology, in his *Die Lehre von der musikalischen Komposition* (1845):

> The second theme, on the other hand, serves as contrast to the first, energetic statement, though dependent on and determined by it. It is of a more tender nature, flexibly rather than emphatically constructed—in a way, the feminine as opposed to the preceding masculine. In this sense each of the two themes is different, and only together do they form something of a higher, more perfect order.[19]

The convention of designating themes as masculine and feminine was still common in pedagogy and criticism of the 1960s, although musicology by and large has since repudiated it—especially its application to sonata movements that antedate Marx's formulation.

However, the fact that themes were not referred to in this fashion until the mid-nineteenth century does not mean that earlier pieces are free of gendered marking: the themes of many an eighteenth-century sonata movement draw upon the semiotics of "masculinity" and "femininity" as they were constructed on the operatic stage, and thus they are readily recognizable in their respective positions within the musical narratives. To identify them as such is not to commit an anachronism: the gender connotations of the opening "Mannheim rockets" or "hammerstrokes" and the sighing second themes in Stamitz symphonies are so obvious as to border on the cartoonish, even if neither he nor his contemporaries actually called the respective themes "masculine" and "feminine."

Nor is it merely a matter of deciding whether or not to label themes as "masculine" and "feminine" in what are otherwise neutral narrative processes. Drawing on the structuralist work of the Soviet narratologists Vladimir Propp and Jurij Lotman, Teresa de Lauretis has demonstrated with respect to traditional Western narrative that:

> The hero must be male, regardless of the gender of the text-image, because the obstacle, whatever its personification, is morphologically female. . . . The hero, the mythical subject, is constructed as human being and as male; he is the active principle of culture, the establisher of distinction, the creator of differences. Female is what is not susceptible to transformation, to life or death; she (it) is an element of plot-space, a topos, a resistance, matrix and matter.[20]

Furthermore, as de Lauretis and other narratologists have demonstrated, regardless of the manifest content of particular stories, these two functions interact in accordance with a schema already established in advance—the masculine protagonist makes contact with but must eventually subjugate (domesticate or purge) the designated [feminine] Other in order for identity to be consolidated, for the sake of satisfactory narrative closure.[21]

This narrative schema is played out quite explicitly in opera.[22] But it is no less crucial to the formal conventions of "absolute" music: indeed, large-scale instrumental music was not feasible before the development of tonality, which draws on the model of these powerful narrative paradigms. In its early manifestations in the late seventeenth and early eighteenth centuries, the course of a movement traces the trajectory from a home base (tonic), to the conquest of two or three other keys, and a return to tonic for closure. Schoenberg, for one, was explicitly aware of the narrative demands of tonality:

> For [our forebears] the comedy concluded with marriage, the
> tragedy with expiation or retribution, and the musical work "in
> the same key." Hence, for them the choice of scale brought the
> obligation to treat the first tone of that scale as the fundamental,
> and to present it as Alpha and Omega of all that took place in
> the work, as the patriarchal ruler over the domain defined by its
> might and its will: its coat of arms was displayed at the most
> conspicuous points, especially at the beginning and ending. And
> thus they had a possibility for closing that in effect resembled a
> necessity.[23]

Thus, the Other may be merely an alien terrain through which the mono-
logic subject of the piece passes (and secures cadentially) on its narrative adventure away from and back to tonic. However, the sonata procedure that
comes to characterize instrumental music of the eighteenth and nineteenth
centuries features a more polarized version of that basic narrative paradigm.
In sonata, the principal key/theme clearly occupies the narrative position of
masculine protagonist; and while the less dynamic second key/theme is *necessary* to the sonata or tonal plot (without this foil or obstacle, there is no
story), it serves the narrative function of the feminine Other. Moreover, satisfactory resolution—the ending always generically guaranteed in advance
by tonality and sonata procedure—demands the containment of whatever is
semiotically or structurally marked as "feminine," whether a second theme
or simply a non-tonic key area.

In his entry on sonata form in *The New Grove Dictionary*, James Webster
is careful to mention the terminology of "masculine" and "feminine"
themes only when he gets to the repertories and theories contemporary with
A. B. Marx. Yet in his opening structuralist account of the sonata paradigm,
he writes the following:

> The second group in the exposition presents important material
> and closes with a sense of finality, but it is not in the tonic. This
> dichotomy creates a "large-scale dissonance" that must be
> resolved. The "sonata principle" requires that the most
> important ideas and the strongest cadential passages from the
> second group reappear in the recapitulation, but now transposed
> to the tonic. The subtle tension of stating important material in
> another key is thus "grounded," and the movement can end.[24]

As abstractly worded as this statement may be, it reveals that the sonata and
likewise tonality are manifestations of the same cultural paradigms as the
mythic narratives schematically laid bare by Propp, Lotman, and de Lauretis. They depend upon the logic that assumes as natural the tonic protago-

nist's necessary subjugation ("resolution," "grounding") of whatever "large-scale dissonance" occupies the second narrative position.

Of course, the Other need not always be interpreted strictly as female—it can be anything that stands as an obstacle or threat to identity and that must, consequently, be purged or brought under submission for the sake of narrative closure. Robert Walser has suggested that the terms of tonality and sonata might be dealt with productively through methods expounded by cultural theorist Fredric Jameson in his analysis of *Jaws*. Jameson argues that the reason the film had such a powerful impact on the public imagination is that its narrative tensions could be interpreted in terms of a wide range of social tensions. In other words, the shark is not necessarily just a shark, but is available as a stand-in for any force (untamable nature, commodity culture, or even—in keeping with classical narratology and the shark's grotesque resonance with traditional iconography—the vagina dentata) that threatens the individual spectator. The danger posed by that "Other" is raised to an excruciating level and then resolved, granting at least momentarily the experience of utopia.[25]

Likewise, the paradigms of tonality and sonata have proved effective and resilient in part because their tensions may be read in a variety of ways. I do not want to reduce two centuries of music to an inflexible formula. Yet the heavily gendered legacy of these paradigms cannot be ignored either. In literature, even if the second narrative slot is not occupied by a woman character, whoever or whatever fills the fatal slot is understood on some fundamental cultural level as a "feminine" Other: to conquer an enemy is to "emasculate" him as he is purged or domesticated. Similarly, chromaticism, which enriches tonal music but which must finally be resolved to the triad for the sake of closure, takes on the cultural cast of "femininity."[26] The "feminine" never gets the last word within this context: in the world of traditional narrative, there are no feminine endings.

These are features of composition and reception that are taken for granted as aspects of autonomous musical practice, as simply "the way music goes." They are usually not considered actively by composers, are not "intended." They simply are the elements that structure his or her musical (and social) world. Yet they are perhaps the most powerful aspects of musical discourses, for they operate below the level of deliberate signification and are thus usually reproduced and transmitted without conscious intervention. They are the habits of cultural thought that guarantee the effectiveness of the music—that allow it to "make sense"—while they remain largely invisible and apparently immutable. Most of the essays that follow concentrate heavily on these conventions, for it is through these deeply engrained habits that gender and sexuality are most effectively—and most problematically—organized in music.

4. *Music as a gendered discourse.* Throughout its history in the West, music has been an activity fought over bitterly in terms of gender identity. The charge that musicians or devotees of music are "effeminate" goes back as far as recorded documentation about music, and music's association with the body (in dance or for sensuous pleasure) and with subjectivity has led to its being relegated in many historical periods to what was understood as a "feminine" realm. Male musicians have retaliated in a number of ways: by defining music as the most ideal (that is, the least physical) of the arts; by insisting emphatically on its "rational" dimension; by laying claim to such presumably masculine virtues as objectivity, universality, and transcendence; by prohibiting actual female participation altogether.[27]

If the whole enterprise of musical activity is always already fraught with gender-related anxieties, then feminist critique provides a most fruitful way of approaching some of the anomalies that characterize musical institutions. Some of this work is already available. For instance, Linda Austern and Richard Leppert have demonstrated that one reason the English have produced so little music is that they—more than their German or French neighbors—have long associated music strongly with effeminacy.[28] The English effectively prevented themselves as a society from participating in musical culture, except as connoisseurs and consumers, and Anglo-Americans have followed suit. As Maynard Solomon writes of Charles Ives:

> [Ives] is both drawn to music and repelled by it. "As a boy [I was] partially ashamed of music," he recalled—"an entirely wrong attitude but it was strong—most boys in American country towns, I think felt the same. . . . And there may be something in it. Hasn't music always been too much an emasculated art?" To ward off such feelings, Ives would eradicate the traces of the "soft-bodied" and the "decadent" in his own work, perhaps employing the techniques of modernism to conceal the atmospheric, lyrical, yielding strata which often underlie his first ideas.[29]

Likewise, the polemics that proliferate around moments of stylistic change are frequently expressed in terms of sexual identity. Early Romanticism, for instance, was in part an appropriation of what the Enlightenment had defined as subjective, "feminine" imagination, and the battles over the relative status of structure and ornamental excess, between rationality and irrationality in early nineteenth-century music were understood as battles over the proper constitution of the bourgeois male. Similarly, the turn from late Romantic hysteria and popular music to the refuge of rigorous Modernism is a gesture partly informed by the desire to remasculinize the discourse.[30]

Even the strange absence of criticism in the discipline may well be related to gender-related anxieties. A particularly poignant manifestation of such anxiety in action is Schumann's celebrated essay on Schubert's Symphony in C Major. The essay carefully establishes a dichotomy between the masculine example of Beethoven and the more sensitive, romantic Schubert; and throughout the essay, Schumann shields himself from Schubert's influence by calling upon Beethoven's "virile power" at moments when he is about to be overwhelmed by Schubert's charm. At the end, after he has succumbed to a rhapsodic account of what it is like to listen to the Schubert symphony, he seeks to recover his masculine authority by abruptly informing the reader: "I once found on Beethoven's grave a steel pen, which ever since I have reverently preserved. I never use it save on festive occasions like this one; may inspiration have flowed from it."[31]

Despite the deeply conflicted nature of Schumann's essay, he does risk revealing himself in print as a man given to strong emotional impulses, perhaps even as one who is as attracted to the seductive grace of Schubert as to the virility of Beethoven. Most music analysts today do not have the nerve to follow Schumann's example — and thus, for instance, the recent outcropping of daunting structuralist graphs used to distance and objectify the passionate music of nineteenth-century opera. For if to admit that music moves one affectively means that one may not be a proper masculine subject, then one's study of music will systematically avoid addressing such issues.[32]

The consequences of such anxieties are enormous — for individual musicians, for the history of music as it unfolds, and for the questions and methods admitted in the course of its academic study by theorists and musicologists. Even though these are extremely difficult and delicate issues, they have to be addressed seriously if music criticism of any sort is to proceed beyond surface details.

5. *Discursive strategies of women musicians.* There have been many obstacles preventing women from participating fully (or, at some moments in history, from participating *at all*) in musical production. Most of these have been institutional: women have been denied the necessary training and professional connections, and they have been assumed to be incapable of sustained creative activity. The music that has been composed by women (despite all odds) has often been received in terms of the essentialist stereotypes ascribed to women by masculine culture: it is repeatedly condemned as

pretty yet trivial or—in the event that it does not conform to standards of feminine propriety—as aggressive and unbefitting a woman.[33]

Within the last two generations, it has finally become possible for relatively large numbers of women to enter seriously into training as composers. Composers such as Joan Tower, Ellen Taaffe Zwilich, Thea Musgrave, Pauline Oliveros, Libby Larsen, and many others have successfully challenged the pernicious and absurd stereotypes that have plagued women for centuries. They prove that women can and do compose first-rate music, and they are fully capable of deploying the entire range of the semiotic code they have inherited—not merely the sweet and passive, but the forceful aspects as well. Many superb women composers insist on making their gender identities a nonissue, precisely because there still remain so many essentialist assumptions about what music by women "ought" to sound like.[34] That they are determined to demonstrate that they too can write MUSIC (as opposed to "women's music") is understandable. Moreover, it is an important political position and strategy, given the history of women's marginalization in this domain.

However, I am no longer sure what MUSIC is. Given that my first three sets of questions are concerned with laying bare the kinds of gender/power relationships already inscribed in many of the presumably value-free procedures of Western music, it becomes difficult to stash that information and simply analyze MUSIC, even if is produced by women. For even though women have managed to enter into composition as professionals, they still face the problem of how to participate without unwittingly reproducing the ideologies that inform various levels of those discourses.

Thus I am especially drawn to women artists who, like myself, are involved with examining the premises of inherited conventions, with calling them into question, with attempting to reassemble them in ways that make a difference inside the discourse itself, with envisioning narrative structures with feminine endings. The work of these women broadens the range of possible musics, as it comments both on the assumptions of more traditional procedures and on the problematic position of a woman artist attempting to create new meanings within old media.

3

How does one go about grounding arguments of the sort these questions would require? The intellectual obstacles that have impeded the development of feminist music criticism are rooted in the assumptions that have long informed and sustained academic musicology in general. It is important to remember that there really is very little resembling criticism *of any sort* in musicology.[35] For many complex reasons, music has been and continues to be almost entirely exempted from criticism as it is practiced within other humanities disciplines: even those scholars who produce work resembling that of the old-fashioned New Criticism of literary studies still count as radicals in musicology. In other words, feminist criticism has not necessarily been singled out for exclusion — to a very large extent, its absence is merely symptomatic of the way the discipline as a whole is organized. Consequently, it is not a matter of simply adding feminist issues to a well-established tradition of critical inquiry: before we can address the questions concerning gender and sexuality discussed above, it is necessary to construct an entire theory of musical signification.

It is an intimidating task to try to unlock a medium that has been so securely sequestered for so long. There does exist, of course, a sophisticated discipline of music theory, but this discipline by and large restricts the questions it acknowledges to matters of formal process as they appear in musical scores. To be sure, the contributions of music theory are indispensable to feminist or any other kind of criticism. Far from setting the score aside and concentrating on extramusical issues, my work is always concerned with explaining how it is that certain images or responses are invoked by particular musical details. But as long as we approach questions of signification *exclusively* from a formalist point of view, we will continue to conclude that it is impossible to get from chords, pitch-class sets, or structures to any other kind of human or social meaning. Indeed, the more deeply entrenched we become in strictly formal explanations, the further away we are from admitting even the *possibility* of other sorts of readings, gendered or otherwise.[36]

Yet music need not be — and has not always been — defined exclusively in terms of its atomic bits. In the seventeenth and eighteenth centuries, for instance, music was typically discussed in terms of affect and rhetoric. Monteverdi wrote letters in which he openly recounted his invention of various kinds of musical signs: ways of representing madness, military ferocity, and so forth. Bach's contemporaries Mattheson and Heinechen wrote lexicons cataloguing affective devices, and composition teachers of the time instructed students on how to produce passionate responses in listeners through rhetorical manipulation. And even though the musicians of the nineteenth century sought to give the illusion that they wrote by inspiration and with disdain for social codes, the documents produced by composers and critics testify to a belief in the emotional power of music, even if they wished that power to be regarded as unmediated and transcendent.

Likewise today most people who have not been trained as academic musicians (who have not had these responses shamed out of them) believe that music signifies—that it can sound happy, sad, sexy, funky, silly, "American," religious, or whatever. Oblivious to the skepticism of music theorists, they listen to music in order to dance, weep, relax, or get romantic. Composers of music for movies and advertisements consistently stake their commercial success on the public's pragmatic knowledge of musical signification—the skill with which John Williams, for instance, manipulates the semiotic codes of the late nineteenth-century symphony in *E. T.* or *Star Wars* is breathtaking. As Galileo is reported to have uttered after he was forced to recant his theories before the Inquisition, "And yet it moves." It doesn't really matter that academic disciplines have tried to insist that music is only music, that it cannot mean anything else. In the social world, music achieves these effects all the time.

Like any social discourse, music is meaningful precisely insofar as at least some people believe that it is and act in accordance with that belief. Meaning is not inherent in music, but neither is it in language: both are activities that are kept afloat only because communities of people invest in them, agree collectively that their signs serve as valid currency. Music is always dependent on the conferring of social meaning—as ethnomusicologists have long recognized, the study of signification in music cannot be undertaken in isolation from the human contexts that create, transmit, and respond to it.

However, this is not to suggest that music is nothing but an epiphenomenon that can be explained by way of social determinism. Music and other discourses do not simply reflect a social reality that exists immutably on the outside; rather, social reality itself is constituted within such discursive practices. It is in accordance with the terms provided by language, film, advertising, ritual, or music that individuals are socialized: take on gendered identities, learn ranges of proper behaviors, structure their perceptions and even their experiences. But it is also within the arena of these discourses that alternative models of organizing the social world are submitted and negotiated. This is where the ongoing work of social formation occurs.

Most members of a given social group succeed in internalizing the norms of their chosen music and are quite sophisticated in their abilities to respond appropriately. They know how to detect even minor stylistic infractions and to respond variously with delight or indignation, depending on how they identify themselves with respect to the style at hand. Yet very few people are able to explain verbally to themselves *how* music affects them.

I am interested first and foremost in accounting for the ways music creates such effects. On the informal level, my work has always been strongly influenced by my own perceptions: the perceptions of a member of this society who has been immersed in musical "high culture" for forty-four years and professionally engaged with it for over thirty. I always begin by trusting that my own reactions to music are legitimate. By "legitimate," I do not mean to suggest that my readings are identical with everyone else's or are always in line with some standard version of what a piece is taken to mean. Indeed, the essays that follow diverge quite consistently from received wisdom.

But neither would I accept the charge that my readings are "subjective" in the sense that they reflect only my own quirks. Rather, I take my reactions to be in large part socially constituted — the products of lifelong contact with music and other cultural media. Thus I regard them as invaluable firsthand evidence of how music can influence listeners affectively, how it can even participate in social formation.[37] If most other music professionals are reticent about confessing music's effects on them, I can at least draw upon my own experiences. Miraculously, thirty years in the profession have not succeeded in destroying my faith in that fundamental storehouse of knowledge.

But if I pay close attention to my own reactions (instead of shoving them to the side for the sake of an objectivity that will always prevent in advance the examination of music's impact), I am also very much concerned with the reactions of others. Since I want to be able to argue that music is socially grounded, I have conducted extensive field research (or, if you prefer, "reality testing") over the past twenty years. That is, I play pieces of music for and invite responses from many other kinds of people: inner-city high school students, professional string quartets, groups of senior citizens, musicology graduate students, literary critics, New Music America audiences. What I have learned is that nonprofessionals are extremely adept at comprehending and even explaining affect and rhetoric in music, while professionals tend to divide into two camps: those who think they are above such nonsense and who supply formal explanations for everything they hear, and those who have not surrendered their conviction that music signifies but who have kept this carefully hidden, rather as though they were adults who still believe in the Tooth Fairy.

But mere gut reactions (my own or those of others) are only the beginning — although without these, it would be impossible to discuss signification at all. My primary concerns are first with justifying those reactions through musical analysis, social history, critical theory, and much else. But once the validity of such reactions is established, I am further concerned with interrogating them: it is important to ascertain that Bizet does, in fact, make our pulses race at the end of *Carmen*, sweeping us ineluctably forward to Carmen's murder, and also to account for how he accomplishes this musically. But then it also becomes necessary to explain why — in Bizet's day and in ours — such a musico-narrative device has been regarded as so compelling and even pleasurable. And the question then arises of whose interest is being served by the public deployment of such devices.

My eclectic tool kit of methods has been assembled over the years out of whatever has seemed handy in unlocking particular musical problems, for music continually (and unpredictably) draws upon everything available in the social domain. In the various essays I have written—feminist or otherwise—I have made use of whatever helped me to make sense of the composition at hand. Thus I have no sense of loyalty to any particular orthodox position. To be sure, my various theoretical acquisitions invite me to make connections that would not be available to those who refuse categorically to look beyond the literal details of the musical notation. But my focus is invariably on the music itself—or, to be more precise, on the music as it operates within human contexts.

4

By far the most difficult aspect of music to explain is its uncanny ability to make us experience our bodies in accordance with its gestures and rhythms. Yet this aspect is also what makes music so compelling. If music were not able thus to move us, the human race would not have bothered creating any of it for formalists to dissect, for musicologists to catalogue, or for sociologists to classify. In a recent song, the Doobie Brothers sing, "Music is a doctor, makes you feel like you want to." And Raymond Williams too has stressed the impact of music on the body, albeit in rather more academic terms:

> We are only beginning to investigate this on any scientific basis, but it seems clear from what we already know that rhythm is a way of transmitting a description of experience, in such a way that the experience is re-created in the person receiving it, not merely as an "abstraction" or an emotion but as a physical effect on the organism—on the blood, on the breathing, on the physical patterns of the brain. . . . it is more than a metaphor; it is a physical experience as real as any other.[38]

Although Williams claims that what he is talking about is "more than a metaphor," the best way of grounding what he is addressing is philosopher Mark Johnson's recent epistemological work on metaphor. Johnson argues convincingly that metaphors are not mere figures of speech (which seems to be how Williams construes the word), but rather are the fundamental means through which we as embodied beings orient ourselves with respect to the world and thereby structure our discourses and our cognition. His work constructs a theory of knowledge that avoids the splits between mind and body, between objectivity and subjectivity that have plagued Western thought since Plato:

> The body has been ignored by Objectivism because it has been thought to introduce subjective elements alleged to be irrelevant to the objective nature of meaning. The body has been ignored because reason has been thought to be abstract and transcendent, that is, not tied to any of the bodily aspects of human understanding. The body has been ignored because it seems to have no role in our reasoning about abstract subject matters.
>
> Contrary to Objectivism, I focus on the indispensability of embodied human understanding for meaning and rationality. "Understanding" is here regarded as populated with just those kinds of imaginative structures that emerge from our experience as bodily organisms functioning in interaction with an environment. Our understanding involves many preconceptual and nonpropositional structures of experience that can be metaphorically projected and propositionally elaborated to constitute our network of meanings.
>
> My purpose is not only to argue that the body is "in" the mind (i.e., *that* these imaginative structures of understanding are crucial to meaning and reason) but also to explore *how* the body is in the mind—how it is possible, and necessary, after all, for abstract meaning, and for reason and imagination, to have a bodily basis.
>
> *Any adequate account of meaning and rationality must give a central place to embodied and imaginative structures of understanding by which we grasp our world.*[39]

I have quoted Johnson at length because I believe that it is only by adopting such an epistemological framework that we can begin accounting for how music does what it does. Certainly the acoustician's sound waves in and of themselves cannot be demonstrated to possess any of the powers Williams describes. Yet when those sound waves are assembled in such a way as to resemble physical gestures, we as listeners are able to read or make sense of them, largely by means of our lifelong experiences as embodied creatures.[40]

Thus to say that one hears sexual longing in the *Tristan* prelude is not to introduce irrelevant "subjective" data into the discussion. Surely that is the point of the opera, and we are missing the point if we fail to understand that. The process by means of which Wagner's music accomplishes this is not at all mystical. In part, his music draws on his own (excessively documented) experiences in the sexual realm, and we as listeners perceive longing in his music likewise because we are human beings with bodies who have experienced similar feelings firsthand. But this is not to suggest that music works on the basis of essences or that this communication between bedroom and ear happens without extensive symbolic mediation. Wagner's music relies heavily on the traditional semiotics of desire available in the musical styles he inherited, and listeners understand his music in part because they too have learned the codes (the minor sixths demanding resolution, the agony of the tritone, the expectation that a dominant-seventh chord will proceed to its tonic, and so on) upon which his metaphors depend.

Moreover, the musical conventions for representing such human experiences are far from timeless or ahistorical. Desire, for instance, was configured differently in seventeenth-century music, in part because Baroque social codes of signification and even norms of harmonic syntax were very different: some of the techniques exploited by Schütz in "Anima mea liquefacta est" resemble distantly those in *Tristan* and can be grasped by the modern listener without special tutoring; but many more of them depend upon the listener's familiarity with the relevant set of grammatical expectations. Musical imagery, in other words, is heavily mediated through the available syntax, sound forces, genres, and much else.

Nor are the bodily experiences engaged by musical metaphors stable or immutable.[41] Indeed, music is a powerful social and political practice precisely because in drawing on metaphors of physicality, it can cause listeners to experience their bodies in new ways—again, seemingly without mediation. The explosion of rock 'n' roll in the mid-1950s brought a vocabulary of physical gestures to white middle-class kids that parents and authorities quite rightly perceived as subversive of hegemonic bourgeois values. Sheltered Northern adolescents picked up on the dance rhythms of the Southern honky-tonk and black R & B, and their notions of sexuality—their perceptions of their own most intimate dimensions of experience—split off irrevocably from those of their parents. Even if it is difficult to account definitively for how music precipitates such transformations, its political potency must be acknowledged. And any human discourse with this much influence not only warrants, but demands serious scrutiny.

As the Wagner and rock examples indicate, much is at stake in the sets of apparently "natural" metaphors that inform various musics. For music is not the universal language it has sometimes been cracked up to be: it changes over time, and it differs with respect to geographical locale. Even at any given moment and place, it is always constituted by several competing repertories, distributed along lines of gender, age, ethnic identity, educational background, or economic class. Because musical procedures are

heavily inflected over history and across social groups, they function extensively within the public domain and are thus available for critical investigation.

Given its centrality in the manipulation of affect, social formation, and
the constitution of identity, music is far too important a phenomenon *not* to
talk about, even if the most important questions cannot be definitively
settled by means of objective, positivistic methodologies. For music is always a political activity, and to inhibit criticism of its effects for any reason
is likewise a political act.[42]

5

The project of critical musicology (of which feminism would be an important branch) would be to examine the ways in which different musics articulate the priorities and values of various communities. Fortunately, we are
not required to reinvent the wheel, for this is, of course, one of the principal
activities of ethnomusicology. Because the musical images produced by
people foreign to us are usually somewhat opaque, discouraging us from
thinking that we can hear straight through to universal meanings, we tend
to be aware that there are many levels of social mediation involved in the
production of other musics.[43] Accordingly, ethnographers regularly analyze
the musical institutions and procedures of non-Western or folk communities
in terms of social organization. But much less work is available that asks
ethnographic questions of Western art music. For it is one thing to recognize
the social basis of the activities of remote societies, and it is quite another to
begin examining the relativity of our own cherished habits of thought.[44]

To do so demands two very different kinds of work: analytical and historical. On the one hand, the techniques and codes through which music
produces meaning have to be reconstructed. Because the music theories
available at present are designed to maintain the illusion that music is formally self-contained, very little exists in Anglo-American musicology to fa-
cilitate such a project. Having to trace over and over again the processes by
which musical elements such as pitch or rhythm can be said to signify is
extremely tedious, especially within a discipline that refuses even to acknowledge musical affect. Yet it is impossible to go on to finer points of
interpretation so long as the question of whether music means anything at
all arises to block any further inquiry.

The chapters in this book focus on substantive issues rather than on this
basic methodological problem — although fundamental questions about musical signification are addressed continually throughout. But elsewhere I
have published three essays devoted to demonstrating how formal musical

details may be connected to expression and even to social ideology. Two of them present step-by-step readings of pieces by Mozart and Bach.[45] The third examines a very particular device in nineteenth-century music: narrative interruptions by the key of the flatted submediant.[46] Admittedly, this last project looks arcane on paper. But the reactions of listeners to flat-six interruptions are almost unfailingly immediate and dramatic, even if they do not know technically how to explain their perceptions of discontinuity. All three of these essays account for musical signification in part through details of the score: by means of historical semiotics, generic expectations, deviations from syntactical or structural norms, and rhetorical devices such as continuity, disruption, intensification, and so forth.

But these three essays also locate generic norms and strategies of deviation within historical and cultural contexts. Genres and conventions crystallize because they are embraced as natural by a certain community: they define the limits of what counts as proper musical behavior. Music theory has often been a more or less legislative branch of music that seeks to rationalize and prescribe the preferences of a particular dominant group. Yet crystallization or legislation also makes those norms available for violation, making music itself a terrain on which transgressions and opposition can be registered directly: as Jacques Attali has argued, music is a battleground on which divergent concepts of order and noise are fought out.[47]

For instance, Monteverdi's violations of Renaissance rules of dissonance treatment succeeded in polarizing authorities and advocates of the new practices, and the resulting polemics reveal quite clearly that much more was at stake than an occasional unprepared discord. When Bob Dylan first walked onto the stage with an electric guitar, he was thought to have betrayed the folk community with which he had been identified and threw into confusion the social categories of the 1960s. In our own day, Tipper Gore's PMRC has brought the censorship of rock both to Capitol Hill and to the recording industry because of the kinds of sexual images she claims the music transmits to her children.

In other words, music and its procedures operate as part of the political arena—not simply as one of its more trivial reflections. So long as music reaffirms what everyone expects, it can manage to seem apolitical, to serve as a mere frill. But as soon as it transgresses some deep-seated taboo, it can bring boiling to the surface certain antagonisms or alliances that otherwise might not have been so passionately articulated. The incidents involving the character Radio Raheem in Spike Lee's film *Do the Right Thing* illustrate this point with extraordinary clarity: Raheem is a loner whose identity is wrapped up in his boombox, on which he incessantly plays Public Enemy's "Fight the Power" at earsplitting volume. When he refuses to turn it off in the pizza shop, the white owner (who displays only photos of Italian-American celebrities on his walls, despite the objections of his all-black clientele) smashes the boombox, triggering the violence that escalates eventually to the looting of the shop, defacement of his cultural icons, Raheem's murder, and a race riot. Struggles over musical propriety are themselves political struggles over whose music, whose images of pleasure or beauty, whose rules of order shall prevail.

Consequently, it is difficult to understand why in certain repertories some images and constructions dominate, why others are prohibited, unless one has a strong sense of social history. The kind of history musicology has typically adopted is that of chronology. There are no power struggles in such histories, to say nothing of sensitive issues such as gender or sexuality. It is in part because history is presented as orderly, settled, and unproblematic that it has appeared to be largely irrelevant to the ways music itself is organized.

Therefore, the other principal task facing a music critic who wants to find the traces of history in musical texts is to discover alternative modes of historiography. Fortunately, a considerable amount of work has already been done toward this end, first through the Frankfurt School critics—exemplified especially in the aesthetic theories and finely nuanced analyses of Theodor Adorno—and more recently through Michel Foucault's "archaeologies of knowledge."

Adorno is the only major cultural theorist of the century whose primary medium was music, as opposed to literature, film, or painting.[48] Thus much of what he accomplished does not require the kind of disciplinary translation that virtually all other critical theorists do. His work, while parochially grounded in the German canon of great composers from Bach to Schoenberg, provides the means for understanding how compositions of the tonal repertory are informed by the fundamental social tensions of their time. His conceptual framework opens up that sacrosanct canon to questions of great social and political urgency.

Writing between the world wars, from the historical vantage point of the horrific collapse of German high culture, Adorno dismisses with contempt those who would regard this music as a set of icons and insists upon treating it as a medium within which the bourgeois contradictions between individual free will and social pressures to conform were played out in increasingly pessimistic ways. The illusion of total order and control cherished by traditional musicologists is stripped away by his readings, which focus unremittingly on historical human dilemmas rather than on transcendent truth. In his hands, the presumably nonrepresentational instrumental music of the canon becomes the most sensitive social barometer in all of culture. It is thereby made available to social criticism and analysis. Without my study of Adorno, I could not have undertaken any of the projects presented in this volume, for I would have had no way of getting beyond formalism. Yet there are many areas of human experience that Adorno overlooks or denigrates as regressive, such as pleasure or the body.

These are precisely the areas Foucault opens up to critical and historical investigation: in book after book, he has demonstrated that such apparent universals as knowledge, sexuality, the body, the self, and madness all have histories bound up with institutional power.[49] Moreover, he theorizes how these have been—and are—variously defined, organized, and constituted by means of cultural discourses such as literature or music. Social critics have typically been scornful of the pleasurable aspects of the arts, favoring those works that could be shown to have the proper political stance; to dwell on the actual details of the artifice was to be seduced by it into false consciousness, to be drawn away from the central issues of the class struggle. However, far from finding pleasure to be trivial, Foucault locates the efficacy of cultural discourses in their ability to arouse and manipulate. Pleasure thereby becomes political rather than private—it becomes one of the principal means by which hegemonic culture maintains its power.

While they offer extraordinary insight into the political machinations of culture, Foucault's formulations often are somewhat pessimistic, for they rarely admit of the possibility of agency, resistance, or alternative models of pleasure.[50] Here the models of political criticism developed by Antonio Gramsci or Mikhail Bakhtin can serve as empowering correctives, in that they recognize and focus on cultural contestation, counternarratives, and carnivalesque celebrations of the marginalized.[51] They conceive of culture as the terrain in which competing versions of social reality fight it out, and thus they permit the study of the ideological dimensions of art while avoiding the determinism that too often renders such analyses reductive.

Inspired in part by Foucault, Gramsci, and others, the practices of history and literary criticism have changed profoundly during the last decade. Historians are increasingly making use of anthropological questions as they interrogate who WE are: why we organize gender and sexuality as we do, how we came to assume certain notions of subjectivity, and how various discourses operate to structure, reproduce, or transform social reality. Consequently, the study of the arts has become a far more central, more urgent enterprise than it was in its Great Books phase. From various angles, writers such as Fernand Braudel, Stephen Greenblatt, Joan Kelly, and Nancy Armstrong have begun to set forth a very different picture of European/ American history—a history no longer just of a privileged people, but of an extended community with beliefs and customs as peculiar as those of any so-called primitive society, a community that structures and reproduces itself by means of cultural discourses.[52]

The essays that follow owe much in terms of method and information to these new directions in historiography. For if we reject the idea that European music is autonomous, then much about the changing world in which it was enmeshed must be reconstructed. Unfortunately for those who want their investigations to be methodologically tidy, the history of that "outside" world is not stable. We are at present in the midst of extensive revisions of the histories of Europe and the United States. Much of what one would like to know about (e.g., attitudes toward sexuality and gender throughout the centuries) is only now being pieced together.

It might be argued that it is foolhardy to jump in to try to account for music before the revised picture of the outside world has been solidified. But if music is one of the cultural terrains on which such issues get worked out, then our picture of the outside world will always be incomplete until music is figured in. Cultural critics have already discovered how absurd it is to write histories of the 1960s without paying close attention to the crucial roles played by music. I suspect that this is true of most other moments in Western history as well.

To the large extent that music can organize our perceptions of our own bodies and emotions, it can tell us things about history that are not accessible through any other medium. This is not to dismiss the importance of verbal documents: indeed, far more than flattened-out historical narratives, historical documents help us to locate music within the ideological struggles that leave their traces on its procedures. Consequently, my essays refer continually to a wide variety of documents and social histories. But for the study of music, music itself remains the best indicator, if we only permit ourselves to listen self-reflexively and to think.

The essays in this collection attempt to sketch out what several of these historical, analytical, and theoretical projects would look like. If the arguments sometimes seem circular—the analyses depend on particular constructions of the social world that are in part constituted by the music at hand—then this only points to the inseparability of music and the social world within which it operates. What usually motivates a project is that an odd musical detail catches my attention; but in order to explain that detail, I am required to undertake extensive historical excavation. And likewise, my historical studies make me aware of the significance of many musical details I might never have noticed otherwise.

My detour into critical and cultural theory has been interpreted by some as an abandonment of musicology. I have at times even been called a sociologist (though never by actual sociologists, who usually take me to be overconcerned with textual analysis). Yet, once again, it has always been music itself that has compelled me into these dark alleys, that has kept me searching for explanations beyond the scope of the autonomous analytical techniques musicology and music theory offered me. For if the principal obstacle to dealing with music critically has been its claim to nonrepresentationality, then critical and cultural theories make it possible to challenge not only the more superficial aspects of music (the setting of song texts, the delineation of characters in operas, the references to explicit literary sources in program music) but, more important, its very core: its syntactical procedures and structural conventions. Thus it is at this level that much of my critique is aimed—at the narrative impulses underlying sonata-allegro form and even tonality itself.

6

This is a collection of essays written between 1987 and 1989. Together they set out the beginnings of a feminist criticism of music. Although the essays address a wide range of periods and repertories (from the beginnings of opera in the seventeenth century to Madonna's most recent music videos), they are not packaged together here arbitrarily.

As I have considered the ways music might be opened to feminist critique, I have found it useful to develop a practice of scanning across many historical periods. For to focus exclusively on a single repertory is to risk taking its formulations as natural: its constraints and conventions become limits that cease to be noticeable. It is only, I believe, by continually comparing and contrasting radically different musical discourses that the most significant aspects of each begin to fall into relief. There are, consequently, extensive cross-references among repertories in the essays—Monteverdi's spectacles are intersected with those of heavy metal, Laurie Anderson's narratives with those of the nineteenth-century symphony. However, to thus violate period and genre boundaries does not mean losing sight of the specificity of sociohistorical contexts. On the contrary, such scanning facilitates the reading of repertories against the grain—it is the best way to lay bare the unquestioned assumptions that guarantee each repertory, to identify the most important historical questions.

The first three essays are concerned with examining compositions in the standard canon from a feminist point of view. The first of these, "Constructions of Gender in Monteverdi's Dramatic Music," concerns the emergence of a semiotics of gender in early seventeenth-century opera. Drawing on Foucault's *History of Sexuality* and his work on the rise of modern institutions of control in the seventeenth century, Gramscian models of cultural hegemony and resistance, and Bakhtin's concept of carnival, I explore how power relationships connected with gender and class are inscribed in these pieces. This essay examines the artificial codes Monteverdi devises for distinguishing between male and female characters, but it also traces the crisis in gender representation that occurred almost immediately as a result of unforeseen contradictions in the cultural terms of gender propriety.

"Sexual Politics in Classical Music" deals with how music (even classical music) is involved in creating particular models of libidinal desire and also how the standard schemata of narrative organization that inform both opera and instrumental music are loaded with respect to gender and power. The compositions it examines in particular are Bizet's *Carmen* (which also requires that treatments of race and class be addressed) and Tchaikovsky's Symphony No. 4, for which I introduce questions of gay criticism: does the fact that Tchaikovsky was homosexual have any bearing on his musical narratives?

"Excess and Frame: The Musical Representation of Madwomen" continues the study of gender representation and musical narrative conventions by exploring how madwomen from Monteverdi's lamenting nymph to Lucia and Salome are portrayed. It takes much of the work on the social history of madness by Foucault, Elaine Showalter, Klaus Doerner, and others and demonstrates how music participates in that history. However, the depiction of madness in music often is used to justify the flagrant transgression of musical convention (transgressions that become marks of status in the "antibourgeois" phase of bourgeois art). Thus this examination of musical dementia leads to a reexamination of the treatments of musical deviation by music theorists, especially Schoenberg. "Excess" concludes with a discussion of the work of Diamanda Galas, a contemporary performance artist/composer who takes onto herself the musical signs of the madwoman and uses them aggressively in political pieces designed to protest variously the treatment of AIDS patients and victims of the Greek junta. Galas's work makes it possible to compare the politics of representation versus self-representation. It also serves as a convenient bridge to the second set of essays.

The essays in the second group focus on recent music by women composers who deliberately problematize their sexual identities within their musical discourses: respectively so-called serious composition,[53] postmodern performance art, and popular music. I have concentrated here on new music for a couple of reasons. First, these essays were originally written in response to specific conference invitations, all of which happened to be concerned with examining contemporary issues. And second, the political climate of the 1980s has been more hospitable to participation and experimentation by women artists than any previous moment in music history. For the first time, there exists something like a critical mass of women composers and musicians. Moreover, the theoretical work of feminists in literary and art criticism has cleared a space where women can *choose* to write music that foregrounds their sexual identities without falling prey to essentialist traps and that departs self-consciously from the assumptions of standard musical procedures.

I believe it may be possible to demonstrate that various women composers in history (Hildegard von Bingen, Barbara Strozzi, Clara Schumann, Fanny Mendelssohn) likewise wrote in ways that made a difference within the music itself. Now that the music of these women is becoming available, we are able to begin examining their strategies for the first time. But the essays included in this volume concern only women artists who we can be relatively sure are engaged in the kinds of deconstructive enterprises I discuss.

The first of these, "Getting Down Off the Beanstalk: The Presence of a Woman's Voice in Janika Vandervelde's *Genesis II*," deals with the artistic development of Minnesota composer Janika Vandervelde who began to recognize certain masculinist traits in many of the techniques she had been taught or had absorbed from her lifelong exposure to classical music. Her response was to problematize these procedures in a piece that counterpointed them explicitly against new ways of organizing time. The result was the piece *Genesis II*, which is discussed at length in the essay.

"This Is Not a Story My People Tell: Musical Time and Space According to Laurie Anderson" takes up many of these same issues, but in the context of postmodern performance art. Drawing upon the feminist work on cinema and narrative of Teresa de Lauretis, Mary Ann Doane, and others, this essay focuses on the problem of the female body in performance, on electronic mediation, and on the compositional procedures of two songs: "O Superman" (*United States*) and "Langue d'amour" (*Mister Heartbreak*).

The final essay, "Living to Tell: Madonna's Resurrection of the Fleshly," moves into the realm of popular music. Yet it continues several of the threads already developed in the previous two pieces, including the deconstruction of inherited conventions and the possibility of new modes of organizing musical time. Like the piece on Laurie Anderson, it also deals with issues surrounding the female body, although—needless to say—this question is far more urgent in Madonna's case. Roland Barthes has written of the text as that "uninhibited person who shows his behind to the *Political Father*."[54] And Madonna's cheeky modes of self-representation habitually greet the anxieties so often ascribed to women's bodies by "mooning" them: she flaunts as critique her own unmistakably feminine ending. Thus, the essay also discusses Madonna's music videos, especially the ways in which their visual scenarios interact with her music.

Despite their obvious differences, these four contemporary women musicians—Galas, Vandervelde, Anderson, and Madonna—are similar in that they have inherited the sometimes oppressive conventions examined in the first group of essays. Each is concerned with carving out a niche for herself within the highly resistant medium of music; each is at least intuitively aware of the premises of the tradition; and each strives to rework those premises such that she can tell new and different stories.

In short, they accomplish within the music itself the kinds of deconstructions I present throughout this book in analytical prose. They too are Material Girls who find themselves in Bluebeard's castle, and they too refuse to abide by the house rules. They have entered resolutely into the forbidden chamber with its dark, hidden codes and have transformed it into a carnival—a playground of signifiers—for their own pleasure. And just as they dare to write compositions with feminine endings, so I conclude this collection with their voices.

Chapter 2
Constructions of Gender in Monteverdi's Dramatic Music

One of the great accomplishments of seventeenth-century culture was the development of a vocabulary by means of which dramatic characters and actions could be delineated in music. The techniques for emotional and rhetorical inflection we now take for granted are not, in fact, natural or universal: they were deliberately formulated during this period for purposes of music theater. Monteverdi's descriptions of how he invented the semiotics of madness for *La finta pazza Licori* or of war for the *Combattimento di Tancredi e Clorinda* reveal how very self-consciously he designed methods for "representing" affective states.[1]

The achievements of the *stile rappresentativo* made possible most of the musical forms with which we still live today: not only the dramatic genres of opera, oratorio, and cantata, but also instrumental music, which is dependent on the tonality and semiotic codes born on the seventeenth-century stage. Indeed, we are so immersed in these and other cultural forms of the early modern era that only recently have their original social purposes been examined critically. Studies such as José Antonio Maravall's *Culture of the Baroque*, Jacques Attali's *Noise*, and Lorenzo Bianconi's *Music in the Seventeenth Century* have begun to lay bare the post-Renaissance politics of "representation" and to demonstrate how opera and other public spectacles of the seventeenth century served as sites for struggles over power. For if audiences can be made to believe that what is presented on stage is literally the re-presentation of reality itself, then questions of what gets represented, how, and by whom become vital political concerns to rulers and the ruled alike.[2]

To be sure, the ideological struggles Maravall, Attali, and Bianconi have in mind are those of the public sphere: those of the Counter-Reformation, the disintegrating courts of northern Italy, or the rise of the absolutist state. But the crisis of authority in the seventeenth century was not confined to the realm of princes and popes: it also impinged on the most intimate dimensions of private life. Michel Foucault's *History of Sexuality* marks the seventeenth century as a pivotal moment when the West started to alter radically its attitudes toward and treatment of human erotic behavior. He writes: "Since the end of the sixteenth century, the 'putting into discourse of sex,' far from undergoing a process of restriction, on the contrary has been subjected to a mechanism of increasing incitement."[3] As Foucault goes on to demonstrate, even if such public discourses are intended to control and contain sexuality, the obsession always to talk—or sing—about sex also has the effect of continually stirring libidinal interests. To a greater extent than ever before, gender and sexuality become central concerns of Western culture in the seventeenth century, and the new public arts all develop techniques for arousing and manipulating desire, for "hooking" the spectator. Witness, for example, the brand of tonality that emerges at this time: a sure-fire method for inciting and channeling expectations that easily supplants the less coercive procedures of modality.[4]

In staged "representations" of the social world, the identification of characters as either male or female is fundamental. The seventeenth-century composer writing dramatic music immediately confronted the problem of gender construction—that is, how to depict men and women in the medium of music. The concept of "construction" is important here, for while the sex of an individual is a biological given, gender and sexuality are socially organized: their forms (ranges of proper behaviors, appearances, duties) differ significantly in accordance with time, place, and class.[5]

It may be possible to trace some of the musical signs for "masculinity" or "femininity" that are displayed in opera back into earlier genres such as the madrigal. Erotic desire undeniably ranks among the central themes of Italian madrigals, and vivid musical images simulating longing, frustration, or fulfillment occur in abundance in this repertory. But such musical images of desire need not be marked as gender-specific. Because madrigal texts typically speak from the masculine subject position that is assumed as normative in Western culture, they are usually treated as neutral or undifferentiated with respect to gender. However, there are texts—especially those drawn from Guarini or Tasso—that are understood to be female utterances, and some musical settings of these seem subtly coded as "feminine."[6] Still, the convention of setting texts as mixed-voiced polyphony tends to make the "realistic" representation of gendered individuals a lesser priority in the madrigal than in opera. Music drama provides the incentive for the full-scale entry of gender construction into music. Opera emerges and continues to function as one of the principal discourses within which gender and sexuality are publicly delineated—are at the same time celebrated, contested, and constrained.[7]

Not surprisingly, musical delineations of "the feminine" or "the masculine" in early opera were shaped by attitudes prevalent in the societies in which the composers lived. And those delineations of gender in turn participated in social formation by providing public models of how men are, how women are—much as film, television, and popular music do today. Some of these early gendered types in music have survived along with the attitudes that first gave them voice and are recognized relatively easily by present-day listeners. But many of the ways in which gender is construed in this music are alien to us and can be recovered only if we know something of the historical context within which they were developed. This may seem counterintuitive, since many of us are still inclined to believe in the immutability of gender and sexuality. But recent research is beginning to establish that even certain fundamental concepts concerning sexuality have changed radically since the seventeenth century, making it extremely treacherous for us today to depend on what we might assume to be universal experiences of the transhistorical body.

To give an example, Stephen Greenblatt argues in *Shakespearean Negotiations* that the dynamic energy characteristic of Shakespeare's erotic dialogues is predicated on a belief that was then prevalent even in medicine and science:[8] namely, that for purposes of reproduction, both male and female partners had to be aroused to the point of ejaculation. If the woman was not brought to such a state of ardor that she emitted her "seed," conception was thwarted—thus the emphasis in many sixteenth- and seventeenth-century cultural documents on feminine desire and mutual arousal. Greenblatt suggests that the rapid repartee in Shakespeare's comedies is meant to simulate this all-important "friction to heat." He also notes that when science discovered that feminine arousal served no reproductive purpose, cultural forms silenced not only the *necessity* but finally even the *possibility* of desire in the "normal" female. Greenblatt's discussion would seem to shed light on the erotic friction celebrated in the trio texture so beloved by seventeenth-century composers from Monteverdi through Corelli—trios in which two equal voices rub up against each other, pressing into dissonances that achingly resolve only into yet other knots, reaching satiety only at conclusions. This interactive texture (and its attendant metaphors) is largely displaced in music after the seventeenth century by individualistic, narrative monologues.

Regardless of whether or not they happen to survive, all modes of gender encoding are social constructs rather than universals. As such they warrant historical investigation. The area of research I am describing is vast and would demand many book-length studies to do it justice. This chapter will focus on one issue: the ways gender is organized in early opera with respect to rhetoric and, by extension, to social power.

1

It has long been recognized that rhetorical virtuosity was one of the central concerns of early monody. But rhetoric was cultivated for purposes far more prestigious than the arts in Monteverdi's time. As Gary Tomlinson demonstrates in *Monteverdi and the End of the Renaissance*, sixteenth-century society regarded rhetorical skill as indispensable for effective participation in public affairs: "Behind the humanist exaltation of oratorical persuasion lay a recognition of the passions as dynamic forces directing human thought and action, and a felt need to control and exploit these forces."[9] Given the personal and political power ascribed to rhetorical prowess, it is not surprising that Renaissance humanists sought to regulate who was to have access to such skills, and thus the "woman question" arose in many humanist treatises on behavior and education.[10] Attitudes concerning women and rhetoric were divided. On the one hand, Saint Paul's injunction that women remain silent still informed etiquette: accordingly, Bembo declared that women under no circumstances were to be trained in rhetoric. On the other hand, Castiglione advocated the same humanist education for female as for male children, although he also made it clear that males developed rhetorical skills in order to operate effectively in the public realm, while females were to exercise their abilities in order to enhance their charm in the private sphere.[11]

For rhetoric in the mouth of a woman was understood as a different phenomenon from that issuing from a man. A man skilled in oratory was powerful, effective in imposing his will in society at large. A woman's rhetoric was usually understood as seduction, as a manifestation not of intellectual but of sexual power.[12] So pervasive were the constraints upon feminine utterances in the public sphere that even those few women who exercised political power had to cultivate images that made their speech socially acceptable: Elizabeth became "the Virgin Queen," and Catherine de' Medici identified herself in official iconography as Artemis.[13] In essence, both women had to disavow or elaborately redefine their sexualities in order to secure credibility and voice.

There are many fine musicological studies that analyze the devices used to heighten the texts of characters—male and female—in early music drama. But most do not differentiate according to gender or consider portrayals up against the contemporary social apparatus that would tend to privilege male utterances and to silence women. However, even a cursory survey of the ways the issues of gender, speech, and power intersect in early opera raises many questions about the politics of representation in the early seventeenth century. For despite the fact that aristocratic patrons had extensive control over the subject matter of their entertainments, the works themselves often appear—at least at first glance—to undercut assumed social hierarchies and call into question the authority of patriarchy and nobility. The remainder of this essay examines the ways Monteverdi deals with the rhetorical options available to male and female characters in his operas.

2

More than subsequent operas, *L'Orfeo* appears to reproduce the stable Renaissance world. It includes instances of the old-fashioned musical genres characteristic of court entertainments; its formal structure is organized in terms of self-contained, ultimately static symmetries and palindromes; and its themes are easily recognized as humanist. As we might expect, it also reinscribes, for the most part, traditional hierarchies of authority: mortal women defer to men and the shepherds to their "semigod." Likewise Orfeo submits—although somewhat more ambivalently—to the deities who ultimately ground this imaginary universe. How does rhetoric operate within this stable order?

Orfeo is, of course, the quintessential rhetorician of mythology and of early music drama. His eloquence was able to sway the passions of humans and gods alike. Writing music for such a character was far more difficult than simply asserting that Orfeo had such powers: Monteverdi was faced with the task of actually moving the passions of listeners, or else the representation would have proved hollow. He created two kinds of rhetoric—two discursive practices—for Orfeo, both of which continue to resonate (though in different ways) in subsequent operas.

The first I will call the rhetoric of seduction—a process of artificially arousing expectations and then willfully channeling the desires of listeners. The sexy, arrogant, charismatic Orfeo is best illustrated in his first utterance—the wedding song "Rosa del ciel." There are three sections to this oration, each with a different rhetorical strategy. In the opening section, Orfeo commands that the sun stand still to listen to him as he spins his virtuosic apostrophe out over a single chord (Ex. 1a). Modern listeners and performers are accustomed to similar recitations over sustained bass notes in later *recitativo secco*, and thus the power of Monteverdi's strategy may be lost on us. Monteverdi's contemporaries were used to modal syntax, in which

Example 1a: "Rosa del ciel," section 1. [Note: Examples transcribed from the edition printed in 1615 in Venice.]

Example 1b: Syntactical reduction

the melodic line carried the relevant information and in which the bass usually supported the mode-bearing melodic pitches on a one-to-one basis.[14] Underlying Orfeo's opening strain is one of the most familiar and most predictable progressions for that time: the generating modal line initiates a descent through the G-dorian diapente from the fifth degree to the mediant and is harmonized in the strongest fashion available (Ex. 1b). Yet instead of simply singing that modal line as his melody (as might be the case in a madrigal or a Caccini monody), Orfeo embellishes its first element to an extreme that is almost unbelievable, given the expectations of the day. Listen-

Example 2a: Syntactical reduction (Romanesca)

Example 2b: "Rosa del ciel," section 2

ers (including Apollo—the sun) must wait until he is ready to move on before the syntactical progression may proceed. We are instilled with a longing to hear motion, yet dazzled by the audacity and control with which he stretches out . . . and out . . . his initial appeal.[15]

The second section teases us—repeatedly moving purposefully through the standard Romanesca progression toward the final, g (Ex. 2a). Twice the listener is encouraged to expect the promised resolution, and twice—after tricking us into investing libidinally in hearing that final—Orfeo interrupts the descent on the penultimate pitch (Ex. 2b). What occurs in the rarefied, suspended animation that follows the ruptures is extremely significant. His initial, self-consciously Petrarchian figures ("Fu ben felice il giorno" and "E più felice l'hora" invoke Petrarch's ecstatic sonnet "Benedetto sia 'l giorno, e 'l mese, e l'anno") are sung with the forthright confidence we might expect of the orator who sang the opening section. But when he approaches the source of his happiness—Euridice and her responses to his sighs—his

Example 3a: Reduction

forthrightness is sidetracked by eros. Gradually that moment of rupture on a becomes the pivot to another pitch center that lies deep within his modal ambitus: d. After the second interruption deflects him toward d, he submits himself to this alternate reality—the site where he abandons his G-dorian orientation to join with Euridice—through an elaborate cadential confirmation of d. He thus delivers a different final from the one promised, but he does it so compellingly (and for such agreeably sentimental reasons) that the listener cannot object. We are seduced along with him as he reports this most crucial event through the stammering resimulation in music of his desire-laden frisson.

The third section begins verbally as though it is but the third member of a rhetorical triad (felice, più felice, felicissimo), but its musical setting marks it as a distinctly new realm. It both absorbs the deferred energy of the previously unfulfilled progressions and serves as a final push for cadence. The organizing context remains G-dorian (Ex. 3a), though this becomes clear only with the reestablishment of the Romanesca-based progressions beginning at "Se tanti cori havessi." Instead of moving methodically toward g as in earlier instances, in this section the progression rushes impulsively, exuberantly through the whole cycle (Ex. 3b). Orfeo pauses only once (at "tutti colmi sarieno") and, as he does so, we learn how truly manipulated we are: we hang on his every pitch as though he constructs reality for us—which indeed he does. Once again at the last moment he surrenders his own final (g) for an unexpected, dramatic yet somewhat self-effacing conclusion on d, thus opening the way to Euridice's answer.

The extraordinary difference between modes of rhetoric traditionally available to men and to women is evident in Euridice's reply. As we shall see in the examples of Proserpina and Poppea, it is feasible for female characters to be rhetorically skilled; but it is significant that both of these counterexamples are mature, experienced women. Euridice, however, is an untouched maiden. If her speech were too compelling, her innocence might well come into question (how did she learn to manipulate—or even to express—desire?). The librettist, Striggio, already creates a kind of speaking

Example 3b: "Rosa del ciel," section 3.
*Pitch missing here in the original print. This solution is provided in the Malipiero edition.

void of Euridice, as she begins haltingly with "I cannot say," then tells Orfeo her heart is with him and he must look to himself for her answers.[16]

Monteverdi has the difficult task of creating music for this moment that is lovely yet self-deprecating, that lacks rhetorical force but that charms us all the more for that lack. He uses several rhetorical devices toward that end (Ex. 4a and 4b). First, whereas Orfeo's speech is intensely teleological, Euridice finds it difficult to move directly toward a goal without apologizing. Her very first, forthright move from d″ to a′ is immediately qualified by a move to g#′. She makes her linear descent (a′ to d′) seem erratic by establishing tiny unexpected tonics here and there — on a′, c″, and g′; yet she does finally reach out and match Orfeo's pledge on D. She backs away immediately, however, as if afraid she has been too forward. Her last phrase is even ambivalent with respect to its own final: if d′ is still her final, then she returns to the equivocal species of fourth (d″-a′) for her conclusion and hovers indecisively on the fifth degree. If, however, G-dorian can still be heard as organizing the entire exchange of vows (with Euridice's reply simply elaborating the intimate domain Orfeo established and circumscribed for this purpose), then this conclusion may be heard as lingering shyly on the penultimate second degree to g′, hesitating to state the bottom-line tonic. In any case, this bottom line is cheerfully supplied for her by the chorus, which leaps in with its boisterous "Lasciate i monti" to seal the marriage contract in G major.

I am not suggesting that Monteverdi wrote inferior music for Euridice or that this is what he thought of women. But his musical construction of "maidenhood" is informed by what his audience would expect to hear as the utterance of a young girl.[17] This tiny speech, painstakingly composed out of the available rhetorical devices to produce *anti-* rhetoric, might well have been more difficult to accomplish than the flamboyant oratory of the Orfeo character.

The rhetoric of seduction is also practiced by a female character in *L'Orfeo*: Proserpina, who intercedes with her consort, Plutone, as an advocate for Orfeo's case. The text of her intercession seeks very frankly to arouse and manipulate Plutone's desire, as she recalls her own courtship and the joy of their marriage bed. She even echoes the Petrarch-inspired "fu ben felice il giorno — e più felice — felicissimo" sequence of Orfeo's early vow. The music Monteverdi gives her resembles closely that of Orfeo's wedding song, as she likewise prolongs her recitations dramatically over suspended basses or fuels her arguments through the logic of Romanesca-type progressions. Three circumstances legitimize Proserpina's rhetorical skill: first, she is communicating with her own spouse — a situation in which sexual pleasure is socially condoned; second, her rhetoric is in the service of Orfeo — her manipulation is for a worthy cause; and third, she appeals directly to Plu-

Example 4a: Reduction

Example 4b: "Io non dirò"

tone, whose replies (at once legalistic in that he tends to sing the bass, and yet arbitrary in that his movements are difficult to predict) make it clear that he maintains patriarchal authority. He yields to Proserpina's wishes, though by his own choice and for his own interests. However, despite the fact that this is obviously a patriarchal relationship (and ignoring for the moment the circumstances that cause Proserpina to be in Hades in the first place), what we have in this scene is quite rare: the mutual and explicit acknowledgment in music by a man and a woman of sexual desire and pleasure untainted by a sense of shame or impending punishment.

The other form of rhetoric displayed by Orfeo is the lament: his expressions of pathos following Euridice's two deaths (the end of Act II and most of Act V). Laments are typically performed in traditional societies by women, and they are often highly ritualized rather than personal. Orfeo here unwittingly participates in a female genre—and without the protective shield of ritual. In his erratic outbursts, he frequently seems to lose control of his own speech, and this turns out to be crucial. For if the glory of opera is its ability to give the illusion of depth to characters (i.e., to deliver both verbal text and also an additional dimension that inflects the text affectively), then a great deal depends on who seems to be wielding that second dimension.

When Orfeo is operating as a rhetorician (at the beginning of his wedding song, in his appeal to Caronte in "Possente spirto," etc.), he appears to direct the musical flow himself. But in the laments, it is Monteverdi rather than the orator himself who carefully constructs the signs of Orfeo's temporary insanity—the disorienting fluctuations in modal center, the rapid changes in rate of declamation, the discontinuous melodic lines, and so on. Madness, like gender and sexuality, is socially organized, and definitions of what it means to be mad vary greatly with respect to time, place, class, and especially gender.[18] Orfeo's version of madness is defined precisely in opposition to his former rhetorical prowess. His speech remains affectively heightened, but now the gestures that once persuaded us have become unglued from their sustaining logic. He can no longer assemble those shards and fragments rationally, and the illusion of secure reality his oratory had previously created is literally deconstructed before our ears.

Instead of willfully seducing the audience, Orfeo's involuntary utterances appeal to the *pity* of the listener, all the more because they seem "authentic," that is, not manufactured for purposes of manipulation. It is these anguished outbursts (not his calculated seductions) that move the gods finally to relent, though at considerable cost: in thus having his innermost thoughts exhibited as public spectacle, the figure of Orfeo is rendered vulnerable. The audience itself has auditory mastery over him, as it is permitted to "eavesdrop" on his private grief; likewise the provisional nature of his powers—his dependence on aristocratic liberality—is laid bare. The traditional hierarchy of class authority may be preserved and reinforced, but Orfeo's masculine authority is severely threatened.

If audience members have invested too much in Orfeo's charisma, these sections—brilliant as they are—are bound to provoke discomfort.[19] Catherine Clément argues that in later opera, men who lose control and display their pain are marked as somehow feminine, and they often are subjected to fates similar to those of tragic heroines:

> But now I begin to remember hearing figures of betrayed, wounded men; men who have women's troubles happen to them; men who have the status of Eve, as if they had lost their innate Adam. These men die like heroines; down on the ground they cry and moan, they lament. And like heroines they are surrounded by real men, veritable Adams who have cast them down. They partake of femininity: excluded, marked by some initial strangeness, they are doomed to their undoing.[20]

Orfeo could stand as a prototype of Clément's feminized hero. And her formulation even echoes Apollo's admonition to Orfeo when he descends to rescue his fallen son:

> Why to rage and grief as prey
> do you thus give yourself, o son?
> It is not the counsel
> of a generous heart
> to serve one's own passions;
> by shame and peril
> I see you already threatened,
> wherefore I descend from heaven to assist you.

Iain Fenlon has noted the strangely cool reception of this opera, which modern musicologists regard as one of the great monuments of music history. We know of only two contemporary performances; and when reminiscing later about his accomplishments in the *stile rappresentativo*, Monteverdi usually cited *L'Arianna* rather than *L'Orfeo* as his first great achievement in the new medium.[21] It is improbable that Monteverdi and Striggio stumbled onto this problem inadvertently. Indeed, they seem to have intended from the beginning that Orfeo be sacrificed, one way or another: they had originally concluded the piece in accordance with classical models, in which Orfeo is ripped to shreds by the Bacchantes. That version sets up a stronger resonance with the figures of Christ or Prometheus, as Orfeo becomes the supreme artist whose talents challenge traditional authority and who is punished severely for his insubordination, his violation of "natural" class boundaries (this at a time when Monteverdi was feeling unappreciated by his patrons). For whatever reasons, the patrons apparently demanded the substitution of a less inflammatory *lieto fine* in which Orfeo is rescued and brought up into the heavens by Apollo. It is this ending that is preserved in surviving musical sources.

Yet even without the expurgated ending featuring the Bacchantes, the mere fact that Orfeo's psyche is thus publicly displayed already strips him of discursive agency and dismembers him. The opera delivers a host of mixed messages: Is Orfeo a hero or a transgressor? virile or effeminate? rational or mad? Along with the other ways of accounting for the lesser success of this opera, I would add that Monteverdi's depiction of Orfeo may well have precipitated a crisis in gender representation for the musical stage—a crisis that perhaps influenced both its own reception and also subsequent operatic conventions. While sexuality and madness remain favorite themes of music drama, they prove to be extremely problematic when enacted by male characters. The "mistake" was rarely repeated, for in operas by Monteverdi and others after *L'Orfeo* (with the intriguing exceptions of the feminized males analyzed by Clément), both forms of rhetoric—seduction and lament—come to be practiced almost exclusively by female characters.[22]

3

The principal Monteverdian wielder of the rhetoric of seduction after Orfeo is the courtesan Poppea, who operates outside both the humanist ethical code that grounded Orfeo and the patriarchal context that legitimized Proserpina. Much has been written about the courtesans of Renaissance Venice and their rhetorical prowess. For instance, Thomas Coryat, an English traveler, wrote in 1608: "Also, thou wilt find the Venetian Courtezan . . . a good Rhetorician, and a most elegant discourser, so that if she cannot move thee with all these aforesaid delights, she will assay thy constancy with a Rhetoricall tongue."[23] Like Woody Allen's "Whore from MENSA," Venetian courtesans were often highly educated so that they could converse intelligently with the elite men who frequented them. It is largely from their ranks that women poets and intellectuals emerged. They were also, of course, skilled in the erotic arts of seduction, so as to be able to sustain two essential illusions: first, that they really meant what they said and did with their clients (even though they performed their services for hire); and, second, that they acted upon their poor passive male victims, who could then disavow responsibility for their erotic adventures (even though it was the men who sought out such women and who sustained these institutions of high-class prostitution).

The traditional repositories of patriarchal authority in *L'incoronazione di Poppea*—the husband, Ottone; the head of state, Nerone; the philosopher,

Seneca—are all depicted as profoundly passive and impotent. Seneca habitually reverts to silly madrigalisms, which destroy the rhetorical effect of most of his statements.[24] Each of Ottone's lines droops flaccidly to its tonic, and Nerone's utterances are almost all reactive—we witness the volatile flux of his emotions as the direct cause-and-effect results of Poppea's manipulation. Only Poppea seems capable of sustained manipulation, and, significantly, many of her speeches use precisely the same devices as did Orfeo's wedding song. The major difference is, however, that we are also given glimpses of the "real" Poppea who pulls the strings so skillfully, so cynically. For instance, immediately after her passionate farewells to Nerone in the first act, we witness her throw off the mask of sincerity and triumphantly gloat over how successfully she has ensnared him. The illusion of "authenticity" (always to some extent manufactured in rhetorical situations) is here unambiguously revealed as contrived deception.

Tomlinson argues in *Monteverdi and the End of the Renaissance* that by this moment in the seventeenth century, humanist rhetoric had lost its authority and had gradually been replaced by the fetishized imagery of Marino and his followers. I am suggesting that as the potency of humanist discourse evaporated, so did crucial assumptions concerning the potency of patriarchy, male domination, and masculine sexuality. The nadir of this decline is dramatized in *L'incoronazione di Poppea*, as Poppea usurps and perverts to her own ends the tools of patriarchal persuasion, making pathetic "victims" of these last refugees of humanism.

Not only is the role of seductive orator often reassigned to female characters in later opera, but similarly most of the lamenters celebrated in dramatic works after *L'Orfeo* (Arianna, Penelope, and Ottavia) are female: all women who have been betrayed by treacherous, absent, or ineffectual male authority and who express their righteous indignation in tirades as blistering as any present-day feminist critique. In contrast to Orfeo's apparent delirium, these women state their appeals in carefully organized speeches that enumerate grievances with the most self-possessed rhetorical skill. As they condemn the male authority that would make them submit to silence, their eloquence is doubly electrifying: the fact that they speak their cases in defiance of the traditional prohibition is as powerful as the arguments themselves.[25]

4

What happened in the course of the early seventeenth century that permitted these kinds of reversals in the representation of gender? How is it that the rhetorical skill so jealously guarded as a male prerogative in the Renaissance

came to be put almost exclusively into the mouths of women in the pre-
dominantly masculine realm of opera? The answers are as complex and contradictory as the tangle of competing ideologies, cultural forms, and social
institutions within which these compositions took shape.

First, the range of behaviors considered appropriate to men began to alter
considerably in the seventeenth century. From this moment on in Western
history, men are encouraged to stifle their feelings, while women are expected to indulge in emotional expression.[26] Both the extravagant sensuality and the extravagant anguish exhibited by Orfeo come to be regarded as
"effeminate."[27] Indeed, I have argued above that even within *L'Orfeo* the
very success of the hero's rhetoric is also his undoing, for the more Monteverdi's representational genius convinces us that we witness Orfeo's actual
agony or erotic transport, the less tenable we find that character's rhetorical
and masculine authority. Such symptoms of vulnerability are increasingly
projected onto women—both on and off the stage. Thus surrendering rhetorical flair to women may be seen as a way of redefining the spectacle's
proper object. In subsequent operas, it is constructions of *feminine* sensuality
and suffering that are exhibited—for the pleasure of the patriarchal gaze and
ear.[28]

Second, the extensive soliloquies by abandoned women and the seduction tactics of Poppea offer what are supposed to be insights into the inner
workings of the female mind. They purport to reveal without mediation
what women are really like: not docile like Euridice, but insubordinate or
threatening unless they can be reconciled (like Penelope) with a strong male
authority. These characterizations are motivated in part by the increasing
social power of women at that time. But they also can be construed as playing on the male fear of women so prevalent in the seventeenth century. For
this was a time when more women than ever were managing to emerge into
the musical profession (Monteverdi had women colleagues at the Gonzaga
court who made ten times his salary)[29] and when images of female eroticism
proliferated in music.[30] It was also, however, a time when some thought
that castrati enacted women better than women themselves,[31] and when
thousands of women were being executed as witches. In this paranoid
world, in which women were often selected as scapegoats for the crumbling
social order, such "powerful" constructions could also serve to justify patriarchal backlash. As a case in point, Nino Pirrotta argues that Monteverdi's audience would have known about Poppea's ultimate fate—that Nero
later murdered the pregnant Poppea by kicking her in the stomach—and
could thus have supplied for themselves the missing patriarchal retribution
to her apparent triumph at the conclusion of *L'incoronazione di Poppea*.[32]

But these constructions of powerful women may also be understood as potentially liberatory, for the shift in gender representation was bound up with the more general crisis in all forms of authority—political, economic, religious, and philosophical—during the first half of the seventeenth century.[33] Significantly, composers and librettists grant the right to launch attacks on traditional authority not only to women characters, but also to servants, who complain constantly about class oppression. Although such grievances are blunted somewhat by being put into the mouths of women and grotesque comic characters, these moments of resistance may reveal— and yet conceal—more general dissatisfaction with powerful social institutions: critiques are safer, after all, when displaced onto marginalized Others.[34]

Displaced or not, complaints from the disenfranchised against traditional authority *were* registered in this public forum with surprising candor. And, indeed, the reforms at the end of the century served to purge opera of precisely these carnivalesque "impurities": to guarantee consistency of style, but also to silence the troublesome voices from the margins.[35] Patriarchy and the nobility returned with a vengeance in later court operas: musical and dramatic structures became formulaic; impulsive tonality was domesticated and even "naturalized" through Enlightenment music theory; the comedians were quarantined; and victimized female characters such as Scarlatti's Griselda were trotted out to sing hymns of faith to male authority.

However, between *L'Orfeo* and *La Griselda*, there existed an anomalous moment in culture when power relationships associated with gender and rhetoric were oddly reconfigured. If, as Maravall, Attali, and Bianconi indicate, operatic spectacles are bound up with the reproduction of aristocratic—and, I would add, patriarchal—interests, they may not actually have served their masters in as monolithic a way as we might expect. Indeed, in Venice, where a degree of free enterprise tempered the administered culture of the courts, it seems actually to have been in the interest of some of the elite to underwrite spectacles that displayed a more varied, more liberal social network.

For instance, Gianfrancesco Busenello, the librettist of *L'incoronazione di Poppea*, was a member of the Accademia degli Incogniti. Bianconi describes this group as "a club of libertine intellectuals whose apparent praise of deceit in reality cloaks *nothing but* an underlying attitude of bitter philosophical scepticism, intolerant of all preconstituted authority (political, moral, rational, religious). . . . Only the pessimistic scepticism and subtle immoralism of the Incogniti can explain the fanciful yet disenchanted mockery of certain scenes of this opera" (my emphasis).[36] The mere fact that some patrons and artists subscribed to the tenets of or even belonged to groups such as the

Accademia degli Incogniti indicates that Venetian social power was organized along substantially different lines from those prevailing in earlier
Mantua, Rome, or in later Naples. Monteverdi's Venetian operas quite
clearly testify to a more complicated web of interests than we have thus far
been able to explain. We need to know a good deal more about what is
"cloaked" by this "underlying attitude of bitter philosophical scepticism"
and intolerance "of all preconstituted authority."[37]

For a variety of reasons, traditional hierarchies of authority were subjected to extraordinary questioning during this period of doubt and shifting
alliances. In the name of "entertainment," many contradictory models of
power slipped by as guileless representations of the world itself—at least until the art police clamped down to dictate what was and was not to be heard
on the stage. And much of this crisis in power was played out dramatically
in terms of gender, which thus became one of the principal sites of contestation in the new cultural media. If we are to make sense of early opera—its
achievements and its discontents—we must begin to unravel that tangle of
gender, rhetoric, and power that first found its voice in the musical conventions of the *stile rappresentativo*.

Chapter 3
Sexual Politics in Classical Music

Sexuality is one of the most intensely pleasurable and yet troubling aspects of human experience. It is at the same time the most personal of realms and also the realm most carefully constrained by social order. It is the terrain where the imperatives of biological survival meet the treasured belief that we humans differ from animals by virtue of our ability to transcend demands of the body. One of the functions of social discursive practices (law, religion, art) is to moderate that gap, to translate into terms of culture the exigencies of the physical.[1]

Literature and visual art are almost always concerned (at least in part) with the organization of sexuality, the construction of gender, the arousal and channeling of desire. So is music, except that music may perform these functions even more effectively than other media. Since few listeners know how to explain how it creates its effects, music gives the illusion of operating independently of cultural mediation. It is often received (and not only by the musically untutored) as a mysterious medium within which we seem to encounter our "own" most private feelings.[2] Thus music is able to contribute heavily (if surreptitiously) to the shaping of individual identities: along with other influential media such as film, music teaches us how to experience our own emotions, our own desires, and even (especially in dance) our own bodies. For better or for worse, it socializes us.

This way of understanding music is commonplace in the area of popular music production and reception. Both musicians and listeners know that one of the principal stakes in this music is the public construction of gender and sexuality. Whether Prince, Madonna, The Smiths, Tracy Chapman, or Guns N' Roses, most pop artists strive to create images that challenge traditional definitions of "masculinity" and "femininity," to present models of sexuality that range from liberatory, to polymorphously perverse, to mutually supportive, to overtly misogynist and violent.[3] The critical controversies that greet each new development demonstrate how very significant this music is—not simply as leisure entertainment, but as a site in which fundamental aspects of social formation are contested and negotiated.[4]

Such critical debates are almost entirely absent from traditional musicology. The standard explanation would be that while popular music admittedly addresses issues such as sexuality, classical music (the standard concert repertory of the eighteenth and nineteenth centuries) is concerned exclusively with loftier matters. Indeed, it is precisely this difference that many devotees of classical music would point to as proof that their preferences are morally superior to those of the pop music fan: their music is not contaminated by the libidinal—or even the social.

I will be arguing in this chapter that classical music—no less than pop—is bound up with issues of gender construction and the channeling of desire. Like its popular counterpart, classical music presents a wide range of competing images and models of sexuality, some of which seem to reinscribe faithfully the often patriarchal and homophobic norms of the cultures in which they originated, and some of which resist or call those norms into question. If musicology took its subject matter as seriously as many pop critics take theirs, a central task would be explaining how mere pitches can be made to "represent" gender or to manipulate desire—as well as ascertaining just *whose* versions of gender or desire thereby get reproduced and transmitted.

Our academic music disciplines tend, however, to avoid questions of signification altogether, to deny the presence even of expressive (let alone erotic) components in music. This denial has a complex cultural history that reaches far beyond the domain of music theory and musicology. As feminist scholarship in every discipline is beginning to demonstrate, the tendency to deny the body and to identify with pure mind underlies virtually every aspect of patriarchal Western culture.[5] Thus, it is not surprising to find that this fundamental mind/body split likewise informs classical music as well as its institutions.[6] Consequently, I will be examining not only particular musical constructions of gender and desire, but also the ways in which the denial of the erotic both operates within specific compositions and also influences their traditional receptions.

I will begin my critique with an opera—Georges Bizet's *Carmen* (1875)—for at least it is reasonably clear in texted and dramatic music that women and men are being depicted, that gender is understood explicitly by composer and listener alike to be an issue. Not surprisingly, I will pay considerable attention to the semiotic constructions of various characters as they are revealed in particular musical numbers. But I will ultimately be more interested in the ways in which inherited conventions of musical representation and formal paradigms predispose this opera to particular narrative treatments of gender and sexuality.

However, the strategy of relying only on texted music is always vulnerable to the charge that one is finally dealing only with words (which we already knew were socially contaminated) and that music itself—in particular the "Absolute Music" of the classical symphonic repertory—remains essentially pure, ineffable, and emphatically not concerned with such mundane issues. Indeed, music theory classes rarely deal with texted music at all; or, if they do, they pointedly ignore the words or dramatic situations, precisely because it is only in the absence of words that music can really be examined "on its own terms."[7] I am especially concerned with deconstructing the Master Narrative of "Absolute Music," with removing that final fig leaf for open critical discussion, for I believe that it is this denial of meaning in the instrumental repertory that has systematically blocked any attempt at feminist or any other sort of socially grounded criticism. Therefore, in the second part of the chapter, I will take the constructions analyzed in *Carmen* back to the rarefied, privileged realm of nineteenth-century instrumental music for a discussion of Tchaikovsky's Fourth Symphony (1877).

As is the case in literature and the visual arts, constructions of gender and sexuality in music vary widely from time to time, from place to place. Several recent studies have begun to chart the radical swings of the cultural pendulum with respect to the social organization of feminine and masculine sexuality within the relatively limited context of the European nineteenth century.[8] There are, in other words, no universals to be sought, although usually some correlation exists among the images and attitudes toward sexuality manifested in the various arts at a given time.

Both of the pieces I will deal with in this chapter are from the mid-1870s, and they share many of the assumptions critics find in literature and painting from that historical moment. Like much late nineteenth-century art, this music is rife with portraits of hapless men who are seduced from their transcendental quest by feminine sensuality, of heroic victims who must either rise to the occasion and destroy—or else *be* destroyed.

But unlike many of the works literary or art critics exhume for examination, neither *Carmen* nor Tchaikovsky's Fourth is simply an artifact from the past. *Carmen*, for instance, has inspired a large number of films throughout the history of cinema, each reworking the opera in terms of the sexual politics and cinematic conventions of the day.[9] To the extent that these pieces still hold places of honor in our classical Top 40 and even infiltrate popular culture, they continue to influence our notions of social organization even today.

1

Bizet's opera is based on Prosper Mérimée's novella *Carmen*, which had been a scandalous success some thirty years earlier. This subject seems to have been suggested to the librettists, Meilhac and Halévy, by Bizet himself; and it was he who pushed the opera through to completion, despite the severe reservations of the managerial staff of the Opéra-Comique for which it was designed. Moreover, Bizet had to struggle to find a singer willing to perform the part (he finally succeeded when he located a singer who was not acquainted with the novella), and he had to fight with directors who were reluctant to carry out his unprecedented "realist" ending in which the lead female character is murdered on stage. This was largely Bizet's project, and he had to suffer the consequences when the opera was (predictably enough) rejected as immoral by its first audiences.[10]

The opera diverges from the novella in several important respects, the most important of which is its extensive restructuring of Mérimée's original narrative strategy. The story in the novella is told by a scholar who almost succumbs to Carmen's charms himself, but who ends up merely serving as an unwitting witness to José's downfall, which he relates in this document some time after the fact. In the final section of the novella (following Carmen's death and José's execution), the narrator attempts to purge himself of Carmen's influence by writing an "objective" ethnographic taxonomy of gypsies, in which he reduces these people—especially the women—to the status of near animals. In the opera, the narrator is eliminated, and José's story—not relayed secondhand as in Mérimée, but enacted before the audience's very eyes—makes up the entire libretto.

Moreover, the novella is structured around a solitary female character, Carmen, who is sought after by two principal men—Don José and the "objective," scholarly narrator—in addition to Carmen's husband and the bullfighter. By contrast, the opera is organized in terms of the traditional Western dichotomy between proper and improper constructions of female sexuality, between the virgin and the whore. This alteration of the basic structural tensions of the story seems partly motivated by the need to simplify: Mérimée's multiple narratives are not feasible on the stage. The authors justified the change by claiming that the family audience of the Opéra-Comique required a positive female figure to stand in binary opposition to Carmen. And it may be that music operates more easily, more "naturally," when arranged according to such dichotomous structures. But whatever the explanation, this shift influences the sexual politics of the opera profoundly.[11]

The character of Micaëla, Don José's childhood sweetheart, represents the stereotypical Angel in the House: the sexless, submissive ideal of the bourgeoisie.[12] Her signs of affection are carefully defined in terms of José's mother, for whom she is but the passive conduit of a maternal kiss. Her musical discourse accordingly is simple, lyrical, sweet: as she sings to José in their initial encounter, her melody lines are diatonic (never deviating into insinuating inflections), her rhythms innocent of physicality. Had José obeyed his mother's wishes and married Micaëla, he would never have experienced the contamination of sexual passion.

The energy in the opera is, of course, located in the musical characterization of Carmen herself: she is the dissonant Other who is necessary for the motivation and sustaining of the plot. Bizet grounds Carmen's music in the physical impulses of exotic, pseudogypsy dance.[13] Significantly, her principal numbers are referred to neither by their texts nor by conventional operatic designation (e.g., aria or duet), but by their dance-type designations: "Habañera" (a Cuban genre from Havana) and "Seguidilla." Her rhythms indicate that she is very much aware of her body. In fact, before she even begins to sing, her instrumental vamp sets a pattern that engages the lower body, demanding hip swings in response.[14] Moreover, these rhythms are so contagious that they make José—and the listener—aware both of her body and also (worse yet) of their own bodies. She arouses desire; and because she apparently has the power to deliver or withhold gratification of the desires she instills, she is immediately marked as a potential victimizer.

Now there ought to be nothing wrong with celebrations of the body and the erotic. But, again, one of the principal claims to supremacy in European classical music (and other forms of high culture) is that it transcends the body, that it is concerned with the nobler domains of imagination and even metaphysics.[15] Thus to have the body "thrust" at us (by Bizet) in a piece of music is to encounter the figure of the temptress in the midst of what ought to have been a pure Platonic field.

Carmen's music is further marked by its chromatic excesses. Her melodic lines tease and taunt, forcing the attention to dwell on the moment—on the erogenous zones of her inflected melodies. In her opening "Habañera," for instance, her descent by half-steps through the tetrachord d-to-a is arranged so that we grasp immediately the outline she implies (and thus are compelled to desire the suggested outcome); but the way she moves through that descent alternately coaxes and frustrates (Ex. 1). What is set up as the normative rhythmic motion from d to c# is halted on c-natural—a tentative pitch with a strong gravitational urge to move onward—where she plays

Example 1: Carmen, "Habañera" mm. 1-8

with our expectations not only by lingering but also by reciting in irregular triplets that strain against the beat. She rubs our noses in this rather funky chromatic inflection to make sure we get it.[16] The b-natural that follows is quick and encourages us to think she will slide immediately now to the expected goal; but the b♭, which ought to have been an inconsequential passing-note on a weak pulse, is given an insinuating nudge by the declamation of the word "*re*-belle." While there is never any question of her tonal or melodic orientation in this phrase, her erratic means of descending through the tetrachord (and, subsequently, the remainder of the scale—sometimes granting the tonic, but often withholding it sadistically at the last instant before implied gratification) reveals her as a "master" of seductive rhetoric. She knows how to hook and manipulate desire. In her musical discourse she is slippery, unpredictable, maddening: hers is the music we remember from the opera. She becomes José's obsession—and likewise the listener's.

However, it is not Carmen but rather Don José who is the central character of this moral fable: it is *his* story that organizes the narrative, *his* fate that hangs in the balance between the Good Woman and the Bad. And his musical discourse is that of the "universal" tongue of Western classical music. In marked contrast to Carmen's music, it is devoted to lofty sentiments rather than to the body. His melodies unfold solemnly, albeit with what Carl Dahlhaus characterizes as "lyric urgency."[17] José is a bourgeois visionary suggesting horizons beyond the present moment, contingent on the indefinite postponement of gratification. Ostensibly his music is transcendental.

But, in fact, José's music is no less invested libidinally than Carmen's. In his "Flower Song," José sings of his stay in prison and of how he would sniff Carmen's flower in order to inspire his fantasies. After a lovely lyric opening, he begins to construct musical images of fevered longing and dread, as he imagines Carmen as demon and then as object of desire. On the words "un seul désir, un seul espoir" (a single desire, a single hope), he sets up a pitch-ceiling that constricts his melodic line (thus recreating in sound the experience of frustration), which he penetrates on "te revoir, ô Carmen" (Ex. 2a). Following this explosive moment, his energy gradually seems to subside almost to a kind of whimpering. But as he sings of submitting himself masochistically to her power ("Et j'étais une chose à toi"), he rises again—this time through an unaccompanied scale—and attains climax on $b^\flat$, the highest, most vulnerable pitch in the aria (Ex. 2b). Strangely, he sings to Carmen of his masturbatory practices right at the moment when she expects them to make love. He reconverts her back into a distanced object of desire even in her presence; he manages to "transcend" only by so doing (though the treacherous chromatic harmonization of his leading tone in mm. 44-45 indicates the extent to which Carmen has undermined his diatonic confidence: her influence almost prevents this hard-won cadence at the last moment). Unlike the dialogues between Escamillo (the Toreador) and Carmen, in which genuine interaction appears to take place, José's moment of greatest passion is his self-absorbed monologue, his internalized metaphysical narrative that has no room for another human voice.

What makes the opera fundamentally a paranoid fantasy is that Carmen's music (constructed by Bizet—there is no woman's voice in this piece) is made to be undeniably more powerful, more alluring than José's well-behaved discourse of masculine European classical music (also, of course, constructed by Bizet). The opera demonstrates vividly how impotent the sublime experience of transcendence is in the face of the lowest common dominatrix. Infuriatingly, the male-constructed Carmen refuses to be contained in accordance with José's fantasies; she says "no" to his "lyric urgency," talks back, makes sexual demands, takes other lovers. She continually resists his attempts at possessing her, manipulates him pitilessly, and even persuades him to desert the army, to become an outlaw for her sake.

Example 2a: Carmen, "Flower Song," mm. 28–34

She is portrayed as monstrous, José as a dangerously weak link in the patri-archal chain of command.

The opera has a happy ending, however, for the powers of transcendence finally save the day from such intolerable insubordination. Just as the local population and the gypsies are framed by the occupying army of which José is a member, so the opera itself is framed by his discourse of classical music. The opening chorus presents the soldiers singing in the style of bored Pari-sian *flâneurs*, amusing themselves by observing and commenting on the

Example 2b: "Flower Song," mm. 38–46

spectacle of "these droll people." As listeners, we are drawn into the privileged point of view of these colonizers and are positioned thus throughout
the opera, as we too are offered the titillating display of flashy gypsy music
as a kind of sideshow. The sideshow threatens to become too seductive for
the good of José (or for the bourgeois listener), however, and the framing
device has to be exerted: despite the undeniably greater popular appeal of
the gypsy dances, the musical conventions regulating structure turn out to
reside on the side of the unfortunate white, male, high-art "victim," whose
duty it is finally to purge all traces of the exotic and chromatic, to restore
social and musical order *at any cost.*

Closure is a far more absolute condition in classical music than in most
other arts. Literary narratives, for instance, often play with degrees of closure. In Mérimée's original novella, Carmen's death is described to the nar-

rator as an event in the past. After the report of her death three-quarters of the way through the novella, the remainder comments on and unravels the closure that her death would seem to have established. Moreover, the reader is never given the illusion of being present at the murder: those irretrievable events are multiply mediated through Don José's self-interested confession and the narrator's hysterical, unreliable transmission to the reader.

By contrast, in most tonal music of the eighteenth and nineteenth centuries, nothing less will suffice for purposes of concluding pieces than complete resolution onto the triad. Equivocal endings, not coincidentally, are few and far between. Yet the fact that most listeners do not know how to account for the overwhelming push for closure they experience in this music means that it often seems like a force of nature rather than a human ideological construct. In order to take fullest advantage of this musical demand for closure, Bizet radically reconfigured for his opera the presentation of Carmen's death: the spectator witnesses the fatal event firsthand — apparently without mediation and as though it is inexorable. Moreover, there is no aftermath to soften its finality.

In the concluding scene outside the bullring, José insists that Carmen submit to his wishes while she continues to pull away. Unlike earlier scenes in which Bizet freely indulged in Carmen's sexy music, this scene is informed by the necessity of tonal closure. As José pleads with Carmen to give in, the harmonic bassline turns into a maddeningly slippery chromatic floor. Not only José but also the listener (who is, knowingly or not, trained in terms of classical tonal discourse through exposure to film scores and television) longs for this flood of chromaticism to be stopped, for stability to be reestablished — even though we know that the triumph of tonal closure means the violent murder of Carmen. Bizet's musical strategies, in other words, set up almost unbearable tensions that cause the listener not only to accept Carmen's death as "inevitable," but actually to *desire* it. At the same moment that the crowd inside the bullring cheers in response to Escamillo's victory over the bull, we outside the ring witness and celebrate victory over an even more treacherous form of beast. Chromatic slippage (carefully defined throughout the opera as "the feminine") is purged once and for all from the discourse as though by natural necessity. The major triad prevails.[18]

Yet the musical materials that articulate this attempt at tonal closure belong not to José, but to his rival. Just before he murders Carmen, José explains that he cannot let her go because she would laugh at him in the arms of Escamillo. But it is Escamillo's signature "Toreador Song" that greets José at his moment of triumph, and the treacherous, exotic motive associated with Carmen throughout the opera punctuates his confession. For José himself has no tune—he is identified solely through his subjective passion, his "lyric urgency." And we get a last pathetic glimmer of José's characteristic discourse as he proclaims his love for Carmen once more just before the final triad.

Moreover, while Bizet does end the opera with a major triad (the traditional sign not only of finality, but also of "happy ending"), he chooses, from the standpoint of tonal convention, the *wrong* triad. For the concluding key of F# (with all its aggressive, spiky sharps) is not the key from which this opera began its trek, and thus it cannot unambiguously establish rational narrative closure. To be sure, it does halt the chromaticism, and the implication is that this is (at least temporarily) all that matters. But conventional closure is incommensurate with the contradictions of this narrative: José's encounter with Carmen may have made the narrative we have witnessed feasible, but it also apparently resists as inadequate any nonviolent resolution. Therefore, the opera terminates with a gesture that provides satisfaction on some levels (the resolution of dissonance, the purging of chromaticism, the return to diatonicism), while it also betrays its essential impotence (the final key is arbitrary, and the thematic terrain belongs to the droll, exotic people who were supposed to remain in their place as a sideshow).[19]

The opera can, of course, be interpreted in a variety of ways, and some alternative readings will be suggested below. But it seems clear that Bizet articulates in *Carmen* a whole range of late nineteenth-century symptoms of cultural paranoia. Several issues other than gender are engaged and brought to violent—if equivocal—closure in the opera, most notably the perceived "threats" of the racial Other and of popular culture. For one of the opera's central themes involves the necessity for white bourgeois codes of behavior (as exemplified by Micaëla) to reign supreme in the face of the apparently more permissive, more sinister lifestyles of the "darker races."

Nineteenth-century Europeans habitually projected onto racial Others the erotic qualities they denied themselves. The racial Other became a favorite "feminine" zone within the narratives of European colonizers; and depending on the circumstances of the narrative, the Other was viewed with desire, envy, contempt, or fear.[20] *Carmen* participates fully in this brand of exoticism, as do a remarkable number of Bizet's other compositions: he seemed to have been able to rise to his creative heights principally when provided with exotic subject matter.[21] He usually expended little effort in trying to ascertain what the music of the ethnic group in question actually sounded like: the identity of the group was not so important as the fact that it was exotic with respect to Europe. Consequently, there is a significant blurring of racial Others throughout the opera, with gypsies portrayed in part through the musical discourse of Cuba (as in the "Habañera"). And Nietzsche reveals how unimportant the specific ethnic setting of *Carmen* was to him as a sophisticated consumer of exoticism. He understood the opera as a whole as having a peculiar "African" aura:

> This music [of *Carmen*] is cheerful, but not in a French or German way. Its cheerfulness is African; fate hangs over it; its happiness is brief, sudden, without pardon. I envy Bizet for having had the courage for this sensibility which had hitherto had no language in the cultivated music of Europe—for this more southern, brown, burnt sensibility. —How the yellow afternoons of its happiness do us good! We look into the distance as we listen: did we ever find the sea smoother?—And how soothingly the Moorish dance speaks to us? How even our insatiability for once gets to know satiety in this lascivious melancholy![22]

The question arises: Can Bizet's subaltern speak?[23] Or does she serve only as a function of exoticism? Dahlhaus has written: "As an opera heroine, Carmen is characterized basically by a negative trait: she is *incapable* of attaining lyric urgency. Carmen can parody lyricism, as in her duet with Don José, but she cannot make it her own" (my emphasis).[24] It is indisputable that there is no actual gypsy present in this music, that Carmen can only speak in accordance with Bizet's design. Yet even within the internal logic of Bizet's opera, it does not seem that Carmen is so much "incapable" of José's discourse as that she has no interest in adopting it, except occasionally for strategic purposes. Dahlhaus's observation not only betrays an ethnocentric assumption that all human subjects aspire to José's ejaculatory "lyric urgency," but it also overlooks an important feature of Bizet's characterization of Carmen.

For part of Carmen's threat is in her ability to wield a variety of musical discourses: she resists being tied down to unitary identity.[25] Her principal musical motif (first heard at the end of the overture and subsequently for most of her dramatic entrances) is made up of the illicit augmented-second interval that had long been the musical sign for the Jew, the Arab, the all-purpose racial Other; this is the motif that finally is forcibly expunged by the final triad of the opera. Moreover, Carmen knows how to seduce José by manipulating his own privileged language: in the "Seguidilla" section, she dictates to him the tune with which he first confesses his passion. And finally, it is Carmen's lower-class pop music (actually the fashionable stuff of the contemporary Parisian cabaret scene rather than genuine gypsy music) that seduces him repeatedly into betraying his superior, transcendental, classical music discourse—with disastrous consequences for everyone concerned.

Thus it is not simply Carmen's sexuality that is at stake in the opera, but also her *discursive* promiscuity. She is one of those "droll people" of the exotic sideshow who are redefined as sinister as soon as they resist containment or demonstrate too well that they can mimic the dominant discourse. And while she displays fluency within José's high art language, she persists in practicing the vernacular, demonstrating that she assigns no particular prestige to his modes of communication. Like her erotic power, her ethnic exoticism and her pop culture songs are seen as grounded in the body, as alluring yet treacherous, as feminine *and effeminizing* to those like José who fall prey to them. Consequently, even though José belongs to the occupying army and to elite culture, it is apparently the lure of the colonial and her pop music that victimizes *him*, that requires that *he* resort to violence in order to defend himself.

This defensive slippage among the "feminine," the racial Other, and popular culture remains prevalent well into the twentieth century and frequently informs modernist attacks on pop music, such as Adorno's otherwise incomprehensible ravings about jazz—the jungle music that engages the body, causing formerly civilized individuals to wallow in self-abasing, masochistic ecstasy, celebrating their own castrations:

> The aim of jazz is the mechanical reproduction of a regressive moment, a castration symbolism. "Give up your masculinity, let yourself be castrated," the eunuchlike sound of the jazz band both mocks and proclaims, "and you will be rewarded, accepted into a fraternity which shares the mystery of impotence with you, a mystery revealed at the moment of the initiation rite."[26]

In *Carmen* and Adorno's jazz criticism, gender, race, and class identity get mapped upon each other, and they seem to become the same threatening issue. Of course, race, gender, and class are *not* the same, and it is crucial that they not be confused. However, the critic must be sensitive to the ways in which traditional Western culture has conflated them and to what ends.

I want to stress once again that *Carmen* is a male—rather than a female— fantasy: a male fantasy, moreover, that was especially characteristic of a particular moment in European history. Even though the figure of Carmen is given extraordinary power within her position in the opera, the conventions of gender and ethnic representation and the narrative schema Bizet draws upon conspire to demand her murder.[27] Yet *Carmen* must not be dismissed as a lesson in simple, straightforward misogyny or racism. A piece that has exerted so strong an influence on subsequent culture cannot be dismissed quite so perfunctorily.

It is important to notice, for instance, that the protagonist Don José is not satisfactorily aligned with patriarchy. Even though *Carmen* ultimately delivers the horrible bottom line of male (white, bourgeois) domination, the opera would not, in fact, work if it were not playing into some of the most agonizing contradictions of Western culture. José (along with the spectators for whose pleasure the piece is designed) would not become embroiled in this mess if he were not experiencing considerable discontent with what ordered, rational patriarchal culture offers him: control over others if (but only if) he repudiates his own body and feelings. As he ventures further and further from the clear-cut binary oppositions of masculine/feminine prescribed as social norms, he experiences that which had always been denied him: pleasure, intense emotional bonding with a woman—indeed, his own sexuality.

Viewed in this way, the opera becomes a bitter critique of European patriarchal forms of gender construction. For the José who is in love with Carmen (despite his persistent cowardice) is infinitely preferable to the pasteboard soldier Micaëla encounters at the beginning. Yet the person he tries to become has no place in the social world he inhabits. Unable to endure freedom as Carmen defines it, he lunges to reimpose control, thus reproducing the very modes of behavior he had sought to escape. In fear and desperation, he attempts to retreat to the black-and-white security of patriarchy; in killing Carmen, he also severely mutilates himself. He also ultimately bungles his realignment with patriarchy as he manages to reach closure only in a key other than the one demanded by convention. Yet he does, still and all, *kill* Carmen; and even if we manage to interpret the text in a way that is reasonably sympathetic with José's ordeal, this fact must never be forgotten or minimized. Someone (a colonial, nonwhite, non–Christian, lower-class female character) actually has to die as a result of José's mind/body crisis.

In some ways the ruptured, anxiety-ridden narratives of the nineteenth century are more interesting than those of the Enlightenment in which easy reconciliations and the jingo of "Liberté, égalité, fraternité" give rise to illusory hopes. José's contradictions are articulated as too fundamental for a rational, negotiated conclusion in the style of Mozart to be feasible. His only solution—the only way he knows to contain the damage—is through arbitrary, violently imposed closure.

Such irreconcilable contradictions were erupting in many domains in 1870s France: the limits and reversals of imperial expansion were beginning to become evident, and both women and the working class were organizing to demand their economic, political, and cultural rights. Liberal humanism's commitment to universal rights was strained when it became a matter of sharing privileges with women, the working class, or the colonized — upon all of whom the privileged were dependent. This tension between liberal overextension and the need to assert control even informs the terms of musical discourse itself: the nineteenth century's indulgence in hedonistic chromaticism and exoticism in music gradually becomes addictive, and the purging of this slippery stuff for the sake of diatonic order at conclusions of pieces such as *Carmen* finally comes to seem intolerably arbitrary — the brute imposition of convention from the outside.[28]

Carmen manages to dramatize every single one of these issues in a way that is most compelling. The renewed popularity of this particular opera in the era of Allan Bloom is not at all surprising, when once again liberal humanism is finding it necessary to declare that its promises of universal emancipation have been taken too far.[29] Ironically, Bloom would see *Carmen* as an unassailable product of high culture, as one of those canonized works of art that testify to the stability of the Golden Age before the intrusion of women's, African-American, and popular-culture studies programs. In point of fact, the opera presents a kind of rehearsal for the twentieth-century crises over class, race, and gender. And it demonstrates all too well the inadequacy of Don José's — and Bloom's — attempted solutions.

2

As I mentioned earlier, many who would grant much of my reading of *Carmen* would also deny that any of this has anything to do with *real* music. Indeed, there are strong implications in polemics concerning "Absolute Music" in the nineteenth century that the materiality of verbal language defiles both texted music (i.e., opera or song) and also programmatic music.[30] Only hard-core instrumental music maintains the ideal of transcendental purity. It is for this reason that the other arts in the nineteenth century come to envy abstract instrumental music and, as Walter Pater put it, to aspire to its condition.

However, the aspects of *Carmen* I have just discussed — namely these particular constructions of gender, the ejaculatory quality of many so-called transcendental moments, the titillating yet carefully contained presentation of the feminine "threat," the apparent necessity of violent closure — are all central to the great tradition of nineteenth-century "Absolute Music." We can easily find both the characterizations and plot lines of *Carmen*, *Salome*, or *Samson et Dalila* exquisitely concealed in the presumably abstract, word-free context of many a symphony.

Before turning to the symphony, I would like to make a couple of comments. First, I am not undertaking a Freudian search for unintentional phalluses. Rather I will be relying on the common semiotic codes of European classical music: the gestures that stereotypically signify "masculine" or "feminine," placidity or violence, the military or the domestic realm, and also the standard narrative schemata that underlie most nineteenth-century instrumental movements. These codes were readily acknowedged during the seventeenth and eighteenth centuries and only became suppressed with the obsession over the authenticity of subjective expression that arose during the Romantic period.[31] But the fact that such codes are now denied both by composers themselves and by professional musicians does not render them inoperative. Indeed, any five-year-old has sufficient experience from watching Saturday morning cartoons to verify most of the signs I will need.

Second, I am not rummaging through this repertory trying to find tiny isolated details or occasional snags I can construe as traces of a masculinist bias. Rather, it seems to me more and more that the whole fabric is at stake. The problem is not that eroticism or even patterns articulating male sexuality are often present in this music. That part is fine by me. Rather it is that in classical music, the erotic continues so often to be framed as a manifestation of feminine evil while masculine high culture is regarded as transcendent. And the pervasive cultural anxiety over women as obstacles to transcendence justifies over and over again narratives of the victimized male and the necessary purging or containment of the female.[32] If the men responsible for high culture could acknowledge their own desires both in life and in artistic production, I would not have to be explaining this dimension of these pieces on such an elementary level. Perhaps if erotic impulses were valued as positive—if, in other words, arousal were not a pretext for anti-woman hysteria—the whole repertory would be radically different, as it is, for instance, in much overtly erotic popular music.[33]

Most opening movements in the nineteenth-century symphony are organized according to a schema called sonata-allegro procedure.[34] Central to this procedure is a confrontation between two key areas, usually articulated by two distinctly different themes. The first theme establishes the tonic key and sets the affective tone of the movement: it is in essence the protagonist of the movement, and it used to be referred to quite commonly (in the days preceding feminist consciousness) as the "masculine" theme. Indeed, its character is usually somewhat aggressive; it is frequently described as having "thrust"; and it is often concerned with closure. Midway through the exposition of the movement, it encounters another theme, the so-called feminine theme, usually a more lyrical tune that presents a new key, incompatible with the first. Given that a tonal, sonata-based movement is concerned with matters of maintaining identity, both thematic and tonal, the second area poses a threat to the opening materials. Yet this antagonism is essential to the furthering of the plot, for within this model of identity construction and preservation, the self cannot truly be a self unless it acts: it must leave the cozy nest of its tonic, risk this confrontation, and finally triumph over its Other. The middle segment of the piece, the development, presents the various thematic materials of the exposition in a whole range of combinations and keys. Finally, at the recapitulation, the piece returns to reestablish both the original tonic key and the original theme. The materials of the exposition are now repeated, with this difference: the secondary theme must now conform to the protagonist's tonic key area. It is absorbed, its threat to the opening key's identity neutralized.

The specific content of each composition casts many possible shades on this paradigm: some are gleefully affirmative, demonstrating quite straightforwardly the triumph of the "masculine" over the "feminine" principle. Many of Beethoven's symphonies exhibit considerable anxiety with respect to feminine moments and respond to them with extraordinary violence: see, for example, the first movement of the *Eroica*. But other pieces, such as many by Mozart or Schubert, tend to invest their second themes with extraordinary sympathy, and this leads one to regret the inevitable return to tonic and the original materials: for example, in the "Unfinished" Symphony, it is the lovely, "feminine" tune with which we are encouraged to identify and which is brutally, tragically quashed in accordance with the destiny predetermined by the "disinterested" conventions of the form.[35]

3

The symphony movement I wish to examine for our present purposes is one whose characterizations and narrative bear an uncanny resemblance to those of *Carmen*, namely, the first movement of Tchaikovsky's Fourth Symphony (1877). The resemblance between the opera and the symphony is not, in fact, coincidental. Tchaikovsky had recently seen *Carmen*, which he described as "joli," though he concluded his account of *Carmen* on a rather more serious note:

> I cannot play the last scene without weeping; on the one hand, the people enjoying themselves, and the coarse gaiety of the crowd watching the bullfight, on the other, the dreadful tragedy and death of two of the leading characters whom an evil destiny, *fatum*, has brought together and driven, through a whole series of agonies, to their inescapable end.[36]

Example 3a: Tchaikovsky, Fourth Symphony. Mov't I, Introduction, mm. 1-7

Tchaikovsky was still very much under the influence of the opera when he wrote this symphony, and the ways he reconstitutes the gender politics of both *Carmen* and of sonata conventions for this movement make it a fascinating study.

Like *Carmen*, this movement opens not with the presentation of the protagonist but with an introduction bristling with military connotations. It is scored for brass so as to resemble fanfares, and its motivic materials are characterized by unison scalar descents that proceed as though inexorable. For all its brutal power, the introduction pivots irrationally between F minor and E major through a common tone, a♭/g#; yet this quality of arbitrary force only makes it seem more terrifying, for it seems resistant to reason (Ex. 3a).

Example 3b: Principal theme, mm. 27-32

Tchaikovsky described this material as "Fate, the force of destiny":

> The introduction is the *seed* of the whole symphony,
> undoubtedly the main idea. This is fate, this is that fateful force
> which prevents the impulse to happiness from attaining its goal,
> which jealously ensures that peace and happiness shall not be
> complete and unclouded, which hangs above your head like the
> sword of Damocles, and unwaveringly, constantly poisons the
> soul. It is invincible, and you will never overcome it. You can
> only reconcile yourself to it, and languish fruitlessly.[37]

Against this oppressively patriarchal backdrop, the principal "masculine" theme enters. In contrast to the more typical heroic opening themes, this appoggiatura-laden, limping theme is hypersensitive, vulnerable, indecisive. It is marked with yearning, with metaphysical angst in search of a moment of rhythmic or tonal stability (Ex. 3b).

After an attempted futile escape to A minor fails, our protagonist desists; and in that off-guard condition, he encounters the second theme (Ex. 4a). This is no simple "feminine" theme. Like Carmen, it is sultry, seductive, and slinky. Its contours are marked with chromatic slippage, and its fragments echo maddeningly in all registers—its very location cannot be fixed. Moreover, unlike the obsessively goal-oriented protagonist, this theme manages to be at the same time both utterly static (even stagnant) and also irrational with respect to its unexpected twists and turns: precisely as is Carmen when she is seducing José.

And the protagonist's immediate fate is similar to José's. His theme reappears inside this sensual, alien terrain, now domesticated and paralyzed. An even more languid theme (in the key area a sinister tritone away from tonic) toys with him, much like a spider with a trapped fly (Ex. 4b). All thought of metaphysical quest is expunged. Yet eventually the hero man-

Example 4a: Transition and secondary theme, mm. 110-19

ages with tremendous effort to come to his senses, to pull himself from this drugged state, and to emerge with a triumphal theme to finish the exposition (Ex. 4c).

I should mention that this account of the second-theme sequence does not completely jibe with Tchaikovsky's. He ascribes nothing negative to this part of the piece, but rather characterizes the second theme as an area of illusory happiness that is doomed to be quashed. On the one hand, like Carmen, this theme can be heard as representing the site of patriarchally prohibited desire. Moreover, it has much in common semiotically with Tchaik-

Example 4b: Combination of principal and secondary themes, mm. 133–41

ovsky's own musical depictions of the exotic Other in the ballets—thus the stereotypical links among the feminine, the oriental, and illicit pleasure are here once again reinforced.[38] On the other hand, like Bizet, Tchaikovsky also portrays the object of desire as sinister, slippery, potentially lethal. As we shall see, Tchaikovsky's own views of sexuality were exceedingly ambivalent at the time he was writing this symphony; but so—as we have already seen—were those of his culture in general. Thus it would be a mistake for us to try to resolve in either direction this contradiction between happiness and dread. These affective qualities are here presented—as in *Carmen*—as inseparable.

Example 4c: Closing theme, mm. 161-65

The protagonist's triumph suddenly falls under the shadow of the military call to arms. After several futile attempts at reconstructing the self, the development turns to the kind of passionate sequential procedure that typically signals the standard move to transcendence.[39] The self-indulgent straining of this passage exceeds many times over the implicit patriarchal standards at this time for rhetorical propriety. As the sequence goes on and on without reaching its climax, the military call suddenly breaks in. A long, violent struggle ensues between the military material and our hero—a struggle that prevents the usual formal articulation of the recapitulation, which is ordinarily the moment where the theme and tonic key reestablish their identity. No solution is reached: rather the energy finally simply dissipates. And as the protagonist lies in helpless exhaustion, the sluttish second theme reenters—in the key of the raised submediant rather than under the hegemony of the protagonist's tonic, as convention would demand—and toys with him, finally depleting him. This time there is no illusory triumphant theme, but merely frenzied escape back into the first theme and to tonic. The military breaks in once again and brutally forces the movement toward its conclusion. At the end of the movement, the first theme is presented in all its anguish, its plaintive appoggiaturas still unhealed, its complicity with violent closure as bitter as Don José's.

The conclusion of this movement is not the end of the symphony; there are three additional movements in the cycle. Yet the first movement has often been heard as containing the dramatic essence of the symphony. Interestingly, Tchaikovsky's own description of the last movement indicates that he understood it not as a resolution to the opening movement's challenge but as the possibility of release through submersion with "the people," that is, through escape and self-erasure:

The fourth movement. If within yourself you find no reasons for joy, look at others. Go among the people. Observe how they can enjoy themselves, surrendering themselves wholeheartedly to joyful feelings. A picture of festive merriment of the people. Hardly have you managed to forget yourself and to be carried away by the spectacle of others' joy, than irrepressible *fate* again appears and reminds you of yourself. But others do not care about you. They have not even turned around, they have not glanced at you, and they have not noticed that you are solitary and sad. O, how they are enjoying themselves, how happy they are that all their feelings are simple and direct! You have only yourself to blame; do not say that everything in this world is sad. There are simple but strong joys. Rejoice in others' rejoicing. To live is still possible![40]

In some important sense, the protagonist is no longer the subject of the symphony at this point: he has abandoned his own narrative to observe impersonal, social events from the outside. Thus, the opening movement may be examined on its own terms as presenting the dilemma that still remains unresolved at the end of the cycle.

Even though his movement has long proved effective with audiences, critics often find it necessary to bash it for failing to measure up to convention. Dahlhaus, for instance, writes:

The "actual" main theme, however, with an urgent pathos curiously held in check by its meter and tempo, is hardly suitable, at least by Beethovenian standards, for establishing a symphonic movement spanning hundreds of measures. The fact that this theme reaches an ecstatic *fortissimo* in the development section emerging directly from the exposition has little or no bearing on its weaknesses as the mainspring of a symphonic movement. . . . To put it bluntly, the grand style fundamental to the genre has been split into a monumentality that remains a decorative façade unsupported by the internal form of the movement, and an internal form that is lyrical in character and can be dramatized only by applying a thick layer of pathos.[41]

Just as Dahlhaus assumed that Carmen was incapable of José's "lyric urgency," so he dismisses Tchaikovsky as incapable of measuring up to "Beethovenian standards" with respect to abstract formal conventions. But Tchaikovsky, I would argue, is not so much trying and failing to follow tradition, as attempting to tell another kind of story with other kinds of characters. He is, in effect, deconstructing the powerful narrative paradigm of adventure and conquest that had underwritten the symphony since its beginnings.

For what we have is a narrative in which the protagonist seems victimized both by patriarchal expectations and by sensual feminine entrapment:

both forces actively block the possibility of his self-development. Such a narrative resonates strongly with Tchaikovsky's biography. As a homosexual in a world of patriarchally enforced heterosexuality, his behavior was always being judged against cultural models of "real men."[42] In fact, 1877 (the year of this symphony) was a crisis year in Tchaikovsky's psychosexual development: he finally yielded to social and paternal pressures to get married, with disastrous consequences for all concerned, and then attempted suicide because of his distress over the marriage and his clandestine sexuality.[43] The extent to which these events colored his perceptions is revealed in his letters, and a strong sense of struggle and alienation likewise marks his programmatic description of the symphony.

This is not to suggest that the piece should be understood *only* as the narrative of a homosexual male, or even less that what I have presented is the only possible reading from a homosexual viewpoint. The piece has long been admired by listeners of various orientations who hear it as resonating with their own emotional experiences, and there is no reason why that should change. Certainly the complexities of the composition ought not to be reduced to a single totalizing label. The movement can also be heard, for instance, as portraying a more "universal" oedipal pattern, or as a nonspecific struggle with both power and sensual enticements, or in any number of other ways.[44]

Nor am I implying that one can necessarily detect anything about the writing itself that inadvertently betrays Tchaikovsky's "deviance." Various colleagues have suggested to me that traces of Tchaikovsky's homosexuality might be found in the unusual modulatory progression by thirds underlying this movement. I am not sure how one would go about making such a connection, although I fear that they are extrapolating from the old semiotic principle that movement by fifth is strong (i.e., masculine), while movement by thirds is weak (i.e., feminine). Once again, it is important to recognize the deliberate nature of Tchaikovsky's key scheme: it is very carefully worked out and is in no way a "lapse." Moreover, even if one might characterize *falling* thirds as passive, this symphony is organized by aggressively rising minor thirds and resulting tritone relationships, which together create an affect of frenzied striving. Moreover, the fact that its path is both systematic and symmetrical makes the strategy all the more oppressive: even though it presses continually upward through unusual key relationships (as though eradicating identity), it finds neither escape nor stability and is returned at the end—as though inexorably—to the opening key. The protagonist of the movement is trapped, not passive.

David Brown too argues that Tchaikovsky's homosexuality is apparent in this symphony, but he argues that it is to be detected in rhetorical excess (which he hears as signs of "morbidity" and "self-loathing").[45] Once again, I think it is crucial that inferences such as these be carefully grounded so that pernicious essentialist stereotypes of homosexuals (excessively emotional, hysterical, self-loathing, etc.) are not unwittingly drawn upon and re-inscribed. On what basis are we to accept the "ruthless climaxes" (186) of the symphony as signs of desperation or hysteria (171), or as "an outlet for emotional drives that could not be channelled into a full physical relation-ship" (182)? We need ways of accounting for these qualities that are sensitive both to Tchaikovsky's situation and also to the highly mediated discursive idiom that is music.[46] As we proceed into gay criticism, we have to be ex-tremely cautious about how we ground these issues.

A major obstacle impeding gay criticism is the difficulty of establishing a reliable "norm" for nineteenth-century symphonies against which to gauge possible inflections by homosexual composers, given the dearth of certifi-ably *heterosexual* symphony composers during this period. Furthermore, there is scant information concerning composers and homosexuality, al-though there is a rich tradition of speculating in music biographies about dubious liaisons with women. This part of the historical record needs to be corrected—though not for the sake of sensationalism. Rather the acknowl-edgment of Western musical culture's debt to homosexual artists might help to counter the homophobia still so prevalent; it would offer an illustrious history for gay individuals today—a source of deserved pride rather than shame; it would end the silly charade of filling biographies with bogus girl-friends; and it would permit much more interesting and human readings of the music. In music as obsessed with gender construction and narrative as the nineteenth-century symphony, it would be truly remarkable if this rather crucial factor were not relevant.

For this is a composition by a man who was tormented by his situation within his homophobic society. As a composer, he inherited a code of signifi-cation that marked themes (as well as human beings) as either masculine or feminine, that predisposed movements (and individuals) to work in accor-dance with certain narrative paradigms. This inheritance did not dictate his creations or, for that matter, his behavior. Rather it provided the terms for negotiation and set the stakes. It was in his power—at least as a composer—to manipulate these *musical* materials to conform to his own specifications, even if his choices in real life were rather more restricted and treacherous.

To deny him the option of having devised unconventional stories—stories that were informed by his own experience (though always, of course, heavily mediated through the technical specificity of formal, har-monic, and orchestrational procedures)—is to continue to silence him by pushing him into some kind of assumed uniform patriarchal grid: precisely that against which he fought his whole life. It is to accept him if and only if he agrees to suppress his sexuality or to keep it concealed from public attention.[47] Or it is to punish him (as Dahlhaus does) for simply having failed to measure up to abstract Beethovenian standards, as though those standards were universal.[48] Given this background, I can view the perhaps not-so-paranoid fantasy of this movement with considerable sympathy: it is not standard misogyny, although it does operate off of (and thus, to some degree, it reproduces) the stereotypical late nineteenth-century characterizations and narratives of misogyny.[49]

<h1 style="text-align:center">4</h1>

My purpose in examining these two compositions is not to indict them for their monstrous feminine images or deadly narrative strategies, though those dimensions of both pieces (and countless others) are horrifying. On the contrary, I wish to argue that these pieces themselves suggest that no one wins within the strictures of traditional modes of organizing gender and sexuality. Tchaikovsky's symphony appears to problematize this no-win situation for the nineteenth-century homosexual male superbly (if pessimistically). And *Carmen* demonstrates that heterosexual males are no less mutilated by patriarchal models of gender construction.

The dilemmas raised in both compositions ought to spark discussion, as controversial novels or pop songs often do. But classical music is perhaps our cultural medium most centrally concerned with denial of the body, with enacting the ritual repudiation of the erotic—even (especially) its own erotic imagery. For in Western culture, music *itself* is always in danger of being regarded as the feminine Other that circumvents reason and arouses desire. Hence the ongoing academic struggle to control music objectively: just as Carmen must be brought in line with patriarchal demands, so the musicologist must silence music, deny that it has meaning, and impose theoretical closure on this discourse that often provokes far more than it can contain. Thus while pieces such as *Carmen* and Tchaikovsky's Fourth Symphony continue to be central to our concert repertory, they are rarely dealt with critically. For obvious reasons, it is easier to treat them as aesthetic objects and take comfort in the resolutions they (perhaps ambivalently) offer than to confront either their misogyny or the disturbing social critiques they enact.

Yet far from destroying our appreciation, examining the treatment of such issues as sexuality in these pieces can cause us once again to take them seriously. Even if they cease along the way to stand as icons guaranteeing that Father Knows Best, they may be able to reclaim the status of documents worthy of cultural debate. And by indicating so clearly the contradictions and shortcomings of the models they reinscribe and yet at the same time resist, they might even contribute to the creation of new models of gender and desire: models that do not pit mind against body, that do not demand shame—or death—as the price for sexual pleasure.

Chapter 4
Excess and Frame:
The Musical Representation
of Madwomen

From Monteverdi's experiments in the *stile rappresentativo* or Donizetti's tragic heroines to Schoenberg's *Erwartung* and beyond, composers have long been attracted to the dramatic subject of madwomen. Opera audiences obviously share their fascination: many operas of this genre maintain positions of honor within the standard repertory, and there are even specialized commercial recordings that contain nothing but Mad Scenes, all conveniently excerpted and packaged together so that the listener doesn't have to endure any of the boring stuff between the "good parts." Nor is the musical madwoman confined to operas with explicitly mad characters: Ethan Mordden's book on the phenomenon of the Diva bears the title *Demented*, because (he explains) "demented" is the highest accolade one can bestow on a prima donna's performance — or at least it was so for a particular time among opera buffs at the Met.[1] The excess that marks the utterances of a Lucia or a Salome as insane is thereby elevated to the status of an essential ingredient — a *sine qua non* — of interpretations by women opera stars, regardless of the specific role.

The mass popularity of madwoman representations, their frank appeals to sensationalism, and their somewhat tacky reception histories tend to make them sources of embarrassment to musicologists and theorists. Some of the pieces in question are dismissed as unworthy of serious critical attention, while others are acknowledged and studied as important masterworks, but with the issues of madness and gender shoved to the side as irrelevant to the music itself. The very aspects of these operas that make them favorites among opera lovers typically are overlooked, disparaged, or explained away: thus Salome's depravity can become an intricately designed configuration of pitch-class sets, and Lucia's lucidity may be recovered through linear and structural graphing. What appeared at first glance to be deviant is revealed to be normative, and all is well.[2]

But the links among madness, women, and music are neither irrelevant nor trivial—although to explain how and why these connections are significant will necessarily take us out of the realm of self-contained musical analysis and into such areas as history and literary criticism. For music is not the only cultural domain in which madwomen show up rather more prominently than one would expect, and their musical manifestations need to be examined at least in part against the broader contexts from which they emerge and in which they are received.

Fortunately, much of the information required for such a task is already available. The work of historians Michel Foucault and Klaus Doerner, for instance, has begun to lay bare the social history of madness in Europe: they have traced the ways in which insanity (which previously was regarded as a universal) has been defined differently by institutions at various times and places, how it has been treated, and so forth.[3] Moreover, Elaine Showalter has demonstrated that during the nineteenth century, madness came to be regarded as a peculiarly female malady—usually as a manifestation of excess feminine sexuality.[4] The socially perceived differences between male and female were, in other words, often mapped onto the differences between reason and unreason. Both official institutions (law and medicine) and also cultural enterprises such as literature were engaged in constructing and transmitting such formulations. And as the frequency of operatic madwomen indicates, music likewise participated in this process.

But music is not simply another medium. Its priorities and procedures differ significantly from those of literature, and thus we cannot apply directly to music the insights gleaned by Showalter or Foucault. It is reductive, for example, to regard characters such as Lucia as mere victims, in part because of the technical virtuosity required of the singer performing such a role. If the prima donna in such operas can be interpreted as a monstrous display, she also bears the glory of the composition: her moments of excess are its very raison d'être.

In this essay, I will examine several famous portrayals of madwomen in music from both cultural and musical points of view. I hope to demonstrate how madwomen such as Monteverdi's nymph, Donizetti's Lucia, and Strauss's Salome are offered up as spectacles within the musical discourse itself: how their dementia is delineated musically through repetitive, ornamental, or chromatic excess, and how normative procedures representing reason are erected around them to serve as protective frames preventing "contagion."

But I also want to consider what may at first appear to be a strange coincidence: namely, that the excessive ornamentation and chromaticism that mark the madwoman's deviance have long been privileged components in Western music—the components that appear most successfully to escape formal and diatonic conventions. When these same strategies appear in instrumental music, they are regarded as indications not of psychopathology but of genius. This essay concentrates on particular musical representations of madwomen. But it also employs the insights gained from those specific examples to illuminate a fundamental contradiction within the social framing of Western music since 1600—namely, its compulsion for theoretical control and yet its craving for strategies that violate and exceed that control: a contradiction that is at times projected onto and dramatically enacted by musical madwomen, but that is by no means restricted to that genre.

Before proceeding to the music itself, however, I want to reconstruct something of the historical contexts within which these pieces took shape, paying particular attention to dominant cultural beliefs concerning madness, women, and spectacle. For it was not only musical style that changed between Monteverdi and Strauss: many social assumptions concerning gender and madness likewise underwent radical transformations during this period, and these extramusical assumptions strongly influenced the various characterizations as well. Indeed, these outside assumptions created the very conditions that made feasible the emergence and popularity of musical madwomen.

1

Michel Foucault's *Madness and Civilization* presents itself as the first "archaeology" of attitudes toward insanity in early modern Europe. In this influential study, Foucault argues that before the seventeenth century, individuals who were regarded as mentally deficient or deviant were usually permitted to wander about freely unless they proved to be dangerous. The seventeenth century saw the emergence and development of many of the institutions and social habits we now take for granted, among them the confinement of the insane. For the first time in European history, the mad were gathered up and incarcerated in precisely the same way as lepers had been in an earlier time. In Foucault's words, in the classical society of the seventeenth century,

> reason reigned in the pure state, in a triumph arranged for it in advance over a frenzied unreason. Madness was thus torn from that imaginary freedom which still allowed it to flourish on the Renaissance horizon. Not so long ago, it had floundered about in broad daylight. But in less than a half-century, it had been

sequestered and, in the fortress of confinement, bound to
Reason, to the rules of morality and to their monotonous
nights.[5]

The rationale for this move was in part beneficent: to protect these poor,
unfortunate beings from the outside world. But it also was motivated by the
modern state's obsession with surveillance, its need to define and control
behavior: "The house of confinement in the classical age constitutes the
densest symbol of that 'police' which conceived of itself as the civil equivalent of religion for the edification of a perfect city" (63).

Yet even though the mad were sequestered during and after the seventeenth century, it was not quite a matter of "out of mind, out of sight."
Quite the contrary: the public display of mad persons became and remained
an extremely popular entertainment well into the nineteenth century. As
Foucault states:

> Here is madness elevated to spectacle above the silence of the
> asylums, and becoming a public scandal for the general delight.
> Unreason was hidden in the silence of the houses of
> confinement, but madness continued to be present on the stage
> of the world—with more commotion than ever. (67)

The indulgence of our civilized ancestors in such freak-show exploitation
of the helpless may seem almost incomprehensible today. However, as
Klaus Doerner explains in *Madmen and the Bourgeoisie:*

> These spectacles had more in common [with displays of animals]
> than merely the bars of cages and the skilful baiting of the
> keepers. They were displays of a wild and untamable nature, of
> "bestiality," of absolute and destructive freedom, of social danger
> which could be demonstrated far more dramatically behind the
> bars of reason, just as that same act showed the public reason as
> the necessity of the control over nature, as a limitation of
> freedom, and as a guarantee of authority. . . . The arrangement
> that presented the insane as wild and dangerous beasts was an
> appeal to the public to accept the moral yardstick of the absolute
> state as its own measure of reason.[6]

In other words, the agencies of the newly consolidating modern state found
it useful to exhibit those whom it defined as deviant, largely as a means of
persuading the public to embrace restrictive legal and behavioral codes—
codes ostensibly designed to protect individuals from their own potentially
fatal excesses.

Nor did the public require much coercion to get them to attend such exhibits: the desire to observe those who had lost all inhibition appealed to the same tastes as executions, bear baiting, or strip shows. The voyeurism that guaranteed the popularity of madhouse displays also inspired innumerable artworks—novels, paintings, and especially operas—that were concerned with representing the spectacle of madness. And in these artistic genres, as in the asylums, we find the double gesture of confinement and exhibition, of frame and display, of moral lesson and titillation.

Foucault and Doerner deal with insanity largely without paying particular attention to gender. But in *The Female Malady*, Elaine Showalter has demonstrated the extent to which attitudes toward madness in modern Europe have been informed by attitudes toward sexual difference.[7] Two of her arguments are crucial for the purposes of this essay. First, she demonstrates that the growing "science" of psychiatry came to differentiate radically between explanations for unreason in men (which ranged from grief or guilt to congenital defectiveness) and the cause (singular) of madness in women, namely, female sexual excess. Over the course of the nineteenth century, psychiatrists obsessed over mechanisms of feminine dementia to the extent that madness came to be perceived *tout court* as feminine—even when it occurred in men.[8] Moreover, they came to perceive all women—even apparently "normal" ones—as always highly susceptible to mental breakdown, precisely because of their sexuality. The surveillance and control that had always characterized the psychiatric profession became focused on the "problem" of Woman, and so it has remained with substantial help from Darwin and Freud.[9]

Second, Showalter reveals that when madness is dealt with in bourgeois artworks (whether in literature, art, or music), it is almost always represented as female.[10] These two features of modern culture—psychiatry and public art—inform each other: the more science tells us that it is women who go mad from an excess of sexuality, the more artists reflect that understanding; but the more art gives us vivid representations of sexually frenzied madwomen, the more society as a whole (including its scientists) takes for granted the bond between madness and femininity. In other words, explanatory models in science and representational artifacts in the arts are often interdependent in processes of social formation.

Cultural anthropologists and historians have demonstrated that there is no essential or ideologically neutral condition that is "the mad." Rather, because each society values certain types of behavior, each defines deviance according to very different criteria. Notions of madness consequently vary across time and space, and especially with respect to gender, and these differences inform representations of dementia in art. Yet representations are never mere transcriptions of reality or ideology. Artistic conventions themselves change across time and space, and the available artistic codes of a given moment likewise inform what gets represented. Thus part of my concern here is with the ways madwomen are "framed" in the sense of constructed: what characteristics mark their musical utterances as feminine and as mad?

There is a second sense in which I am interested in "framing." As one surveys the genre of madwomen in art, a very interesting formal tick emerges. In two of the most famous paintings celebrating psychiatry — *Pinel Freeing the Insane* and *Charcot Lecturing on Hysteria at the Salpêtrière* — the madwoman is being exhibited not merely as one who suffers some disorder, but also as a sexually titillating display.[11] She is a beautiful woman whose chief sign of abnormality is her indecency: her bared breasts of which she herself seems to be incognizant, but of which her painter and the viewer of the painting are most certainly aware. Moreover, within the confines of the represented scene itself are male displayers of the madwoman. As scientists they are in control. They represent the normal, the bars of reason that protect the spectator from the monster. They are, as Doerner points out, necessarily present within the discourse itself.[12] The frame of masculine rationality is constantly visible to guard against the male-constructed (or framed) image of the madwoman. It is apparently only within the security of that double frame that feminine madness can be presented for public delectation.

One of the conventions governing representations of madwomen in most media is that they are silent.[13] They are seen but are rarely given the power of language, are almost never given the opportunity to speak their own experiences. But music, of course, is radically different in this regard. If musical representations of madwomen likewise are often pruriently conceived and doubly framed, they must — because of the special capabilities and demands of the medium — actually give voice to symptoms of insanity. Since the seventeenth century, dramatic music has offered the extraordinary illusion of knowledge beyond the lyrics, beyond social convention. When Orfeo or Otello sings, for instance, we grasp not only the meanings of his texts (which we could actually do better through spoken theater), but also another dimension in addition to the words, which is understood to be the character's subjective feelings. The music delivers a sense of depth and grants the spectator license to eavesdrop upon the character's interiority.[14]

But the apparent power of music to make us as listeners privy to the inner thoughts of characters becomes problematic when that character is a madwoman, for the risk arises that what we hear may so influence us — so move the passions — that we will be seduced into unreason ourselves. Since Plato, music has been regarded as a very tricky medium that can corrupt, effeminize, bedazzle, and delude. Most listeners do not know how to account for the effects music has on them, and thus they often understand those effects as manifestations of their own subjectivities, as their own inner truths. Thus a composer constructing a madwoman is compelled to ensure that the listener experiences and *yet does not identify with* the discourse of madness. It becomes crucial, therefore, that the musical voice of reason be ever audibly present as a reminder, so that the ravings of the madwoman will remain securely marked as radically "Other," so that the contagion will not spread.

The three portraits I will examine—Monteverdi's nymph, Donizetti's Lucia, and Strauss's Salome—date respectively from 1638, 1835, and 1905, and thus their stylistic premises are extremely different. To the extent that style defines what counts as rational, what as irrational, these three characterizations are indelibly marked by the musical tensions of their day. As exceptions that prove the rules, they tell us a great deal about the styles from which they are constructed. Madwomen strain the semiotic codes from which they emerge, thereby throwing into high relief the assumptions concerning musical normality and reason from which they must—by definition—deviate. And by threatening formal propriety, they cause frames of closure or containment (which usually operate more or less unnoticed) to be enacted most dramatically.

2

They cannot represent themselves, they must be represented.
        Karl Marx, *The Eighteenth Brumaire of Louis Bonaparte*

In study after study, Foucault's work posits the seventeenth century as the era when most modern institutions and discourses emerged, including those organizing power, knowledge, insanity, and sexuality. The most significant of the new discursive practices in music—the *stile rappresentativo*—was dedicated to inventing musical constructions of affect, but also class, gender, and madness. Monteverdi alone created several different versions of musical madness,[15] the most famous of which is the *Lamento della Ninfa*, a chamber piece that appears in his eighth book of madrigals.[16]

The core of this three-part composite is the prolonged soliloquy sung by the nymph, and it is for this segment that the piece is justly famous. The particular brand of madness generating the lament is that of obsession: the nymph is fixated on memories of a lover who has abandoned her—who has awakened her sexually and has left her with no outlet for that excess, no recourse but madness. Her responses and reminiscences range widely with

Example 1a: "Lamento della Ninfa," refusal of cadence

respect to affect (self-pity, anger, grief, envy, erotic longing, hopelessness, etc.), and yet she is unable to escape that solitary fixation.[17]

This obsessive quality is created musically through an unvarying cycle of four bass notes that seem to progress rationally through the A-minor tetrachord, only to double back inevitably to starting position. Against this backdrop, the nymph's vocal lines sometimes acquiesce, sometimes struggle—though always in vain. It is a mark of Monteverdi's powers of imagination that we never hear the ostinato bass the same way twice: it is constantly being reinflected by the nymph's dramatic moments of resistance (her dissonant refusals of cadences implied in the bass, the futile attempts at cadencing on g; see Ex. 1a and b) or of sudden collapse (Ex. 1c). Monteverdi presents us here with a stark experience of madness and also of uninhibited female desire as both were construed within seventeenth-century style and ideology, and it counts as one of his most powerful portraits.

So effective is this ostinato-lament that we often forget its frame. Indeed, it may be an indication of how very successful the frame is, that it manages

Example 1b: "Lamento," Attempted cadence on G

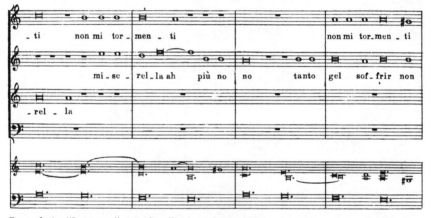

Example 1c: "Lamento," nymph collapses and trio imposes continuity

to escape our memories of the piece. For the chamber piece is not composed solely of this lament, but of three distinctive sections of which this is but the middle unit. The piece is not even in A minor, but rather C major, with the lament positioned as an extravagantly prolonged envelope on the region of the tentative sixth degree. And while the nymph is the principal attraction of the piece—it is her energy, her subjectivity we are invited to witness and experience vicariously—she does not control the proceedings. She is carefully mediated by a trio of men who introduce her and remain ever present until the nymph's conclusion, following which they offer a short coda that brings the composite to secure closure.

In their introduction, the trio sings complacently, twice reaching easy cadences on C, thus establishing their rationality and credibility. As they begin describing the pathetic nymph, they empathize with her various states, painting in music her sorrow, her rupturing sighs, and her trampling of flowers (a sure sign of her derangement is that she thus disregards these standard emblems of femininity). Finally, with the line "thus lamenting she went forth," they turn the piece over to the main event—the representation of the nymph proper. Foucault states in the earlier quotation that madness was allowed "to flourish on the Renaissance horizon," "to flounder about in broad daylight." And the premise of the libretto of this piece is that the three men have observed the nymph doing just that—flourishing and floundering in her madness on the Renaissance landscape. Yet as they "represent" her to us, they enact the confining frame that turns her into a seventeenth-century exhibit.

Throughout the nymph's lament, the three men make their presence audible as they continually mark her utterance as their own recollections: they punctuate her first line with "she said," thus undercutting the potential immediacy of the spectacle; they complete syntactical units in the music when the nymph falters, ensuring rational continuity despite her (Ex. 1c); and they insert their own sympathetic responses ("miserella") to her ordeal, thus insisting upon their humane intentions even while they display her publicly (Ex. 2a). At the end, they return us to secure, normative reality with another couple of complacent cadences on C major (Ex. 2b).[18]

This elaborate framing device is crucial to the organization of the composition. The intrusive trio of men is extraneous to the dramatic immediacy of the lament—indeed, it even works to the deliberate detriment of verisimilitude. Yet they serve a vital function: they protect and reassure us throughout the featured simulation of insanity. For the madwoman is one of the most terrifying archetypes in Western culture, and she is fascinating precisely because she is terrifying. We the spectators are curious to know about her (in order to accumulate possible human experiences, in order to control), but we do not want to be endangered by a creature who is beyond reason and who may inflict unmotivated injury or spread her disease. The density of auditory reminders of this masculine presence is directly related to the anxiety potentially generated by the confrontation with this frightening and unpredictable force.

Moreover, the three men establish and maintain a masculine subject position throughout. Just as the psychiatrists in the paintings mentioned earlier situate their disheveled hysterics as objects of the male gaze, so the trio situates the nymph's outburst as a display designed by men, chiefly for the consumption of other men.[19] The mediating filter of masculinity creates something like the grilles that used to be put over the windows of asylums at the time when gentlefolk liked to witness the spectacle of insanity for entertainment. These grilles permitted voyeuristic access and yet ensured security. Thus the double framing effect: the nymph is a male construct (com-

Example 2a: "Lamento," Trio attempts to reassure and to impose closure

posed by Monteverdi and the poet Rinuccini), and the piece's frame is dramatically enacted so as to provide maximal evidence of her containment. She will not bite or even trample flowers. It is safe to observe her distress — her rage against her faithless lover — with "aesthetic" pleasure.

3

The transformation of Walter Scott's Lucy Ashton into Lucia di Lammermoor provides an especially interesting example of the particular demands and potentials of music in the service of representation.[20] In the novel, Lucy plays but a very minor role — as bait in an ill-fated class struggle between a boorish, ascendant bourgeoisie and an impoverished but noble remnant of the aristocracy. Lucy and her family are precariously balanced between their upwardly mobile aspirations and the quagmire of uncultivated peasantry from which (by implication) they have only recently emerged. Large parts of the novel revel in the Scottish dialect of servants and crones, in opposition to the standard English of Ravenswood and the Ashtons. Lucy rarely

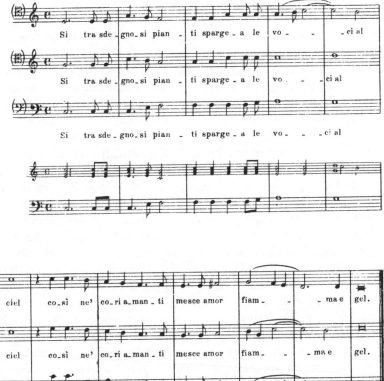

Example 2b: "Lamento," Conclusion

speaks in the novel—she is regularly characterized as quiet, even as "feeble minded." And after her mind snaps, she delivers but a single (though highly significant) line: "So, you have ta'en up your bonny bridegroom?" she croaks as the veneer of bourgeois gentility drops from her, exposing mercilessly her underclass origins. The rest is silence.

By contrast, Lucia and her inner self are the entire point of Donizetti's opera. Scott's Tory politics are eradicated, replaced by a love story reminiscent of *Romeo and Juliet* and a type of mental breakdown more indebted to

Ophelia's than to Lucy Ashton's. Far from losing her ability to manipulate her well-bred musical discourse, Lucia's madness is manifested in her move into increasingly extravagant virtuosity. In her celebrated Mad Scene, Lucia (like Monteverdi's nymph) displays her deranged mind without inhibition as she variously relives erotically charged moments with Edgardo, imagines that they are exchanging vows in marriage, and anticipates her own death, burial, and afterlife in heaven. She has lost touch with outer reality and lives now in a world made up entirely of the shards of her fears, hopes, and dreams.

Yet it is not the text that makes hers the quintessential Mad Scene, but the way in which her music is continually far in excess of the meanings of the lyrics and the rigid formal strictures of *bel canto* style. Indeed, from her very first scene in the opera, in which she sings of her encounter with the specter and of her love for Edgardo, Lucia is only tenuously connected to reality: her music is always given to excess and needs only the shock of her wedding night to unleash its full monstrosity. The other characters in the opera happily conform to the periodic phrases, the diatonicism, the melodic lyricism of this rather restricted sociomusical world. But Lucia always has far too much energy for these narrow confines. Her excess breaks forth at all the weak moments or seams in the form—in roulades between eight-bar phrases, in cadenzas between verses. And when the form of the piece refuses to accommodate her, she spills out in the only direction available: upward into coloratura delirium. Her exuberant singing leaves the mundane world of social convention behind as she performs high-wire, nonverbal acrobatics that challenge the very limits of human ability. And in the Mad Scene, she finally abandons formal convention altogether to enact a collaged fantasia. When she returns to formal continuity for her final "Spargi d'amaro pianto," it is a sign that she has successfully moved into another realm of consciousness, and the discrepancy between her morbid text and her ecstatic dance music betrays how far beyond the bounds of normal reason she has fled.

This is not the way the Mad Scene is always interpreted. For instance, the entry on Donizetti in *The New Grove* states: "Some of the Mad Scene remains on a purely decorative level. . . . The brilliant cabaletta "Spargi d'amaro pianto" shows a curious indifference to the mood of Cammarano's text. . . . Lucia lacks the excuse of morbid euphoria for her roulades."[21] To be sure, Donizetti's music and his librettist's text do not match with regard to affect: the situation and the lyrics suggest that morose music might be more suitable. However, whatever one thinks of Donizetti as a musical formalist, he did have an uncanny sense of theater, and it is unlikely that he would have capped this, his most celebrated scene, with a mistake. And if one reads Lucia's behavior as a manifestation of the sexual excess the nineteenth century ascribed to madwomen, then these "decorative" and "euphoric" details make strong dramatic sense.

During the first fifteen bars of "Spargi," the harmonic vocabulary is remarkably diatonic, conventional, predictable. In the abstract, one might even be tempted to call it "rational," if the singer were not clothed in a blood-splattered gown, and if we had not just witnessed the extravagant discontinuities and ornamentation of the earlier sections of the Mad Scene. Thus her apparent musical lucidity at this point in the action, paired with the seemingly carefree style of her waltz meter, is all the more chilling. She seems to be submitting to the sociomusical frame she has resisted throughout the opera. But the nonfit between the morbid lyrics and musical setting (with its flirtatious grace notes and skips) signals that something is wrong. In measure 32 there is a sudden pivot from the key of the dominant, B♭ major, to the key of its lowered submediant, G♭ major. And it is at the moment of this flat-six excursion that the kind of madness Donizetti seems to have in mind bursts forth in all its splendor (Ex. 3).

Admittedly, such chromatic modulations were relatively common in music of this time. Yet their frequency does not lessen their significance, but rather serves as an index of how effective such rhetorical devices were — and still are. The flat-six modulation creates a sudden, dramatic shift into what is perceived as an alien region: a realm of fantasy, illusion, nostalgia, unreason, or the sublime, depending on semiotic context.[22]

In measure 30, Lucia ascends unexpectedly to a chromatically altered g♭. This pitch challenges the boundaries temporarily, but then Lucia demurs to the lower a-natural and submits to the expected diatonic cadence in B♭ major. In retrospect, it seems that the g♭ was but a local inflection merely interjecting a brief shadow of sensitivity, weariness, yearning. However, without warning she pushes her cadential b♭ up to c♭ as the bass descends to A♭ — a pitch that immediately undermines the sovereignty of B♭ major and that disorients us for the moment. Two measures later we will understand that the A♭ chord was ii in a forceful ii — V — I progression in G♭ major. We are probably relieved at discovering in retrospect the logic of this pivot, but perhaps at the same time a bit disconcerted at having been so easily seduced into Lucia's perverse logic.

G♭ major holds firm for seven measures, following which Lucia returns to her original E♭ major for the remainder of the aria. Her process back to tonic is noteworthy in at least two respects. First, she ascends by step as she did before, though this time she ends on a brilliant g-natural harmonized by E♭ — she succeeds in breaking through the clouds "foreshadowed" by the earlier g♭. And second, she uses a trilled b♭ as a whimsical springboard

Example 3: Lucia di Lammermoor, Mad Scene: "Spargi d'amaro pianto"

from which to launch each pitch of the ascent. If listeners are occasionally disoriented by her logic, Lucia is absolutely confident of her steps and can even take time out to tease her lines sensually, willfully. Once again she folds into a conventional cadence, only to reemerge and leap beyond the now-expected g-natural to a high b♭, at which point she bursts into euphoric spirals of erotic transport. The excess here overspills its bounds completely as she anticipates her reunion with Edgardo in heaven and, formally speaking, her cadence.

In the repeat of the cabaletta—in which lavish ornamentation (now standardized by performance tradition) is added—the flat-six pivot is even more erotically charged. For instead of backing off from the sensitized g♭ in measure 30, she pushes up through it chromatically to the high b♭. If the original rendition was demure and submissive, this one is defiant and exhibitionistic, almost brazen. And from that high, vulnerable pitch, she moves on without a breath to the pivotal c♭, which is now almost unbearably exposed. The *rallentando* indicated in the score can make this moment both delicious and excruciating, especially if the singer clings to that high pitch before she plunges down the octave and pushes (*stringendo*) toward the return of tonic and ever more dazzling roulades.

Of course, much depends on the performance: the scene can be (and frequently is) sung as a formal *vocalise* or as the lament of a pathetic distracted virgin. But it is also possible to use details of this sort to create an extraordinary portrait of a woman who, in her madness, has transgressed all conventions of propriety and whose exuberance is both awesome and frightening.[23] If the performance of conventionalized ornaments is potentially this effective, imagine the impact if a performer were to invent new roulades—if she were allowed to rage at will without our being able to predict her every move in advance! We have lost a great deal in terms of dramatic impact in our substitution of traditional solutions for improvisation in *bel canto*, though we have also thereby secured certainty (Ex. 4).

As extravagant as it may be, there are important ways in which Lucia's music is carefully framed within the opera. In the middle of this, the most ecstatic and uninhibited demonstration of feminine jouissance they are ever likely to hear, the chorus of wedding guests breaks in with the refrain: "It is no longer possible to refrain from weeping." They attempt in vain to lead her into a more suitable affective key, C minor, for what they perceive as a tragic event. Indeed, the wedding guests respond to and accompany Lucia very much as the trio of men did Monteverdi's nymph. There is even a lead-in, in which her former tutor, Raimondo, sets the scene, and the emphatic quality of the cadential harmonies bracing and interpolating the scene is

Example 4: Traditional ornaments for "Spargi d'amaro pianto" [from Luigi Ricci, *Variazioni—Cadenze—Tradizioni Per Canto*]

likewise there to remind us of social reality—the base from which Lucia has broken free into her world of unfettered imagination. Yet the conclusion of the Mad Scene itself suggests that Lucia (unlike the nymph) has triumphed, for despite the chorus's desperate attempts to maneuver once again toward a C-minor cadence, it is Lucia's E♭ major and her jubilant high e♭ that prevail. To be sure, another whole scene follows this one, and it serves in part to insulate the Mad Scene. But that final scene, in which Edgardo commits suicide, can also be understood as evidence of Lucia's contagion. The frame itself has become contaminated, has gone mad.

I usually avoid using biographical information to substantiate points—and, indeed, I think that the argument that Lucia's disorder is a sexual one can be supported well enough on the basis of social context, changes from the literary model, and (most important) the details of the musical score. However, I cannot resist bringing to bear what seems to be extremely important evidence that the composer himself associated madness with sexual excess. When Donizetti was mad and dying of syphilis in a Parisian asylum, one of the principal symptoms of his degenerating state (to the great consternation of his friends and keepers) was uncontrollable sexual frenzy. Special care was taken to ensure that he—a celebrity—would not be subjected in this condition to the gaze of curiosity seekers, who were still frequenting madhouses for entertainment.[24] To be sure, if Donizetti had died in excellent mental health at age ninety, I would still argue that this composition works on the basis of the madness/sexuality nexus. That his demise was so like that of some of his heroines, however, is uncanny. He apparently knew whereof he composed.

Yet I would not want to read Lucia solely as an instance of feminine dementia, despite the obvious links between her plight and notions linking madness and sexual excess. For in her revolt against patriarchal oppression and musical conformity, she is also a romantic hero whose energy defies stifling social convention. This would help to account for why the class issues of Scott's novel have been so thoroughly transformed in the opera. Lucia's resistance to social oppression can be celebrated not only as a woman's refusal of an arranged marriage, but also as a refusal of any sort of imposed social contract. Her tragic end potentially enflames the resentment of injustices of all kinds, yet the fact that her dilemma seems domestic rather than overtly political meant that it could (and did) pass through the censors. To have enacted a similar rebellion with a male figure at this time would have been risky. And, because she is mad, Lucia cannot, of course, be held responsible for deliberate resistance. Thus she can be victim and heroine simultaneously—in short, a martyr.[25]

Elaine Showalter has argued that

> to watch these operas in performance is to realize that even the
> murderous madwomen do not escape male domination; they
> escape one specific, intolerable exercise of women's wrongs by
> assuming an idealized, poetic form of pure femininity as the male
> culture had construed it: absolutely irrational, absolutely
> emotional, and, once the single act is accomplished, absolutely
> passive.[26]

Yet Flaubert had Emma Bovary respond to a performance of *Lucia* by ex-
claiming, "Oh why had not she, like this woman, resisted?"[27] The gender
politics of this opera are so heavily mediated by musical factors and subtexts
of Romantic rebellion that it is finally very difficult (as well as undesirable)
to arrive at a definitive reading. But however one chooses to read it, *Lucia di
Lammermoor* is far too interesting and complex to dismiss as either a mere
crowd pleaser or an unambiguous instance of misogyny. Whatever it
means, that high e♭ that triumphs at the end of the Mad Scene does not spell
passivity or simple bravura.

4

The nineteenth century saw great turmoil in the area of sexual politics.
Women increasingly demanded the right to education or admission into
professions, were less and less willing to accept passively the prescribed role
of "angel in the house" as their inevitable fate.[28] Historians such as Peter
Gay have traced how female ambition and resistance were understood as
pathological by threatened male culture, which retaliated by producing in
art a large number of monstrous, vampirish women preying on poor helpless males.[29] By far the most sensational and celebrated of these castrating,
bloodsucking harpies is Salome — Oscar Wilde's creation who proliferated
like a hydra head in paintings, art nouveau illustrations, and, of course,
Strauss's opera.

Sander Gilman has written brilliantly on the various layers of
homophilia/homophobia, anti-Semitism, and misogyny present in this
opera.[30] Thus I will focus only on the musical delineation of Salome's transgressions and her eventual recontainment. Salome's madness is explicitly
linked to excessive female sexuality. One review of the premiere called it "a
medical theme in Biblical clothing," which Gilman glosses as probably
meaning "gynecological."[31] Salome's insatiable sexual hunger finally demands not only the mutilation of John the Baptist, but also an autoerotic

scene in which she manages to attain climax with the aid of his dismembered head.

Musically, Salome's pathology is signaled by her slippery chromatic deviations from normative diatonicism. In this she is a sister to figures such as Isolde and Carmen, who likewise play maddeningly in the cracks of tonal social convention.[32] Of course Isolde is not presented as a dominatrix in quite the way the others are. Still, she does befuddle and seduce poor Tristan by means of her chromatic excess, and she too (like Lucia and Salome) achieves transcendence in the absence of the phallus. Isolde gets the last word in this most unconventional opera: *Tristan und Isolde* has a feminine ending of sorts. Yet she does not survive the frame, for after her climax she expires through a spectacular effusion of irrational bliss.[33]

However, not all offending women in opera die off by themselves, and the framing device that controls the proceedings must sometimes be imposed forcibly for purposes of closure. The increasingly paranoid and masochistic cultural agendas of the late nineteenth century tend to give full rein to the perceived horror of female sexual power, flirting with the possibility that it cannot be stopped except by exerting closure violently from without. Many pieces are constructed to simulate lion-taming acts in which the lion mauls the trainer. The fun of seeing the show is knowing in advance that the lion is dangerous, though presumably under control. To witness the beast break through the first line of defense adds the thrill of actual risk—and also the necessity of martial recontainment. Carmen and Lulu are killed like vampires with stakes through the heart. The triumphant, C#-major conclusion of Salome's "Liebestod" is greeted by Herod's command that his guards crush her to death beneath their C-minor shields. The perverse, overripe sexuality of her transport is interrupted by the arbitrary bludgeoning that brings the piece to an abrupt halt. The monstrosity of Salome's sexual and chromatic transgressions is such that extreme violence seems justified—even demanded—for the sake of social and tonal order.

However, that final gesture indicates that the frame itself has lost its hegemonic authority, that the treacherous chromaticism to which European composers and audiences had increasingly become addicted could no longer be rationally contained. Indeed, from the very first line of the opera, we are made aware that Salome's sexual presence has already contaminated the entire court. The tonal fabric festers with chromatic slippage—the half-step between major and minor mediants flickers as an erotic fetish; occasionally a line coalesces into a moment of diatonic desire, only to sink back into the flood of diffused perversity. Jokanaan tries bravely to assert untainted C-major stability in several of his pronouncements, but even his music is driven to frenzy by his environment.

Thus as satisfying as the final purging of Salome's chromaticism might be on some levels, Herod's (and Strauss's) appeal to social convention for narrative and tonal closure can be seen as an act of extraordinary hypocrisy: after Salome's lurid excesses have been exploited throughout the piece, the bid suddenly to frame her as diseased and radically Other is a bit disingenuous. This imposition of closure also represents stylistic cowardice at a time when resistance against convention was most highly prized among artists. Thus resorting to such violent solutions — to last-minute repudiations of erotic indulgence — signals weakness and desperation. Yet not to impose closure — however "inorganic" — was apparently to risk everything. The chromatic excess of the madwoman became even more intense with Elektra, and she finally escaped her would-be captors altogether in Schoenberg's *Erwartung*, where the secure frame of tonality has been murdered, where atonality reigns in supreme, unchallenged lunacy.[34]

5

At this moment, a very interesting subtext of music since Monteverdi becomes explicit. If we review the portraits of famous madwomen in music, we find that the signs of their madness are usually among the favorite techniques of the avant-garde: strategies that for each style hover at the extremes, strategies that most successfully exceed the verbal component of dramatic music and that transgress conventions of "normal" procedure.[35] These same techniques are used without comment in our most complex, most intellectually virtuosic instrumental music. An ostinato underpins the heroic struggles of Bach's chaconne for solo violin, which enacts the same kinds of resistances, strains, and obsessive returns as Monteverdi's pathetic nymph. The excessive ornamentation, formal discontinuity, and virtuosic display that represent Lucia's deluded mind characterize the extravagant cadenzas of concertos. Here the increasingly crazed harpsichord solo of Bach's Brandenburg No. 5, or the acrobatics of Liszt come especially to mind.[36] And in the nineteenth-century symphony, Salome's chromatic daring is what distinguishes truly serious composition of the vanguard from mere cliché-ridden hack work.

In other words, the very qualities regarded as evidence of superior imagination — even of genius — in each period of music are, when enacted on stage, often projected onto madwomen. In explaining the musical appeal of the subject of madness, Donal Henehan states:

> Even as late as Mozart's time the forms of music were so rigid that the only way the average composer could wriggle out of the

restraints even momentarily was to seize upon certain genre pieces such as the storm. A storm is not expected to follow strict logic, so the composer could break away for a moment and upset the furniture. The Mad Scene offered similar freedom, both formally and expressively.[37]

In opera, the madwoman is given the music of greatest stylistic privilege, the music that seems to do what is most quintessentially *musical*, as opposed to verbal or conventional. She is a pretext for compositional misbehavior.

This says something very interesting and important about music as it is "framed" in Western culture. Roland Barthes has written that

> the body passes into music without any relay but the signifier. This passage — this transgression — makes music a madness. . . . In relation to the writer, the composer is always mad (and the writer can never be so, for he is condemned to meaning).[38]

In contrast to this position, I have always maintained in my work that music is a socially organized enterprise — is likewise "condemned to meaning." Its structures, narratives, semiotic codes, and so on are developed, negotiated, resisted, transmitted, or transformed within a completely social arena. There are social strictures at any given moment that attempt to impose propriety over this scary stuff, whether through Renaissance rules of voice-leading, Rameau's codification of diatonic tonality, or narrative principles of sonata procedure. Yet ever since Glarean praised Josquin for disregarding the rules, artists have been socially encouraged to violate the regulations that would reduce music to mere words and dead forms. This vital dialectic between what Jacques Attali calls order and noise has given rise to all of the music we care about, and it is always socially grounded.[39]

But to the very great extent that Western culture is logocentric, music itself always gives the impression of being in excess, of being mad — and thus Barthes's statement. Moreover, musicians themselves have often tried to have it both ways: to indulge extravagantly in whatever is regarded as lying beyond the pale (as the heavy metal band Iron Maiden puts it, to "play with madness"), but asserting all the while that everything they do is actually ordered, rational, under control. And during the nineteenth century, this paradoxical blend of madness with order, of "feminine" excess with structural rigor came to be known and celebrated as "genius."

Christine Battersby's *Gender and Genius* painstakingly traces the evolution of the concept of "genius" and its attendant ideologies from its beginnings in antiquity (when the word was associated chiefly with male procreativity) to the present (when whatever it is, is supposed to be "scientifically" measurable through IQ tests). As she demonstrates, the word came to be applied in the Romantic era to artists, who were thought to be different from other men precisely because they incorporated "feminine" imagination with "masculine" reason, madness with craft.[40] Battersby warns that this appropriation by males of "the feminine" did not have the result of exalting actual women or granting them a role in cultural production. In the words of Otto Weininger:

> The man of genius possesses, like everything else, the complete female in himself; but woman herself is only a part of the Universe, and the part never can be the whole; femaleness can never include genius.[41]

Yet although women were explicitly excluded from the category of "genius," images of feminine receptivity, organic generation, and childbirth nonetheless abound in nineteenth-century accounts of the creative process. Likewise, characterizations of Romantic artists as holy madmen were commonplace.

Associations of femininity and/or mental imbalance with creative genius occur in writings about music as well. Heinrich Schenker's theories concerning genius, for instance, are thoroughly informed by the formulations of Schopenhauer and others, and he often describes creativity in terms of divine insemination, of feminine passivity and gestation on the part of the artist rather than conscious intention.[42] And Jeffrey Kallberg, in his study of the nineteenth-century critical association of femininity with the genre of the nocturne, located the following extraordinary statement: "The poetic side of men of genius is feminine, and in Chopin the feminine note was over emphasized—at times it was almost hysterical—particularly in these nocturnes."[43]

As this last quotation betrays, the contradictions inherent in the social framing of the composer-genius as androgynous mad(wo)man became ever more stressful over the course of the nineteenth century. The battle between what were understood as the mad feminine side and the rational masculine component was played out stylistically in massive assaults on "normative" procedures, until very little remained to attack. What I am describing is a network of uncomfortably slippery metaphors; but, slippery or not, these are the metaphors that both nourished the transgressions of the fin de siècle avant-garde and also helped to precipitate its unparalleled moment of crisis. For the dilemma confronting musical syntax in the early years of this century was not just an intellectual or formal problem: it was inextricably tangled up with anxieties over sexual identity and gendered distinctions between reason and madness.

We have seen how arbitrary the final frame of *Salome* seems, given the unrelenting resistance to tonality enacted for the full duration of the opera. The fantasy played out in *Erwartung* (1909) is that the contagion of chromaticism is ultimately fatal, that the monstrosity that had gradually been unleashed within musical syntax can no longer be arrested. The rationality of tonal closure that had always come like Dudley Doright to the rescue is revealed as arbitrary, as unmotivated, as imposed from without.

Based on a dramatic monologue by Marie Pappenheim, *Erwartung* presents the ravings of a deranged woman as she searches anxiously for her lover. She eventually discovers his body, which she only gradually realizes is dead. She speaks lovingly to him at first, but then lashes out at him for his infidelities. It seems that she herself is probably his murderer and that we are witnessing her return to the scene of the crime, the memory of which she has repressed at the expense of her sanity.

In his musical setting of *Erwartung*, Schoenberg dispenses with tonal reference or goal orientation altogether, as the woman's paranoid utterances range from catatonic paralysis to chaotic flailing. The first sense of framing I have been tracing—the semiotic construction of the madwoman through discontinuity and extreme chromaticism—is still intact in *Erwartung*; but the protective frame—the masculine presence that had always guaranteed the security of rationality within the music itself—is absent, ostensibly murdered by our madwoman. If the nineteenth century had been enacting a musical game of "chicken" in which ever greater risks were run before pulling back to safety, Schoenberg here careens right over the edge. The bloody tide of insubordinate women so dreaded by European males early in this century here appears to overwhelm the social order completely.[44]

6

Women in the real world who were diagnosed as mad at the end of the nineteenth century were turned over to a new group of professionals called analysts, whose business it was to detect the logic hidden behind aberrant behaviors. The extreme transgressions of early twentieth-century music similarly called forth a new breed of music professional, also known as analysts.[45] There had, of course, been instances of music criticism before this time: musicians such as Glarean or Schumann had written essays explaining what was of value, what was effective, what was unusual in pieces of music. But the new analysts were interested not so much in celebrating the idiosyncrasies of individual pieces as in demonstrating that moments of apparent madness are, in fact, ultrarational. Indeed, analysts tend to flock precisely to those passages that most flaunt their excessiveness.

Heinrich Schenker, one of our fathers of analysis, was concerned with finding a method for objectively distinguishing manifestations of *responsible* excess from pieces that were genuinely deviant, for early modernism had demonstrated to him that some forms of chromaticism were in fact deadly. His graphs are at their most obsessive when dealing with a moment in a beloved piece that seems to defy rational explanation, and he succeeds when he can reduce the offending passage back to diatonic normality or (in the case of his redemptive graphs of Chopin's nocturnes) to structural virility.[46] He delivers the Good Housekeeping seal to those pieces that were just joshing, that deep down inside were rigorously ordered, and the Surgeon General's warning for those such as Wagner or Mahler that are truly bad for your health.

Arnold Schoenberg's route to analysis was considerably more ambivalent, for he was not only a theorist: he also aspired to play the role of the transgressor par excellence. Much of his ambivalence is readily apparent in his 1911 treatise, *Theory of Harmony*, in which he repeatedly asserts his desire to escape the strictures of tonality. What Schenker continued to hold as sacrosanct—rational tonal procedure, dissonance regulation, and laws of necessary closure—Schoenberg perceived as oppressive conventions, rather than immutable or natural. Yet throughout his treatise, Schoenberg also reveals how terrifying it was to identify himself with those forces that had traditionally served to destabilize tonal certainty—dissonance, chromaticism, excess—but which were inevitably quashed in accordance with narrative propriety. In effect, he affiliates himself with what had always been defined as the "feminine" side of all the binary oppositions governing tonal procedures and narratives.

Repeatedly in *Theory of Harmony* Schoenberg lays bare the inherited binarisms he detests. But he is careful in his highly troped language to avoid the obvious and conventional mapping of these musical pairs onto gender. He chooses rather to define the oppositions in accordance with images of resistance against oppressive political authority. And from that vantage point, Schoenberg seems safe, for he is aligning himself with the properly masculine business of revolution:

> Of course the idea of closing with the same tone one began with
> has something decidedly right about it and also gives a certain
> impression of being natural. Since indeed all the simple
> relationships derive from the simplest natural aspects of the tone
> (from its first overtones), the fundamental tone then has a certain
> sovereignty over the structures emanating from it just because
> the most important components of these structures are, so to
> speak, its satraps, its advocates, since they derive from its

splendor: Napoleon, who installs his relatives and friends on the European thrones. I think that would indeed be enough to explain why one is justified in obeying the will of the fundamental tone: gratefulness to the progenitor and dependence on him. He is Alpha and Omega. That is morally right, so long as no other moral code obtains. Yet, another can indeed prevail! If, for example, the supreme lord becomes weak and his subjects strong, a situation that arises only too often in harmony. Just as it is hardly inevitable that a conqueror will endure as dictator, so it is no more inevitable that tonality must take its direction from the fundamental tone, even if it is derived from that tone. Quite the contrary. The struggle between two such fundamentals for sovereignty has something indeed very attractive about it, as numerous examples of modern harmony show. And even if here the struggle does end with the victory of the one fundamental, that victory is still not inevitable. . . . The ceremonious way in which the close of a composition used to be tied up, bolted, nailed down, and sealed would be too ponderous for the present-day sense of form to use it. This precondition, that everything emanates from the [fundamental] tone, can just as well be suspended, since one is constantly reminded of it anyway by every tone. And whenever we let our imagination roam, we certainly do not keep ourselves strictly within boundaries, even though our bodies do have them.

Many examples give evidence that nothing is lost from the impression of completeness if the tonality is merely hinted at, yes, even if it is erased. And—without saying that the ultra-modern music is really atonal: for it may be perhaps that we simply do not yet know how to explain the tonality, or something corresponding to tonality, in modern music—the analogy with infinity could hardly be made more vivid than through a fluctuating, so to speak, unending harmony, through a harmony that does not always carry with it certificate of domicile and passport carefully indicating country of origin and destination.[47]

Here we have a thorough remapping of the conventional tonal narrative, which is now interpreted as arbitrary and authoritarian. Those moments he wishes to preserve, the "vagrants" who travel without passports, are precisely those large-scale dissonances—"feminine" keys, themes, and chromaticism—that motivate the narrative of tonality and sonata. It is the frame itself that had always seemed to guarantee security ("tied up, bolted, nailed down, and sealed") that is now unmasked as the enemy—as the musical incarnation of what Althusser would call an Ideological State Apparatus.

Schoenberg does not always write of those transgressive moments in strictly revolutionary tropes. A kind of sexual license—the right to indulge in excess, to play out forbidden desires—likewise is at stake:

> Thus it can also be imagined how the chance occurrence of a dissonant passing tone, once established by the notation, after its excitement had been experienced, called forth the desire for less accidental, less arbitrary repetition; how the desire to experience this excitement more often led to taking possession of the methods that brought it about. But, should the excitement of the forbidden lead to uninhibited indulgence, that essentially despicable compromise between morality and immoderate desire had to be drawn, that compromise which here consists in a looser conception of the prohibition as well as of that which is prohibited. Dissonance was accepted, but the door through which it was admitted was bolted whenever excess threatened. . . .Preparation and resolution are thus a pair of protective wrappers in which the dissonance is carefully packed so that it neither suffers nor inflicts damage. (48)

Despite his careful presentation of his agenda in political terms, these other tropes often break through to reveal other realms of experience fueling his battle. More important, these tropes are not limited to his theoretical writing—they also informed and helped to legitimate his experimental compositions. Schoenberg had argued that the only genre within which he could bring about his longed-for "suspended tonality" was opera, for symphonic forms depend on the restrictive conventions for purposes of coherence (370). In order to escape tonality's narrative stranglehold and still make sense, he needed another organizing metaphor—one made explicit by the libretto and dramatic action.

And, not surprisingly, his metaphorical surrogate in *Erwartung*—the piece in which he committed his supreme violation, his break with tonality—was once again the figure of the madwoman. The political revolutionary of *Theory of Harmony*, who boldly demands sexual license, is nowhere to be seen. Schoenberg's celebrated "emancipation of the dissonance" is self-consciously presented as the liberation of the female lunatic, of the feminine moment of desire and dread that had driven most nineteenth-century narratives. If he managed in his theoretical writings to construct transgression as a heroic deed, his artistic enactment of that transgression in *Erwartung* betrays his inability to dismiss or transcend traditional binarisms and their gendered associations. The repressed returns with a vengeance. For the principal affect of the composition bears little resemblance to the joy of a hero who has just succeeded in overthrowing a dictator; on the contrary, it conveys a mixture of guilt, confusion, and alarm. Stripped of the possibility of resolution or the intervention of hegemonic control, desire in its rawest, most murderous form runs rampant through the piece. Schoenberg's fantasy of emancipation is realized on the stage as a paranoid nightmare.

As a rebel seeking to justify his unparalleled violations of established order, Schoenberg had debated in *Theory of Harmony* whether or not to invent a new system to account for apparent improprieties, to convert them to logic. At one point he wrote: "If the laws issuing from tonality, the laws of the autocrat, were rescinded, its erstwhile domain would not thereby necessarily sink into chaos but would automatically, following its own dictates, make for itself laws consistent with its nature" (152). His thought in 1911 was so opposed to systems per se that he was reluctant to posit a new one. However, when he revised this passage in the 1922 edition, he added the following phrases: "that anarchy would not ensue, but rather a new form of order. I may add, however, that this new order will soon begin to resemble the old, until it becomes completely equivalent to the old; for order is as much God's will as change, which persistently leads back to order" (152).

To have enacted his fantasy of uninhibited transgressions of *Erwartung* seems to have been unnerving, and consequently Schoenberg soon diverted his energies from anarchy to the analytic search for hidden order. No less an authority than God seemed to demand that he abide by some kind of regulation, yet he could not turn back to what he had himself revealed as the lie of tonality. After this period of anarchy, Schoenberg wrote little music until he emerged with a systematic theory that permitted him to have it both ways: his technique of serialism succeeds in underwriting what sound like dissonant ravings with supreme rational control.[48] Or, as he put it in "Composition with Twelve Tones":

> The desire for a conscious control of the new means and forms
> will arise in every artist's mind. . . . He must find, if not laws or
> rules, at least ways to justify the dissonant character of these
> harmonies and their successions. After many unsuccessful
> attempts during a period of approximately twelve years, I laid
> the foundations for a new procedure in musical construction
> which seemed fitted to replace those structural differentiations
> provided formerly by tonal harmonies. I called this procedure
> *Method of Composing with Twelve Tones Which are Related Only
> with One Another.*[49]

From this moment on, the rational frame guaranteeing social order comes to permeate the dissonant discourse of the madwoman, and the chromaticism of feminine sexual excess no longer poses a threat: henceforth it is appropriated—even generated—by the highest achievement of intellectual discipline. One can now experience that frenzy, that illicit desire, without either the panic that attends chaos or the traditional demand for narrative closure, because the composer and analyst can prove that every pitch is always already contained. In contrast to the tortured prose of *Theory of Harmony*, Schoenberg's explanations of serial theory are serene and orderly, as are his many accounts that demonstrate his essential continuity with (rather than violation against) tradition. And most analysts of serial music no longer acknowledge or even recognize the transgressive impulse that first gave rise to "atonal" and then twelve-tone practices.

But the period between Schenker's tonality and Schoenberg's serial music remains a repertory of great theoretical anxiety, for this is the music (composed in deliberate opposition to the old system and without the security of a new one) that might genuinely be crazy.[50] As music theorists, we are so compelled to find evidence of order in all these traumatic pieces that we sometimes resort to the corrective surgery of pitch-class amoebas—to drawing loops around groups of pitches in order to demonstrate that they are actually arranged rationally.[51] Atonal compositions—like patients throughout most of psychiatric history—are usually silent during the process of analysis, for it is only apparently in the absence of those coils of seductive or demented sound that order can be detected and objectively charted.[52]

That analysis is an indispensable ingredient in our study of music is beyond question. Yet we need to supplement bare formal analysis with information concerning the historical conditions that give rise both to particular repertories and also to the metatheoretical discourses that serve to frame and explain away the "problematic" aspects of music. If—as is clearly the case—a fascination with madness and transgressive behavior motivates much of the music we care about, then surely we need to take that into account before we jump in with our graphs. Otherwise, what precisely are we doing? Whose rationality are we attempting to establish, and why?

7

It is important to keep in mind that the analytical devices for taming the monstrous in music are brought to bear not on actual madwomen—or even on the products of madwomen. They are marshaled to ward off the boogeymen constructed by the same people who also construct the frames and then stand in horror of their own inventions, rather like Dr. Frankenstein and his creature. For the nymph, Lucia, Salome, and the antiheroine of *Erwartung* are first and foremost male fantasies of transgression dressed up as women. Real women—mad or otherwise—do not enter into this picture at all. We sit on the sidelines and watch as mainstream culture concocts such figures, then envies, desires, fears, and finally demolishes and/or analyzes them. This process might be a rather amusing spectacle in its own right, if such travesties were not taken so often to reveal how women really are. In French the word *folle* means both madwoman and drag queen. And so far, we have only been dealing with the latter. Thus I want to conclude by considering a very different sort of example.

In the course of the nineteenth century, female novelists seized the power of self-representation that had traditionally been denied them. And as Gilbert and Gubar's *The Madwoman in the Attic* demonstrates, many of them reappropriated for their own uses the image of the madwoman for expressly political purposes.[53] For a variety of reasons, there have been few women in music in comparable positions until very recently. There are no nineteenth-century musical equivalents of Gilbert and Gubar's madwomen, for whom both the semiotic constructions and the narrative frames were designed by feminists.

But there is at present a woman composer who produces extraordinary simulations of feminine rage. Diamanda Galas emerged within the post-modern performance art scene of the seventies, and like other performance artists she enacts her pieces upon her own body.[54] This is politically very different from the tradition of male composers projecting their own fantasies of transgression as well as their own fears onto women characters and performers. Galas is not interested in the narrative of raising the specter of the monstrous, flirting with madness, and then reimposing control—the narrative in which the double discourse of violation and protection are at stake. Rather, she enacts the rage of the madwoman for purposes of pro-testing genuine atrocities: the treatment of victims of the Greek junta, atti-tudes toward victims of AIDS.[55] Her simulations are not peep shows.

This does not mean that she enacts some essence of femininity or of in-sanity. On the contrary, she identifies herself as a virtuoso of extended vocal techniques and as a composer. Galas has even published accounts of her compositional processes in *Perspectives of New Music*.[56] Her pieces are con-structed from the ululation of traditional Mediterranean keening, and from the kinds of whispers, shrieks, and moans one somehow recognizes as po-tentially human but that have always been represented for our genteel aes-thetic consumption through Lucia's coloratura or Salome's chromaticism.

For instance, in "Free among the Dead," her setting of Psalm 88 from the AIDS trilogy, the parameters most responsible for the power of her music are those most resistant to traditional forms of analysis: ear-splitting volume, a broad spectrum of bizarre timbres, the semiotics of extreme anguish, and a structure that builds intensity through sheer repetition—unlike the carefully modulated, ever-changing responses to the ostinato by Monteverdi's nymph. Or when she sings "Swing Low, Sweet Chariot" entirely in the range above the staff, she applies to the familiar spiritual the signs of crazed virtuosity usually associated with figures such as the Queen of the Night or Lucia. She thereby converts it into a searing protest song, even as she also comments on the conventional link between the coloratura range and madness. If one were to transcribe such pieces onto paper, the scores might look fairly controllable, for the sources of her musical power—including the fact of its sheer noise—would thereby be silenced. (The pitch relationships of "Sweet Chariot," for instance, would remain identical to those of the standard tune.) But paper is not her medium, and producing esoteric structural correspondences is not her aim.

What Galas does is undeniably risky, given the tendency for women in Western culture always to be understood as excessive, sexually threatening, mad. She can be read as simply reaffirming the worst stereotypes available. But she can also be read as extremely courageous as she confronts these stereotypes head-on, appropriates them, and rechannels their violent energies in other directions. Her images enter into public circulation, challenging the premises of the prestigious male-constructed madwomen preserved within the musical canon and giving voice to what has always been represented as radically "Other."[57]

Diamanda Galas's music reveals how very constructed the classic madwomen of music have been—how sanitized, how made to conform to various male cultural fanatasies, and finally how framable. As she seizes the signs of dementia in order to give voice to political outrage, she defies and dispenses with the conventional framing devices that have aestheticized previous portrayals of women and madness. She thereby heralds a new moment in the history of musical representation.

Chapter 5
Getting Down Off the Beanstalk:
The Presence of a Woman's Voice in
Janika Vandervelde's *Genesis II*

Once upon a time, there was a young composer who received a commission to write orchestral music to accompany the dramatic narration of "Jack and the Beanstalk" for a children's concert. Like most beloved fairy tales, "Jack" deals with very basic life issues: the beanstalk is accidentally planted when Jack's mother callously rejects his newly acquired magic beans. Overnight the beanstalk becomes erect, grows very big, and penetrates the clouds, permitting Jack to ascend and conquer the Giant/Father. A more obvious oedipal situation is difficult to imagine.

The music for "Jack" was produced in accordance with the abstract principles of musical order dutifully absorbed by the composer in school: namely, the narrative schemata manifested in tonality and its classical forms. The piece had *thrust*, and it had the requisite climax three-quarters of the way through. Because this was a piece of program music, its sequence of images was designed to correspond to moments dictated by the fairy tale: the quality of thrust entered the serene landscape of the piece only with the beanstalk's dynamic tumescence, and the violent climax (both desired and dreaded) coincided with Jack's triumphant defeat of the giant.

The music depicting the beanstalk's erection and penetration is a highly venerable gesture—one that marks the heroic climax of many a tonal composition. A kind of pitch ceiling consolidates, against which melodic motives begin to push as though against a palpable obstacle. As frustration mounts, the urgency of the motivic salvos increases; they move in shorter and shorter time spans, until they succeed finally in bursting through the barrier with a spasm of ejaculatory release. This musical gesture appears prominently in many of our favorite repertories. It guarantees our identification with the music, for its buildup hooks us, motivating us to invest personally in sequences of seemingly abstract musical events; and we are re-warded for having thus invested in its patterns of yearning when they reach cathartic fulfillment, which mysteriously becomes our own experience of libidinal gratification.

In rock concerts this gesture is celebrated theatrically with the eruption of onstage flashpots and the vigorous wagging of guitars and mike stands. But it is not confined to rock: this same gesture also marks the transcendental moment of what Dahlhaus extols as "lyric urgency" in Don José's "Flower Song," as well as the buildup to the recapitulation in Tchaikovsky's Fourth Symphony.[1] Moreover, despite the fact that serious composers by and large rejected tonality (and, presumably, its attendant narratives) at the beginning of this century, theorist Patrick McCreless has demonstrated that this be-loved gesture nevertheless lived on to serve as the payoff in large numbers of posttonal compositions.[2] And the neotonality of John Adams and David Del Tredici has promoted its unembarrassed reassertion in compositions that once again give concert audiences what they want to hear.[3] The gesture is only slightly more graphic and literal in pornographic films, in which key structural moments of tension and release likewise are conventionally em-bodied through what is called the "money shot"—close-up footage of a dis-charging penis.[4]

To have represented the beanstalk in these terms was virtually inescap-able, given the story and the centrality of this musical convention to narra-tive success. And, not surprisingly, "Jack and the Beanstalk" turned out to be quite successful with its audiences: the children responded with predict-able waves of enthusiasm in keeping with the narrative flow of the music, which they could follow perfectly given their experience with climax-punc-tuated Saturday morning cartoons. As she watched the children's volatile reactions, however, the composer felt somewhat uneasy about what she had wrought (for our composer, incidentally, is a woman). To be sure, she had constructed for the children perhaps the most delicate version of this surefire gesture imaginable: it is painted in pastel orchestral hues, and its penetration of the clouds is but a gentle poke. Yet despite her kid-glove treatment of the emphatically male fairy tale, the end result was that the same old phallic im-ages once again reared their ubiquitous heads.

This is the story of Janika Vandervelde: the story of an artist who chose to get down off the beanstalk, to deny herself the automatic surge of power it reliably delivers, to analyze its contours, and to embark on a journey in search of alternative ways of organizing sound, ways that correspond more closely to her own values and experiences. By extension it is also the story of any composer—female or male—who has become dissatisfied with implied contents of received artistic conventions and procedures, especially the standard narrative of tonal striving, climax, and closure.

1

To date, most discussions concerning women in composition have centered on the issue of equal opportunity. The idea is that given the same access to training and education, women too will emerge as composers, *indistinguishable from their male colleagues*. They will, in other words, be granted the beans from which springs the mighty beanstalk. Since this is the most common variety of seed being dispensed by music schools in music history, theory, and analysis classes, it is not surprising that many women and men trained in those contexts tend to be unaware of the ideological traces encoded in much of that training. The exigencies of the powerful narrative of tonality and the various formal schemata it spawned are simply taken to be the way the world goes, especially since this narrative is also the one endlessly re-inscribed in film, novels, and television. Unwittingly, young women composers often find themselves committed to the further "dissemination" of more and more beanstalks.

For what are the alternatives? A time-honored strategy practiced by many other groups marginalized by a musical mainstream is that of creating a stylistic synthesis: appropriating components of that mainstream but blending them with elements of their own readily recognized idiom. I have argued elsewhere that Bach's eclecticism is a product of such a syncretic practice—an idiosyncratic fusion of Italian and French musical discourses within a specifically German dialect.[5] The musics of black and Hispanic Americans likewise reflect various forms of self-empowering engagement between the white mainstream and ethnic traditions.[6]

However, for white, middle-class women aspiring to the role of "composer," this strategy is not automatically available. History does not offer a separate women's musical culture, complete with styles or performing institutions of its own, from which position a female composer can bargain or negotiate. There is, in other words, no traditional woman's voice.[7]

Worse yet, there is a bogus tradition of "how women sound" in European classical music—a code developed and transmitted by men, in which women are either docile and passive (Monteverdi's Euridice, Bizet's Micaëla, Mozart's Pamina) or else man-devouring harpies (Monteverdi's Poppea, Mozart's Queen of the Night, Bizet's Carmen, Strauss's Salome).[8] Because these pernicious musical images of women—the madonna or the whore—have been the only ones available, generations of women training to be performers or composers have learned not to let themselves "sound like women" in their playing, conducting, or composing. In order not to resemble the passive ideal of femininity, we have learned how to perform or write (how often have we gloried in this compliment!) *with balls*; and yet we have also learned not to play *too* aggressively for fear of terrifying—as composer/performer Diamanda Galas does so audaciously with her dominatrix garb and her "madwoman" shrieks and gutteral moans—our patriarchal mentors.[9] Thus not only do women not have a musical language of their own upon which to rely, but they often have internalized a strong distaste for the idea of permitting their identities as women to be apparent in their music. The category "woman" in music is already colonized and is overcrowded with caricatures concocted by male artists.

Women in literature, dance, and the visual arts have faced and overcome similar difficulties. When these same issues were first raised in 1971 by Linda Nochlin's "Why Have There Been No Great Women Artists?" many women who were already established in the arts publicly attacked Nochlin and the possibility of a "women's art."[10] And even so prominent a feminist writer as Erica Jong has written about her inability as a young writer to identify with female characters in novels or to imagine writing from a woman's point of view.[11] Nevertheless, there do exist women artists who have been preoccupied with creating works that insist upon—rather than mask—the fact that they were produced by women. Literature saw the emergence of such a countermovement as early as the nineteenth century (with Jane Austen, the Brontës, Emily Dickinson, and, later, Virginia Woolf), dance in the early twentieth (Isadora Duncan, Martha Graham), and the visual arts in the last fifteen years or so (Judy Chicago, Barbara Kruger).[12]

There are many reasons why women composers have been reluctant or unable to pursue parallel explorations, including the tremendous pressures of educational and entrepreneurial institutions to conform to certain dominant norms. But an even greater barrier has been the much-celebrated "nonrepresentational" character of music.

It is currently fashionable in literary-critical circles to claim that *no* art is, in fact, representational, by which it is meant that art is always a fabricated construct merely posing as the mirror of reality, and that to view a work of art as representational is to take uncritically its biased formulation to be unmediated reality itself.[13] While I would not wish to argue with this claim, there are at least elements in literature and the visual arts that closely resemble aspects of the world in which we live: identifiable objects, human figures, colors, characters, narrative events, and so forth. When we come to these works in order to interpret them, we can refer to those elements in a common language that nonprofessionals can comprehend. And when a woman artist or writer chooses to create in a mode that expressly draws upon her experience as a woman, she can, for instance, do so by appropriating, subverting, or calling into question traditional images or characterizations of women. The viewer or reader can usually enter into the work at least at the level of recognizing the objects, colors, characters, situations—even if understanding its more subtle dimensions requires a high degree of critical judgment and interpretive skill.

Music, by contrast, rarely has dimensions that are readily identified with aspects of the material or social world. Moreover, the theoretical discourse about music tends to treat musical shapes as self-contained entities and systematically blocks consideration of its content.[14] If music is music is only music, then how does the woman composer enter into composition *as a woman*? I have a colleague who has claimed that the only evidence he would accept for the presence of a woman's voice in music is the demonstration that there can be "tits on chords."

When Minnesota composer Janika Vandervelde decided, partly in response to the "Beanstalk" episode, to produce an alternative to the dominant discourse she had internalized in the course of her training, she was up against that kind of institutional skepticism. She chose to answer the challenge—not only in the more obvious area of vocal music in which verbal texts can bear the burden of signification, but also in the resistant, privileged, "nonrepresentational" bastion of instrumental music. The result has been a series of "Genesis" pieces in which Vandervelde continues to explore and to expand her range of alternative images and narrative schemata. Her strategies and their wide-ranging implications seem to me so remarkable that I will devote the core of this essay to a reading of her composition for piano trio, *Genesis II*.[15]

2

Genesis II opens with what Vandervelde intends as a musical image of childbirth: the pulsation of a fetal heartbeat, the intensifying strains of labor, and the sudden emergence into a fresh and calm new world (Ex. 1).[16] The very presence of this image is remarkable, for while Western culture has produced images celebrating such "universal" human concerns as war, it has avoided dealing with the dynamic moment of birth. This seems odd because, given that we all are born, this phenomenon is genuinely universal. But its absence is also predictable since the birthing process is exclusively female, and cultural themes by and large have been determined by patriarchal interests.[17]

Example 1: *Genesis II*, Prologue, mm. 25–42

The fresh new world that comes into being as a result of this prologue contains two kinds of music, each organizing time in a different way. On the one hand, we are presented with a minimalistic "clockwork" pattern in the piano: a pattern that repeats cyclically but which, because it is internally

Example 2: *Genesis II*, "Clockwork," mm. 1-16

marked by asymmetries of rhythm and pitch, is endlessly fascinating—
almost like the facets of a crystal that seem to change with each turn (Ex. 2).
It creates a sense of existence *in* time that is stable, ordered, yet "timeless."

We are continually made aware of the present moment, as the asymmetries of the pattern attract the ear down into its intricate cross-rhythms; yet the completion of each cycle yields a sense of satisfaction and security, and we experience the possibility that the pattern might be replicated indefinitely, infinitely. It sets up no expectation for change.

And on the other hand, we have the string parts in the ensemble. Once past the first section, in which they coexist peaceably with the clockwork, they present us with the goal-oriented gestures of self-expression and striving that typically characterize Western concert music: gestures that are explicitly *not* content with living in the present moment but that seek to expand horizons and to defy social convention, gestures that trade the very hope of future stability for a never-ending chase after the elusive chimeras of progress, change, and finally the transcendence and obliteration of time.[18]

These two contrasting types of music are extremely rich in metaphorical implication. The cyclic properties of the clockwork resonate with the patterns of nature: seasonal yet timeless, always fascinatingly different and yet always the same. Up against the natural ebb and flow of the clockwork, the string parts are clearly marked with the gestures associated in tonal music with self-determination, with the ongoing struggle of human endeavor.

But human endeavor need not be understood in those terms. Indeed, it is principally the culture—which includes, of course, the music—of post-Renaissance Europe that casts itself in this fashion.[19] Knowing this unlocks another crucial dimension of Vandervelde's piece: the *historical*. Before the general crisis of the late sixteenth century, European culture was shaped by ideals of harmony, balance, stability. It is no coincidence that *Genesis II* 's clockwork is reminiscent of medieval music: both are marked by relatively noncoercive modal techniques that delight in the present moment, rhythms that are grounded in the physicality and repetitiveness of dance, and the kind of carefully regulated contrapuntal interplay that Renaissance theorists associated with the harmony of the spheres, of nature and humankind, of soul and body.

With the general crisis of the seventeenth century precipitated by—among many other factors—the Reformation, colonial expansion, humanism, the scientific revolutions of Copernicus and Galileo, and Cartesian philosophy, the ideal of culture changes from stability and balance to extravagant, individualistic assertion.[20] The musical principles responsible for images of Renaissance *harmonia* are defiantly ruptured, and a new secular spirit of passionate manipulation emerges. The theatrical genres of opera, cantata, and oratorio immediately move to the center of vocal composition; the virtuosic solo violin sonata leads to the creation of specifically instrumental forms that dispense with verbal discourse altogether and that work purely on the basis of aggressive rhetorical gestures; goal-oriented tonality develops to provide the illusion of narrative necessity that underlies the new music of the modern era.[21]

It is precisely that moment in the history of Europe that is enacted so richly in *Genesis II*. This is *the* critical moment, for it is this crisis, this set of choices, that unleashed both the triumphs and the horrors of the world we live in today. And it is to Vandervelde's credit that her composition catches the listener in the troubling, contradictory responses of desire and dread, that it suggests no easy solutions, that it does not even dictate the forces with which one should identify.

There are listeners who quickly tire of the "minimalistic" clockwork and who identify more readily with the narratively organized string parts when they break away—people who hear the clockwork as mechanistic, or as a beautiful yet inanimate crystalline formation, against which the strings become the specifically human voice. Others (and here I count myself) are attracted to or identify with the gentle ebb and flow of the cyclic clockwork and are unnerved by the violence wreaked upon it by the impulsive, self-expressive strings.

In either case, once the harmonious world of the opening clockwork is shattered by the goal-oriented strings, the two elements are set on an inevitable collision course. The possibility of peaceful coexistence and reconciliation disappears, even as a final goal toward which the piece might be working. As de Lauretis has written concerning traditional narrative paradigms, "Story demands sadism, depends on making something happen, forcing a change in another person, a battle of will and strength, victory/defeat, all occurring in a linear time with a beginning and an end."[22] And once narrative conventions are invoked by the strings, this whole set of generic expectations concerning continuation and conditions for closure is inevitably mobilized.

According to conventions of musical narrative, it is the first item that gets to count as protagonist—the opening tonic key, the characteristic initial theme by which we tend to identify the composition. This is usually the most aggressive of the themes, the active agent whose adventure we are called upon to witness. And its narrative foil—the second ("feminine") theme/key—is generally more static: within the context of the protagonist's story it serves first as obstacle, then finally as that which is vanquished or absorbed.

But in *Genesis II*, the order is inverted. The aggressive strings are intruders into a musical landscape that had set up no expectation for change, no suggestion that a narrative was lying in wait. They seize the role of dominator and subject the composition's unfolding to the sadistic demands of story. Yet there is no outcome that could satisfy the impulse of the strings, for they have no stable identity to which they could return for formal consolidation. They are characterized always as striving, always resisting the possibility of stasis. The promise of closure that normally motivates such patterning is antithetical to the particular exigencies of the strings as they are constituted in this composition. In this context, closure can mean nothing but a crash landing.

Midway through the piece the violin and cello quicken their pace: in their push for climax, they disrupt even the clockwork's well-regulated cyclic pattern. The confrontation between the two elements culminates in a violent explosion, after which the triumphant strings—now all by themselves, lonely yet gloriously autonomous—perform a tortured, self-alienated Romantic cadenza (Ex. 3a).

When the clockwork returns, it is in a crippled, corrupted state: its once-pure modal landscape is now permanently marred by a "wrong note" (Ex. 3b). Cautiously at first, then with increasing recklessness, the strings once again mount their offensive—now with the angular, antagonistic musical gestures of twentieth-century Modernism. They succeed finally in harnessing and usurping the patterns of the clockwork, which causes the piano part (the locus of the clockwork up until this time) to disintegrate into agitated arpeggiation. The resulting disorder leads to a second, even more overwhelming explosion.

If the piece concluded here with this "Apocalypse—Now!" gesture, it would yield something of the same thrill as do many of the self-destructive beanstalks of the late nineteenth-century symphonic repertory. For instance, the home stretch of Mahler's "Resurrection" Symphony is ushered in with the chorus shouting in unison the text "I will die in order to live." And with the last line, "that with which you have struggled will lead you to God," the listener is drawn through a minefield punctuated with detonations to the glory of the final triad. It isn't even the "correct" final triad, for we began this symphony in C minor and ought to be ending in C major rather than this overwrought E♭ major. Yet our desire for both transcendence and closure is so intense at this moment that it all seems worthwhile, even if it means the annihilation of identity.[23]

But *Genesis II* does not end with its explosion. Vandervelde follows the detonation by the scattering of withered fragments, and—silence. A post-nuclear silence within which the listener is left to ponder the cost of the excitement generated by the strings. And then she pulls back and presents a second prologue characterized by sustained, pulsating energy: the embryonic promise of a new and perhaps different scenario. She is a Scheherazade who leads us to the brink of disaster and then deftly, disconcertingly turns to

Example 3a: *Genesis II*, String cadenza, mm.1-29

another story. She reveals a nightmare of possibilities and then wakes us up, relieving us by telling us it was all a dream but also warning us that these are our choices, that the collision course is in fact in motion, and that we must do something to prevent the devastation glamorized by this dynamic paradigm so very central to our culture's consciousness. It is for us to imagine what the second prologue's promised continuation might be like.

Vandervelde is not the only composer who presents us with deconstructions of this sort: much of Steve Reich's music likewise suggests the possibility of *being in time* without the necessity of striving violently for control. Philip Glass often plays with the same two qualities of motion as

Example 3b: Genesis II, "crippled" clockwork, mm. 42-54

Vandervelde—that is, both the cyclic and the teleological—and he even executes comparable collisions. For instance, in the last act of *The Photographer*, he repeatedly gives us a typical Mahlerian buildup-to-cadence, only to loop back at the point of promised climax to the beginning of the buildup. A similar dynamic underlies several segments of Glass's music for the film *Koyaanisqatsi*.[24] We learn from such passages how very programmed we are to *desire* violent annihilation through the tonal cadence, and our frustration at not attaining the promised catharsis reveals to us the extent to which we are addicts in need of that fix.

One need not be a woman, in other words, to be gravely concerned with getting down off the beanstalk. But the deconstructive methods of postmodernism—the practice of questioning the claims to universality by the "master narratives" of Western culture, revealing the agendas behind traditional "value-free" procedures—are also beginning to clear a space in which a woman's voice can at last be heard *as a woman's voice*.

What has this piece to do with gender? It should be clear by now that

Genesis II calls into question much more than simple male/female roles in society. Indeed, the piece addresses a very basic level of Western culture's metaphysical foundation, a level at which many of the essential binary oppositions underlying our value system are laid distressingly bare: culture/nature, progress/stability, individuality/community. As has been implied throughout this reading of *Genesis II*, one can read its tensions in terms of the various excessive qualities of modernity—the capitalist undermining of more mercantile economic processes, imperialist invasions of "primitive" societies, scientific quests that replace ecologically grounded philosophies of nature with threats of nuclear destruction, the programs of urban renewal that destroy traditional communities.[25]

But the piece is also available to be read in terms of male/female—the opposition that is probably the most ancient and most fundamental of all and that lurks behind all the others mentioned. In a sense, Vandervelde's *Genesis II* is a rewriting of her music for "Jack and the Beanstalk": the difference is that the composer of *Genesis II* is aware that many of her inherited musical gestures are phallic, for she consistently puts them into contexts that cause them to reveal themselves as such. And she no longer paints them with pastels.

I have had Vandervelde present *Genesis II* to several of my classes. Interestingly, many women students recognize in the clockwork an image of female erotic pleasure—pleasure that is not concerned with being somewhere else, indeed, pleasure that need not even be thought of as tied specifically to sexual encounter, but pleasure that permits confident, free, and open interchange with others. They also recoil in horror when the clockwork is subjected to the assault of the violent string parts. By contrast, many of the men in the classes often report having heard the clockwork as a "void," and they tend to be relieved when the strings rush in to "make something happen."[26] Usually the two groups gaze at one another in bleak disbelief, as though they have just discovered that they are irreconcilably of different species. The men sometimes admit to having assumed that women enjoyed and identified with that venerable musical narrative as much as they. In short, they take that narrative schema to be universal in its appeal. Hearing the composition and the unexpected, shocking responses of the women lays bare the lie of that cultural belief—a lie that many of the conventions of classical music and liberal humanism have helped to perpetuate.

For the tonality that underlies Western concert music is strongly informed by a specific sort of erotic imagery. If music of earlier times presented models of stable order in keeping with the view of the world the Church and courts wished to maintain, music after the Renaissance most frequently appeals to libidinal appetites: during the historical period in which the legitimation of culture moved from the sacred to the secular realm, the "truth" that authorized musical culture became expressly tied to models of sexuality.

When composers in the seventeenth century first turned to the invention of erotic metaphors, they drew upon two distinctly different versions. On the one hand, there were images of pleasure—a quality of timeless, sustained hovering. This quality could be produced through the popular device of ostinato, in which each potential moment of closure is simultaneously the moment that guarantees continuation. The erotic obsessions of Monteverdi's nymph, of Purcell's Dido, or of the duet between Poppea and Nero at the conclusion of Monteverdi's *L'incoronazione di Poppea* are the most celebrated examples of this device. A similar quality could be produced through carefully wrought modal ambiguities that deny the possibility or desirability of closure. Schütz's meditations on texts from the Song of Songs, such as "Anima mea liquefacta est" (*Symphoniae Sacrae II*), create pitch-worlds in which the point is to prolong a kind of pleasure/pain until it melts away in exhaustion.

On the other hand, there were images of desire—desire for the satisfaction of what is experienced as an intolerable lack. The principal innovation of seventeenth-century tonality is its ability to instill in the listener an intense longing for a given event: the cadence. It organizes time by creating an artificial need (in the real world, there is no reason one should crave, for instance, the pitch D; yet by making it the withheld object of musical desire, a good piece of tonal music can—within a mere ten seconds—dictate one's very breathing). After that need is established (after the listener has been conditioned to experience the unbearable absence of some musical configuration), tonal procedures strive to postpone gratification of that need until finally delivering the payoff in what is technically called the "climax," which is quite clearly to be experienced as metaphorical ejaculation.

It is interesting to note that when these two versions of erotic metaphors first emerged, they were distinguished from each other along lines of gender association. The images of pleasure (and of pleasure/pain) were most often projected onto women: the text of "Anima mea liquefacta est" is uttered by a woman dissolving in her longing for her lover, and most of the famous ostinato pieces were performed by female characters. Male characters could also indulge in this discourse, though when they did so, they indicated that they were giving themselves over to the stupor of erotic transport. Thus Nero's drunken ostinato in praise of Poppea betrays his fundamental absence of patriarchal integrity, his "effeminacy."

Compositions that juxtapose the two qualities of being-in-time are perhaps most telling, for their dramatic effects depend upon the listener's ability to distinguish between them and their respective meanings. Thus Monteverdi's "Altri canti d'Amor" (Book VIII) begins with one of the most luxuriant, dissonance-filled of ostinati ("Let others sing of love—the sweet caresses, the sighing kisses . . . "), and then breaks off abruptly to the most self-consciously masculine of styles for a musical staging of military valor ("But I will sing of Mars"). And Alessandro Grandi's setting of "O quam tu pulchra es" alternately pushes aggressively for cadence and lapses back into passive languor.

Images of desire were more often wielded by male characters, who thereby could demonstrate their rationality, their rhetorical prowess, their ability to set and achieve long-term goals.[27] And it is principally this set of images that wins out historically. The ostinato and the voluptuous pleasure/pain images disappeared after the seventeenth century, as did the early baroque's fascination with female sexuality. The rhetoric of desire and conquest prevails thereafter to such an extent that they come to seem universal—not surprisingly, in the century of the Enlightenment and its categories.

This universalization of what had been marked earlier as only one of several versions of the erotic occurred as well in literature. Robert Scholes has written that

> the archetype of all fiction is the sexual act. In saying this I do
> not mean merely to remind the reader of the connection between
> all art and the erotic in human nature. Nor do I intend simply to
> suggest an analogy between fiction and sex. For what connects
> fiction—and music—with sex is the fundamental orgastic rhythm
> of tumescence and detumescence, of tension and resolution, of
> intensification to the point of climax and consummation. In the
> sophisticated forms of fiction, as in the sophisticated practice of
> sex, much of the art consists of delaying climax within the
> framework of desire in order to prolong the pleasurable act itself.
> When we look at fiction with respect to its form alone, we see a
> pattern of events designed to move toward climax and
> resolution, balanced by a counter-pattern of events designed to
> delay this very climax and resolution.[28]

The pattern Scholes observes does indeed underwrite both the literature and the music of the eighteenth and nineteenth centuries, as well as much of what continues to be produced in the twentieth. But he is guilty of both essentializing and universalizing what is in fact a particular version of "the sexual act." As a woman I can recognize—and can sometimes even enjoy—such a pattern, both in music and elsewhere in less metaphorical circumstances. But it is only one of many possible erotic experiences I know.

Moreover, it is not the only or even necessarily the most intense form of erotic pleasure available to men. Yet it is the form that is most concerned with the exclusive control of sexuality by the male. And that control is, in fact, threatened by the kind of sensual eroticism that involves openness or vulnerability. In other words, the omnipresence of this formal pattern in literature and music is part of a larger cultural tendency to organize sexuality in terms of the phallus, to devalue or even to deny other erotic sensibilities (especially that of the female), to impose and maintain a hierarchy of power based on gender.[29]

Moreover, it is a version of the erotic that has as much to do with a whole variety of European-American ideological discourses as with sexuality per se. The more qualities such as rationality, power, and domination are fused onto models of the erotic, the more the standardized experience of the erotic comes into line with the discursive practices associated with imperialism, capitalist expansion, and scientific risk-taking. (Thus John Donne exclaims on gaining access to his mistress's genitals, "O my America, My new found lande, My kingdome, safeliest when by one man man'd.")[30] And conversely, imperialism, capitalism, and science come to resonate with and to be justified in accordance with narratives of sexual desire. The mapping of these various terrains upon one another has produced a world rife with phallic posturing. And literature and music do not simply reflect that world; they help to create and transmit it by reinforcing as pleasurable (and as inevitable, as universal) these habits of thought.

A significant factor that contributes to the violence of tonal procedures is that the actual reward—the cadence—can never be commensurate with the anticipation generated or the effort expended in achieving it. The cadence is, in fact, the most banal, most conventionalized cliché available within any given musical style. Moreover, its appearance always spells a kind of death—the cessation of the energy flow that up until that point in the piece had seemed to organize all subjectivity. At the end, the imaginary object of desire remains elusive, and attaining its cadential surrogate necessarily disappoints. But that surrogate is finally all that tonal music (for all its undeniable ability to arouse) has to offer.[31]

If the degree of frustration created by its postponement is relatively minor, the cadence when it finally occurs may seem simply like the inevitable effect of rational causes. Haydn and Handel, for instance, rarely invented stories that "demand sadism." But Beethoven and Mahler quite regularly push mechanisms of frustration to the limit, such that desire in their narratives frequently culminates (as though necessarily) in explosive violence. This may be one of the factors that cause this latter group to be received as more serious, more virile, more consequential: they don't pull punches, they go all the way to the mat.

For instance, the point of recapitulation in the first movement of Beethoven's Ninth Symphony unleashes one of the most horrifyingly violent episodes in the history of music. The problem Beethoven has constructed for this movement is that it seems to begin before the subject of the symphony has managed to achieve its identity: we witness the emergence of the initial theme and its key out of a womblike void, and we hear it collapse back twice more into that void. It is only by virtue of the subject's constant violent self-assertion that the void can be kept at bay: cadence in the context of this movement spells instant death — or at least loss of subjective identity. Yet the narrative paradigm the movement follows demands the eventual return to the beginning for the recapitulation.

In a more conventional sonata movement, recapitulation would signify simply the reconsolidation of thematic and tonal identity — a kind of formal homecoming that marks the end of a successful adventure. But for the subject of the Ninth, to return to the beginning is to actually regress to a point further back than its own conscious beginnings: it is to be dissolved back into the undifferentiated state from which it originally emerged. And if its hard-won identity means anything, the subject cannot accept such dissolution, even if it is toward that conventional moment of reentry that the whole background structure of the movement has inexorably driven. The desire for cadential arrival that has built up over the course of the development finally erupts, as the subject necessarily (because of narrative tradition) finds itself in the throes of the initial void while refusing to relent: the entire first key area in the recapitulation is pockmarked with explosions. It is the consequent juxtaposition of desire and unspeakable violence in this moment that creates its unparalleled fusion of murderous rage and yet a kind of pleasure in its fulfillment of formal demands.

This explosive rage fuels most of the remainder of the symphony. The important exception is the third movement, which serves as a kind of negative image to the rest. If the first two movements are monomaniacal, the Adagio is dialogic. It stands strangely aloof from the striving narrative of the other movements: perched as it is on the never-never-land degree of flat-six, it may be arcadian recollection, the imaginary sublime, or a dream of utopia. It offers the image of a world in which pleasure is attainable without thrusting desire, where tenderness and vulnerability are virtues rather than fatal flaws. But it can never be reality, as its infinite regress through a spiral of flat-six relationships indicates. And its seductive lure must finally be resisted. The return to the real world at the outset of the final movement quashes the alterity of the Adagio with startling violence — violence that might seem excessive, if we did not understand culturally that to linger in that pleasurable, semiotically and structurally feminine zone would be an act of intolerable transgression. Like Faust we know (as proper patriarchal subjects) that to murmur, "Verweile nur, du bist so schön," is to be utterly damned.

The "triumphal" end of the symphony is likewise problematic, for how could any configuration of pitches satisfactorily ground the contradictions set forth over the course of this gargantuan composition? As the conclusion is approached, the promised (though, by definition, inadequate) cadences repeatedly are withheld at the last moment; and finally Beethoven simply forces closure by bludgeoning the cadence and the piece to death. For if death is inevitable in tonal music (and the reticence to resolve in this piece makes that connection quite pointedly), then one may as well make the most of it.

Adrienne Rich arrives at a remarkably similar reading of this composition in her poem "The Ninth Symphony of Beethoven Understood at Last as a Sexual Message":[32]

> A man in terror of impotence
> or infertility, not knowing the difference
> a man trying to tell something
> howling from the climacteric
> music of the entirely
> isolated soul
> yelling at Joy from the tunnel of the ego
> music without the ghost
> of another person in it, music
> trying to tell something the man
> does not want out, would keep if he could
> gagged and bound and flogged with chords of Joy
> where everything is silence and the
> beating of a bloody fist upon
> a splintered table.

The point is not to hold up Beethoven as exceptionally monstrous. The Ninth Symphony is probably our most compelling articulation in music of the contradictory impulses that have organized patriarchal culture since the Enlightenment. Moreover, within the parameters of his own musical composition, he may be heard as enacting a critique of narrative obligations that is every bit as devastating as Rich's or Vandervelde's. But if Beethoven resists the exigencies of formal necessity at the moment of recapitulation in the opening movement and at the beginning of the final movement, he also finally embraces and perpetuates them, and even raises them to a much higher level of violence. And once his successors in the nineteenth century tasted that combination of desire and destruction, they could not get enough of it.

In most post-Renaissance Western music and in virtually all of its critical literature, the climax-principle (like the phallus of the classical Greek column) has been transcendentalized to the status of a value-free universal of form. Despite the prevalence of this pattern, it is rarely even viewed as sexual (let alone masculine) any longer—it is simply the way music is supposed to go. Yet when musicians describe a compelling performance, they commonly describe it as "balls-to-the-wall" or say that it had "thrust," and they accompany these words with the gesture of the jabbing clenched fist and the facial grimace usually reserved for purposes of connoting male sexual aggression. There is, to be sure, much more to classical music than the simulation of sexual desire and fulfillment. Still, once one learns how to recognize the beanstalk, one begins to realize how pervasive it is, how regularly it serves as a hook for getting listeners libidinally invested in the narratives of compositions. And when it turns violent (as it does more often and more devastatingly in nineteenth-century symphonies than in heavy metal), it becomes a model of cultural authority that cannot be exempted from social criticism.

The clockwork of *Genesis II* provides us with another erotic image: one that combines shared and sustained pleasure, rather than the desire for explosive closure. In the aggressive string parts, the piece also presents the phallic beanstalk image in ways that demonstrate both its exciting appeal and its destructive force. As I mentioned earlier, many of my male students respond immediately and enthusiastically to the violent thrusting of the strings. Some of them only begin to question their enthusiasm after the women have shared their observations (just as many men fail to recognize the phallic dimension of their favorite classics until women, who are situated rather differently with respect to that "universal" experience, point it out).

There are potential problems with the premises of *Genesis II*. It could be argued that insofar as the composition does in fact present the beanstalk image, it grants us our fix and encourages our cravings for such configurations (what rock band Guns N' Roses hails as our "appetite for destruction"). The same can be said of virtually any attempt at dramatized deconstruction, especially when the images being deconstructed are prurient or violent: once they are presented, there they are—available for conventional consumption.

It might also be argued that *Genesis II* has simply reversed the terms of a pernicious binarism: if it is objectionable that in traditional narratives the "feminine" moment must be resolved out as a "large-scale dissonance," then is anything gained by maintaining the same schema but locating the "masculine" as the dissonance? Reversal of terms is not exactly what is at stake in Vandervelde's composition. Rather, she permits the beanstalk to run its familiar self-destructive course and then returns to the serenity of the prologue. But these are her creatures, and they do act in accordance with her design. Another potential problem with *Genesis II* is that it may encourage essentialist readings: to map femininity onto nature, cycles, and timeless stability and masculinity onto culture, linear time, and agency is to risk re-inscribing these associations that very much need to be interrogated and resisted.

But the significance of Vandervelde's achievement is not *simply* that she has revealed as phallic and sexually violent many of the "value-free" conventions of classical form (though there is nothing like the appropriation by a woman of beanstalk gestures to make us realize that there are unwritten cultural rules of gender propriety). Nor is it that she has introduced for the first time some universal, essential woman's voice. For even though our obsession for classifying all music stylistically might make us want to jump impulsively at the chance to codify the distinctive characteristics of a "women's music," there can be no such single thing, just as there is no universal male experience or essence.[33] What Vandervelde has accomplished is an approach to composition that permits her—expressly as a woman—to inhabit a traditional discourse, to call into question its gestures and procedures *from the inside*, and to imagine from that vantage point the possibility of other narrative schemata.

At this moment in history, no one needs to be taught how to salute the beanstalk: our culture is saturated with such lessons in both popular and "high art" media. What we do need, however, are alternate models and images of experiencing pleasure and other, less controlling ways of organizing sexuality, and—by extension—science and even political life. And *Genesis II* is devoted to producing such an alternative. With repeated listenings we can learn to appreciate—even to love—the constant erotic energy, the ecstasy of the clockwork. Perhaps enough to persuade us likewise to get down off the beanstalk.

Chapter 6
This Is Not a Story
My People Tell:
Musical Time and Space
According to Laurie Anderson

In her composition "Langue d'amour"—just after she has retold the Adam and Eve story and just before she moves into the ecstatic stasis that ends the piece—Laurie Anderson says:

> This is not a story my people tell. It's something I know myself.
> And when I do my job I am thinking about these things.
> Because when I do my job, that's what I think about.[1]

She thus casually evokes a typical ethnographic situation, in which a native informant delivers authentic folklore to an anthropologist.[2]

The ethnographic reference here is deliberate. In the book version of *United States*, the text of "Langue d'amour" is given in French, interspersed with English translations. The obvious referent here is Claude Lévi-Strauss, the French structural anthropologist, the great collector and interpreter of myths who has been a prominent intellectual figure since the late 1960s. Moreover, the text is accompanied by close-up stills of a non–Caucasian male—an Other of unidentified origin—who appears to be telling a story. In the last three frames, the camera slides away from the ostensible "subject," revealing that he is situated among some tropical trees. The final frame includes only a tree.

Several familiar conditions for the production of meaning are here put self-consciously into play: we are apparently being offered the testimony of the "primitive" as recorded by a Western ethnographer, who delivers to us a raw, seemingly incoherent myth before it is cooked—made palatable and rational—through the imposition of objective structural analysis. This homage to elite French theory invites one to assume that Lévi-Strauss's el-

Plate 1: Laurie Anderson, "La Langue d'amour" (or "Hothead")

egant binarisms can easily reduce this (like all other cultural artifacts, regardless of content) to stable universal oppositions, can thus make sense of
items such as the elusive details of the snake's stories.

But there are problems here: Who are the individuals referred to as "my
people"? Who is this speaking, and why are her stories different? First,
within the photographs themselves, the jungle that had seemed to be mere
background—the detail that seems to guarantee the on-site veracity of the
ethnographic event being recorded—suddenly looms up to share the frame
with the foregrounded human and then supplants him altogether. Nor is our
narrator a trustworthy informant: by her own admission, she is refusing to
deliver what is always understood to be the desired anthropological
commodity—authentic, transparent access to "the stories my people tell."
Even the language of naive storytelling is corrupted by the slang phrases of
popular culture, such as "happy as a clam" or "hothead": clichés that are
plenty meaningful but that disrupt our ability to hear the story as the pure
voice of the "folk."

And tropical vegetation and anthrospeak notwithstanding, this is not a
primitive myth at all, but rather a pointed retelling of *our own* Western narrative of origin. Moreover, despite the ethnographic photographs of the
male subject, the story is being told by a woman and from a woman's point

Like there was a little fire inside his mouth and the flame would come dancing out of his mouth. And the woman liked this very much.

Et après cela elle se mit à trouver l'homme ennuyeux par ce que quoiqu'il advint, il était toujours aussi heureux qu'un poisson dans l'eau.

And after that she was bored with the man because no matter what happened, he was always as happy as a clam.

Que dit le serpent? Oui, que disait le serpent?

What did the snake say? Yes, what was he saying?

OK. Je vais vous le dire.

OK. I will tell you.

Le serpent lui raconta des choses sur le monde.

The snake told her things about the world.

Il lui parla du temps où il y eut un grand tiphon sur l'île et où tous les requins sortirent de l'eau.

He told her about the time when there was a big typhoon on the island and all the sharks came out of the water.

Oui, ils sortirent de l'eau et ils vinrent droit dans votre maison avec leurs grandes dents blanches. Et la femme entendit ces choses et elle tomba amoureuse.

Yes, they came out of the water and they walked right into your house with their big white teeth. And the woman heard these things and she was in love.

Et l'homme vint et lui dit: "Il faut qu'on s'en aille maintenant," et la femme ne voulait pas s'en aller par ce qu'elle était une brulée. Parce qu'elle était une femme amoureuse.
179

And the man came out and said: "We have to go now," and the woman did not want to go because she was a hothead. Because she was a woman in love.

Toujours est-il qu'ils montèrent dans leur bateau et quitterent l'île.

Anyway, they got into their boat and left the island.

Mais ils ne restaient jamais très longtemps nulle part. Parce que la femme ne pouvait trouver le repos.

But they never stayed anywhere very long. Because the woman was restless.

C'était une tête brulée. C'était une femme amoureuse.

She was a hothead. She was a woman in love.

Ce n'est pas une histoire que raconte mon peuple. C'est une langue que je sais par moi-meme.

This is not a story my people tell. It's something I know myself.

Et quand je fais mon travail je pense à tout cela.

And when I do my job I am thinking about these things.

Parce que quand je fais mon travail, c'est ce à quoi je pense.

Because when I do my job, that's what I think about.

Oooo là là là là.
Voici. Voilà.
Oooo là là là là.
Voici le langage de l'amour.
Oooo là là là là.
Voici. Voilà là là.
Voici le langage de l'amour.

Yeah. La. La. La. La.
Here and there.
Oh yes.
This the language of love.
Oooo. Oh yeah.
Here it is. There it is. La la.
This is the language of love.

Ah! Comme ci, comme ca.
Violà. Violà.
Voici le langage de l'amour.
Voici le langage de l'amour.
Attends! Attends! Attends! Attends! Attends! Attends!
Ecoute. Ecoute. Ecoute.
Oooo là là là là.
Oooo là là là là.

Ah! Neither here nor there.
There. There.
This is the language of love.
This is the language of love.
Wait! Wait! Wait! Wait! Wait! Wait!
Listen. Listen. Listen.
Oooo. Oh yeah.
Oh yeah. Yeah.

Voici le langage de l'amour.
Voici le langage dans mon coeur.
Oooo là là là là.
Voici le langage dans mon coeur.
Voici le langage de l'amour.
Voici le langage dans mon coeur.
Voici le langage dans mon coeur.

This is the language of love.
This is the language of my heart.
Oooo. Oh yeah.
This is the language of my heart.
This is the language of love.
This is the language of my heart.
This is the language of my heart.

of view. With the lightest of touches, Anderson sets up what seems at first glance the standard binary oppositions underpinning Western knowledge: anthropologist/primitive, human/nature, truth/fiction, authenticity/corruption, Western/non-Western, male/female. Then she tilts them slightly, so that they begin to slip. Their bedrock certainty just evaporates.

1

Laurie Anderson's work always involves several discourses all operating simultaneously, all interconnected in unpredictable, sometimes contradictory ways. It is virtually impossible to separate out any one aspect of her pieces for examination without violating her own insistent violation of the genre boundaries that organize the traditional art world. Most critics of drama, film, performance art, and postmodern culture accept, and even celebrate this in their analyses of her work. But while such multimedia approaches are indispensable when one deals with Anderson, one prominent aspect of her work—the music—almost always gets slighted in such accounts for the simple reason that nonmusicians have difficulty verbalizing about music and its effects.

Unfortunately, the academic musicians who know how to talk about music have shown little interest in Anderson's work. Most of the analytical techniques that have been developed in academic music theory slide right off her pieces. Because much of her music is triadic, the harmonic theory designed for the analysis of the standard eighteenth- and nineteenth-century repertories might seem relevant. But all harmonic theory can do is to label the pairs of alternating chords that often serve as the materials for her pieces. Musicians often dismiss Anderson's music as being nothing more than this, as though it were intended for beginners in ear-training classes: "O Superman" gives the boneheads eight minutes to hear the difference between two chords. Next week, a three-chord structure. After a year, maybe a Mozart sonata. Finally, Schoenberg or Carter. For these are, of course, the stories— the *authorized* stories—"my people" tell, in both concert hall and classroom.

In this essay I want to focus on the musical dimension of Anderson's work. If her music resists analysis as we practice it in the academy, it is not necessarily because her pieces are faulty according to universal, objective criteria, but rather because her premises are different. As it turns out, Anderson's musical experiments—the stories she tells herself when she does her job—can tell us quite a bit both about the discursive conventions of the standard repertories and also, by extension, about music theory as it is practiced in the academy. Because they resist many of the categories of traditional music theory, her pieces demand that we develop a new set of analytical questions. Accordingly, this essay concentrates on some very basic issues: the organization of space and time in Anderson's music and musical performances.

2

American musicology and music theory have rarely been interested in examining the temporal and spatial dimensions of music per se. The scarcity of literature in this area is emphasized by Robert Morgan's pioneering article, "Musical Time/Musical Space" (1980), which develops some useful ways of considering various kinds of spatial relationships within music.[3] However, except for a brief aside in which he mentions pieces that deliberately exploit spatial arrangements within performance sites, Morgan's comments address only the metaphorical space within compositions: qualities of high and low, of relative distance, of surface and background. Many aspects of Anderson's pieces can fruitfully be discussed in these terms, and I will return to them later. But there other spatial issues at stake in music—issues that are not only neglected but actively repressed by most professional musicians and theorists. And Anderson forces us to become aware of these submerged—though crucial—issues.

The most significant of these concerns the physical source of sound. In many cultures, music and movement are inseparable activities, and the physical engagement of the musician in performance is desired and expected. By contrast, Western culture—with its puritanical, idealist suspicion of the body—has tried throughout much of its history to mask the fact that actual people usually produce the sounds that constitute music. As far back as Plato, music's mysterious ability to inspire bodily motion has aroused consternation, and a very strong tradition of Western musical thought has been devoted to defining music as the sound itself, to erasing the physicality involved in both the making and the reception of music.[4] Renaissance nobles sometimes hid their musicians behind screens to create the impression that one was listening to the Harmony of the Spheres;[5] Schopenhauer defined music as the trace of the metaphysical Will itself (theorist Heinrich Schenker later revealed precisely how the Will said what it said); and orchestral musicians dress in black so as to minimize the embarrassing presence of their physical beings. The advent of recording has been a Platonic dream come true, for with a disk one can have the pleasure of the sound without the troubling reminder of the bodies producing it. And electronic composition makes it possible to eliminate the last trace of the nonidealist element.[6]

The genre known as performance art arose in the 1960s and was in part a reaction against this erasure of people from art.[7] One of the principal features of performance art is the insistence on the artist as a performing body. Gone is the division of labor in which a composer constructs an object and passes it on to a performer who executes faithfully the demands of the master. In performance art, artist and performer are usually one, and the piece is that which is inscribed on and through the body. The radical separation of mind and body that underwrites most so-called serious music and music theory is here thrown into confusion.

Anderson's treatment of the body in performance is far more complex than the in-your-face transgression that characterizes some performance art. First, her compositions rely upon precisely those tools of electronic mediation that most performance artists seek to displace. In order to put this aspect of her work into perspective, it is important to recall that most modes of mechanical and electronic reproduction strive to render themselves invisible and inaudible, to invite the spectator to believe that what is seen or heard is real.[8] By contrast, in Laurie Anderson's performances, one actually gets to watch her produce the sounds we hear. But her presence is always already multiply mediated: we hear her voice only as it is filtered through Vocoders, as it passes through reiterative loops, as it is layered upon itself by means of sequencers. For some pieces, she attaches contact mikes to drum machines and produces sounds by striking various parts of her body; for others, she speaks through a pillow speaker located inside her mouth.[9] The closer we get to the source, the more distant becomes the imagined ideal of unmediated presence and authenticity. Mary Ann Doane has written about the anxiety provoked in film when a voice is not securely grounded in a particular body to ensure unity.[10] Anderson deliberately plays with those anxieties. She insists on and problematizes her mediation.

The problem this extreme mediation calls up is sometimes referred to as "Man versus Machine," and in fact many reviewers of Anderson's work have assumed that she too is merely critiquing the alienating influence of the media on human authenticity.[11] But to interpret her work in terms of that standard dichotomy is to ignore her obvious fascination with gadgetry. As she has remarked: "It's true that there is a lot of alienation in songs like 'Big Science' and 'O Superman.' All of my work that deals with machines, and how they talk and think, is inherently critical. That's certainly the bias. But I think many people have missed an important fact: those songs themselves are made up of digital bits. My work is expressed through technology—a lot of it depends on 15 million watts of power."[12]

If her work refuses the options offered by the traditional Man-versus-Machine dichotomy, it is in part because she is not a Man. The fact that hers is a *female* body changes the dynamics of several of the oppositions she in-vokes in performance. For women's bodies in Western culture have almost always been viewed as objects of display. Women have rarely been permit-ted agency in art, but instead have been restricted to enacting—upon and through their bodies—the theatrical, musical, cinematic, and dance scenar-ios concocted by male artists.[13] Centuries of this traditional sexual division of cultural labor bear down on Anderson (or any woman performer) when she performs, always threatening to convert her once again into yet another body set in motion for the pleasure of the masculine gaze. It may be possible for men in the music profession to forget these issues, but no woman who has ever been on a stage, or even in front of a classroom, can escape them. This raises the stakes enormously and makes much more significant Anderson's insistence on her self-representation within the performance space.

When Anderson involves herself with electronics, she confuses still other habits of thought grounded in gender difference. For it is supposed to be *Man* who gives birth to and who tames the Machine. Women in this culture are discouraged from even learning about technology, in part so that they can continue to represent authentic, unmediated Nature. To the extent that women and machines both occupy positions opposite that of Man in stan-dard dichotomies, women and machines are incompatible terms. But as Anderson wrestles with technology, she displaces the male subject who usu-ally enacts that heroic feat. And by setting up an implied alliance and iden-tification with the machine, she raises the conventional anxiety of the self-directed robot—the living dolls of science fiction or gothic stories of the uncanny, but a living doll who is self-created, who flaunts her electronic constructedness.[14] As she says in her piece "Closed Circuits," "You're the snake charmer, baby. And you're also the snake."

For all these reasons, musical space in Laurie Anderson's music is multi-ply charged. No longer merely a metaphorical concept, the space within which her music occurs is the arena for many kinds of cultural struggles. It is electronically saturated at the same time as it insists on the body—and not simply the neuter body that has been erased from consideration in music theory, but the problematic female body that traditionally has been the site of the spectacular.

In order to balance out these various tensions, Anderson assumed an an-drogynous persona while working on *United States*.[15] Her androgyny downplays her sexuality, which, given the terms of the tradition, always threatens to become the whole show. By contrast, pop singer Madonna takes control of her erotic self-representation, insisting on her right to con-struct rather than deny her sexuality.[16] But Anderson too has commented—

in imagery strikingly like Madonna's — on the possibility of deriving power from being a *knowing* "object" of the male gaze: "Women have rarely been composers. But we do have one advantage. We're used to performing. I mean like we used to tap dance for the boys–'Do you like it this way, boys? No? Is this better?' "[17]

But whether a woman performer denies or emphasizes her physical presence, it is always read back onto her. Anderson is sometimes criticized, for instance, for presenting gestures "from which spontaneity and joy [read: sexuality] have been banished," or for preventing the audience from identifying with her — for withholding the kind of nurturing presence we expect women performers to deliver.[18] She walks a very thin line — foregrounding her body while trying not to make it the entire point. As she puts it: "I wear audio masks in my work — meaning, electronically, I can be this shoe salesman, or this demented cop, or some other character. And I do that to avoid the expectations of what it means to be a woman on a stage."[19]

3

I would like to move now into the music itself, provided that we not forget the problematized theatrical space within which these sounds are produced. For many of the same dilemmas Anderson faces as a woman on stage confront her again when she decides to compose. How does a woman composer negotiate with established musical discourses? What options are available, and what do her choices signify?

Music is generally regarded as a neutral — a *neuter* — enterprise, again because of the desire not to acknowledge its mediation through actual people with gendered bodies. Some women composers accept this position and write music that is indistinguishable from that of their male colleagues.[20] Many of them chafe at the suggestion that their sexual identity might have something to do with their music, and understandably so: for centuries it has been thought that if women did write music, it would sound frail and passive — that is, would sound the way dominant culture assumed women were and should be. In the last few decades, many women have risen in the area of composition to command the respect of both male and female peers. Respect not as women composers, but as composers. Period. I want to stress here once again that I very much admire the accomplishments of these women.

However, Laurie Anderson is a performance artist whose priorities lead her not only to acknowledge but to insist upon her gender identity in her work, in the music as well as the more theatrical components. But it is not at all obvious how to make gendered differences audible in music, nor is there a single theoretical position on this matter. Some feminist artists endeavor to create images of feminine eroticism in order to celebrate their own experiences and to seize control of the representation of the female body, which has been so thoroughly colonized by pornography throughout Western art history.[21] This option often produces exuberant, liberatory work, but it threatens to reinscribe the old patriarchal notion that women are simply and essentially bodies, are reducible to their sexualities. Poststructuralist feminists tend to resist what they see as the simplistic celebration of the body and concentrate instead on demonstrating how certain binary oppositions in Western thought—oppositions such as male/female, mind/body, culture/nature—organize social reality. They argue that essentialist identifications of women with sexuality, the body, and nature only play back into the hands of the oppressive mainstream.[22] However, the other side often sees poststructuralist feminists as repudiating the potential strengths of gender difference and occupying the same disembodied, joyless, neuter position as the most sterile of mainstream enterprises.

Recently, theorists such as Teresa de Lauretis and Denise Riley have argued that women need to derive strategies from both of these apparently mutually exclusive positions: to practice deconstructive analyses of the tradition when necessary, but also to try to imagine new social realities—worlds in which the celebration of the erotic need not reduce women back to sex objects, in which the intellect and the body can be mutually supportive and collaborative. As de Lauretis puts it:

> Now, the movement in and out of gender as ideological representation, which I propose characterizes the subject of feminism, is a movement back and forth between the representation of gender (in its male-centered frame of reference) and what that representation leaves out or, more pointedly, makes unrepresentable. . . . Thus, to inhabit both kinds of spaces at once is to live the contradiction which, I have suggested, is the condition of feminism here and now: the tension of a twofold pull in contrary directions—the critical negativity of its theory, and the affirmative positivity of its politics—is both the historical condition of existence of feminism and its theoretical condition of possibility.[23]

While much of Anderson's music predates such theoretical formulations, I want to argue that her work has enacted such a solution by continually shifting back and forth across boundaries, sometimes focusing on social critique and sometimes on developing new models of pleasure.

4

"O Superman," the 1981 hit single from the extended work *United States*, is a good example of Anderson in deconstructive mode.[24] It is dedicated to Massenet and refers obliquely to his *Le Jongleur de Nôtre Dame*, a fairly obscure opera from 1902. Anderson's piece invokes Massenet's opera in two ways. First, the opera contains an aria that begins "O souverain, ô juge, ô père," which is transformed into Anderson's opening line, "O Superman. O Judge. O Mom and Dad." Second, the climax of the opera occurs when the juggler, pursued by an angry mob, backs up against a painting of the madonna and is saved when her arms draw him into the picture. The relevance of this imagery to Anderson's piece is quite obvious ("so hold me, Mom, in your long arms . . . your military arms . . . your petrochemical arms"), though typically difficult to unravel. Her engagement with this text offers yet another level of critique, though one available only to those with esoteric musicological knowledge. Ironically, it is precisely those people who are most invested in "high culture" who are likely catch to this reference, only to have yet another beloved object deconstructed.

The musical constant in "O Superman" is a pedal on middle c on a single syllable: "ha ha ha." In performance, one watches as Anderson generates this sound and establishes its technological reiteration through a delay mechanism. It gives the impression of being expressively authentic, as though it exists outside of or prior to language, and it evokes powerful though contradictory affective responses; alternately it may be heard as sardonic laughter or as anxious, childish whimpering. It runs for the duration of the composition, changing only when it is thrown temporarily out of kilter through phasing. Its apparent shifts in meaning are due solely to context, for the sound itself is frozen into place electronically.

Two alternating chords inflect the pedal harmonically: an A♭ major triad in first inversion and a root-position C minor triad. It is her dependence on such minimal musical materials that makes some musicians dismiss Anderson as unworthy of serious analytical discussion. But like many other aspects of Anderson's work, the music often is carefully organized in terms of austere binary oppositions, the kinds of oppositions that structuralists such as Saussure and Lévi-Strauss revealed as lying at the foundations of Western thought and that poststructuralists have been concerned with deconstructing.[25] The binary opposition she has chosen is not innocent, and as the piece unfolds we learn a good deal not only about "O Superman," but also about the premises of Western musical discourse and our own postmodern condition.

The triadicity of "O Superman" invites listeners to read its materials in terms of the traditional codes of tonal procedure. Indeed, some critics hear Anderson's music as a simplistic return to the familiar, reassuring comforts of tonality in reaction against the intellectual rigors of serialism. Yet as easy as it may be to label the individual moments in the piece, we run into trouble as soon as we try to fix the two chords in terms of a tonal hierarchy. The pedal is first harmonized by A$\flat$ major, which serves as the reference point for much of the piece. The C minor harmonization appears initially as a brief inflection that is quickly altered back to A$\flat$.

There are a few details, however, that make the relationship between the alternatives a bit uneasy. First, the only difference between the two chords is the choice between the pitches a$\flat$ and g. The dramatic action of the piece hangs on that flickering half step. Second, the A$\flat$ chord is in first inversion and is thus somewhat flimsy, while the presumably decorative C minor chord is very solid. Third, the semiotics of tonal music associate major with affirmative affective states (hope, joy) and minor with negative states (sadness, depression). And as the piece swings between these two stark triads, one is encouraged to hear the alternation as a happy/sad dichotomy. But the fact that the major alternative is always unstable (because it is in inversion) and the minor always stable suggests that security ultimately lies with the negative option. Thus although the major triad was established first (and therefore has some claim to the status of "tonic"), it is increasingly heard as an inflection poised to resolve to C minor.

In other words, even though we are given only two closely related triads, it is difficult to ascertain which is structural and which ornamental. Consequently, the affective implications of the opposition become confused. Usually in tonal narratives, we are led to desire affirmative, major-key states while dreading the minor. And we are likewise accustomed to defining structural stability in terms of the initial tonic and to expecting that dissonances will be resolved out for purposes of narrative closure. But what about a piece that mixes up these two mechanisms of desire and dread, when clinging to hope spells unstable illusion and certainty comes only with accepting dread?

To be sure, this crossing of affective and narrative wires occurs occasionally in the standard repertory, though only in pieces that themselves are calling into question the premises of tonality and its conventional forms. Haydn's String Quartet, op. 33, no.3, for instance, risks presenting the opening tonic in first inversion, and at the moment of recapitulation it is the mediant minor that seems to have prevailed—though this turns out, of course, to be simply a musical pun. The definition of tonic is never seriously in question, and the narrative schema of sonata procedure easily remedies whatever anxiety might have been generated by the confusion. The principal key is quickly reinstated, and all is well. There are also pieces in which an intolerable minor tonic is fled to the affirmative if unstable and untenable major key on the sixth degree. Beethoven's Ninth Symphony, several of his late quartets, and Schubert's "Unfinished" Symphony come to mind here. In these pieces, stable dread and unstable hope form the contradictory poles structuring the narratives, although inasmuch as the pieces are tonal, we know in advance that they must conform finally to the tonic.[26]

Anderson's piece is in some ways like a performed-out analytical reduction of the axes upon which many such tonal pieces turn. Nothing extraneous is present—she gives us only the binaries that underlie and inform the more complex narratives of the tonal repertory. But the fact that the hierarchical relationship between her two chords is undecidable means that there is not even the potential security of the tragic ending. We may not like Schubert's rejection of the pretty theme and the affirmation of brutal reality at the end of the "Unfinished" Symphony's first movement, but that ending at least confirms the necessity of dissonance resolving to consonance, or the inevitability of second themes yielding to first. The formidable metaphysics of tonality and sonata form win out over romantic illusion, and there is considerable security in knowing that something—even if that something is harsh and tyrannical—guarantees meaning.[27]

Anderson's monologue causes us to map the alternations with certainty at first: Man/Machine, Home/Alienation, and so on. But then things become confused, as Mom becomes Machine, and the clichés of American patriotism become codes of totalitarian control. Finally we are left with the ambiguity of the initial sound and the undecidability of the binarisms. Duration and accent turn out to count enormously in this piece, for it is only through relative temporal and textural emphasis that one or the other of the chords achieves prominence, thus offering us a point of reference, at least for the moment. The most awful part of the piece begins with the words "So hold me, Mom," when both chords finally appear in root position, both equally oppressive. Near the end, after the singing has concluded, predictable periodic phrasing occurs for the first time. An inexorable bass ostinato enters, and over it the two chords switch on and off mechanically. These fade until finally we hear only the original track: laughing or whimpering, human or electronic—all or none of the above.

It is in thus questioning the metaphysics of traditional tonal music that Anderson performs some of her most incisive work. For having invoked the kind of dualistic axis upon which conventional tonal narratives rely, she deftly unhinges it. At stake in the verbal text of "O Superman" are issues such as self versus Other, home versus the public sphere, autonomy versus external control. As her performance splits her off into multiple identities, as the security of Mom becomes indistinguishable from National Security, and human becomes indistinguishable from technological, many of the constants upon which we habitually depend are thrown into turmoil. In her music, as the structural is confused with the ornamental, as the musical semiotics of desire and dread, of hope and disillusion, of illusion and reality get mapped and remapped, inscribed upon and erased from the same two chords, the tidy structures of formal analysis—those assurances of unitary control—become hopelessly tangled.

5

Robert Morgan has suggested that one of the great attributes of tonal music is its ability to create the impression of "depth" beneath the musical surface.[28] Because we are familiar with tonal procedures, we are able to take pleasure in the note-by-note events in a piece of music and still follow the long-term structural mechanisms underlying it. Anderson tempts us to hear that kind of depth in this piece: to interpret one or the other of the chords as simply ornamental. But while this illusion is continually being raised in "O Superman," it is just as continually voided. Thus what we finally have is neither narrative nor depth, but only our craving for both in the face of what is perhaps only the digital technology that guarantees postmodern electronic life.[29] Anderson deliberately activates beloved narratives and demonstrates to us that we are still highly invested in them, even though they may be bankrupt. Or worse.

One of the charges often leveled against postmodern theory and art is that it is nihilistic—that it flaunts its cynical refusal to believe in anything. Jean Baudrillard has decried this as the age of the simulacrum, in which codes and signs that used to signify are set loose to play in flashy if meaningless media assemblages.[30] Fredric Jameson has characterized postmodern artworks as "blank pastiche."[31] And Anderson's deconstructive enterprises certainly can be read as celebrating the crisis in Western meaning currently being experienced.

However, not all plays of signifiers are nihilistic and not all pastiches are blank. Discovering that social reality has been humanly organized through binary oppositions can call forth widely different reactions: for those who have benefited from the illusion that culture and knowledge were grounded in truth (rather than social ideology and privilege), postmodern deconstruction is a calamity.[32] But for those who have been kept in their places by those reigning oppositions, deconstruction can be cause for celebration. The cultural theory of black philosopher Cornel West emphasizes this point repeatedly.[33] And feminist theory likewise delights in taking apart the strictures that have held women in positions of passivity, that have prevented them from participating as full agents in social, economic, or cultural spheres. As Anderson has said: "I also think that women are excellent social critics, basically because we have nothing to lose, anyway. It's like we're not in a position of power, so we don't risk a lot by being critical of it."[34]

Depending on your point of view, then, Anderson's strategies of simultaneously evoking and denying classic structural dichotomies are nihilistic, transgressive, or exuberant. It depends on whose meaning is being displaced. Her music may sound simple up against the sophisticated devices of music theory, but the self-contained rigors of music theory can seem almost endearingly naive up against Anderson's music, the multivoiced popular culture with which it has fused, and the social reality that is being negotiated through such new voices and forms.[35]

6

But deconstruction is only one of Anderson's interests. "Langue d'amour" appeared in both *United States* and later, in a more elaborate version, on the 1984 album *Mister Heartbreak*. Its musical materials too are elemental. Four pitches (d, e, g, and a) cycle through the bass in a synthesized sound that evokes drumming. The pitches occur in any sequence—order and hierarchy don't matter here. Likewise, although there are strong pulses, there is no regular metric organization. The piece encourages physical motion, but it refuses to regiment that motion. Surface events in the piece are unpredictable, yet because they take place within an enclosed musical space that is securely bounded by these few pitches, nothing unexpected happens. Narrative is thus sacrificed for the sake of sustained pleasure.

Layered on top of the mix are the sounds of what are identified as electronic conches—teasing glissandos that slide upward, smearing the certainty of diatonic articulation. Even Anderson's voice is split off into several registers at once by means of the Vocoder—unitary identity is exchanged for blurred, diffused eroticism. Eventually the decisiveness of verbal speech is abandoned for a prolonged moment of musical jouissance, in which the murmured text—"Voici, voilà la langage de l'amour" and "La, la, la, la"—puns continually on "tongue": the tongue of love, the tongue that flickers in and out of the snake's mouth, the tongue inciting feminine ecstasy.

This is most emphatically *not* a story my people tell, if by "my people" is meant official Western musical culture. For feminine pleasure has either been silenced in Western music or else has been simulated by male composers as the monstrous stuff requiring containment in *Carmen* or *Salome*.[36] In-

deed, Anderson's text invokes the primal story of feminine containment—
the biblical account of Man's seduction by Woman, the hurling of Mankind
into history and narrative. That original story has informed our culture ever
since. Retelling it from Eve's point of view quietly eliminates the pathos,
the lethal mixture of desire, dread, and violence that compels narrative
structure. When I play this piece in my classes, male students often complain that it makes no sense, that nothing happens in it, that it is creepy and
vague. In short, it lacks narrative. But the women tend to beam at each
other in recognition of something they have never heard formulated in music and yet feel they have always known. For when they do their jobs, this
is what they are thinking about.

There are a few pieces in the standard repertory that attempt to build
nonteleological models of time, for instance, Debussy's *Prélude à l'après-midi
d'un faune* or the third movement of Beethoven's Ninth Symphony. Given
the programmatic dimension of the Debussy and the overall context of this
movement of the Beethoven, both of these pieces seem to be concerned
with presenting antinarratives. Yet *L'après-midi d'un faune* manages to shape
itself only by moving as though toward climax, even though that climax is
ultimately refused. And the final movement of the Ninth hurls us more violently back into narrative than any other piece I know. The peaceful third
movement seems almost to have been a transgression, an obstacle to the
transcendental quest that fuels this symphony.[37] As the "man" says in
"Langue d'amour," "We have to go now." In Anderson's piece, by contrast, there is no transgression, no remorse, no impulse to return to narrative. There is only pleasure.

By suggesting that Anderson produces images of feminine pleasure in
this piece, I do not mean that there is something essential about the female
body and its experiences or that her artistic processes are irrational. On the
contrary: what Anderson is doing is very complex, both musically and intellectually. It relies heavily on her deconstructions of the presumably neuter
terms of Western music, and it requires that she manipulate the materials of
music so as to produce alternative metaphors. For if many people have experienced the "structure of feeling" conveyed by Anderson, she has had to
work very hard to organize pitches and rhythms such that listeners recognize it in the music.[38] But having isolated and analyzed the elements that
have underwritten patriarchal narratives of control throughout history, she
now has a space within which to assemble those elements in accordance
with a different organization of time.[39]

While women have been marginalized with respect to Western culture
for most of its history, our perspectives from the margins have offered some
advantages. For example, we have been privy both to the public displays

and explications of official masculine culture—including the ways male art-ists construe women—as well as to experiences not accounted for within that official culture, but which Anderson and a few other women are begin-ning to map.

So far as we know, only one man—Tiresias, the seer in Greek myth-ology—has had the opportunity to experience both feminine and masculine realms: he was permitted to live in the body of a woman for several years, and then was changed back into a man. When asked who had the greater erotic pleasure, he answered that women's jouissance was seven times that of a man. For divulging this information he was struck blind. I do not want to repeat his mistake by insisting on the superiority of Anderson's erotic im-agery in "Langue d'amour." So I will conclude with this:

Think of it.

Think of it as.

Think of it as a new way.

Think of it as a new way of structuring time.

Chapter 7
Living to Tell: Madonna's
Resurrection of the Fleshly

A great deal of ink has been spilled in the debate over pop star Madonna's visual image and the narratives she has enacted for music video. Almost every response in the spectrum has been registered, ranging from unambiguous characterizations of her as "a porn queen in heat"[1] or "the kind of woman who comes into your room at three a.m. and sucks your life out,"[2] to formulations that view her as a kind of organic feminist whose image "enables girls to see that the meanings of feminine sexuality *can* be in their control, *can* be made in their interests, and that their subjectivities are not necessarily totally determined by the dominant patriarchy."[3]

What most reactions to Madonna share, however, is an automatic dismissal of her music as irrelevant. The scorn with which her ostensible artistic focus has been trivialized, treated as a conventional backdrop to her visual appearance, often is breathtaking. For example, John Fiske's complex and sympathetic discussion of the struggle over meaning surrounding Madonna begins, "Most critics have nothing good to say about her music, but they have a lot to say about her image."[4] He then goes on to say a lot about her image, and he too has nothing whatsoever to say about the music. E. Ann Kaplan's detailed readings of Madonna's music videos likewise push the music to the side and treat the videos strictly through the techniques of film criticism.[5]

This essay will concentrate on Madonna, the musician. First, I will locate her within a history of gender relationships in the music world: I hope to demonstrate that Madonna has served as a lightning rod to make only slightly more perceptible the kinds of double binds always presented to a woman who attempts to enter Western music. Second, I will turn to her music and examine some of the ways she operates within a persistently repressive discourse to create liberatory musical images. Finally I will present a brief discussion of the music videos "Open Your Heart" and "Like a Prayer," in which I consider the interactions between musical and visual components.

Throughout this essay, I will be writing of Madonna in a way that assigns considerable credit and responsibility to her as a creator of texts. To be sure, the products ascribed to Madonna are the result of complex collaborative processes involving the input of co-writers, co-producers, studio musicians, video directors, technicians, marketing specialists, and so forth. As is the case in most pop, there is no single originary genius for this music.

Yet the testimonies of co-workers and interviewers indicate that Madonna is very much in control of almost every dimension of her media persona and her career. Even though certain components of songs or videos are contributed by other artists, she has won and fiercely maintains the right to decide finally what will be released under her name. It may be that Madonna is best understood as head of a corporation that produces images of her self-representation, rather than as the spontaneous, "authentic" artist of rock mythology. But a puppet she's not. As she puts it:

> People have this idea that if you're sexual and beautiful and provocative, then there's nothing else you could possibly offer. People have *always* had that image about women. And while it might have seemed like I was behaving in a stereotypical way, at the same time, I was also masterminding it. I was in control of everything I was doing, and I think that when people realized that, it confused them.[6]

I am stressing Madonna's agency in her own self-representation in part because there is such a powerful tendency for her agency to be erased completely—for her to be seen as just a mindless doll fulfilling male fantasies of anonymous puppeteers. This particular strategy for dismissing Madonna has always seemed odd to me because the fantasies she enacts are not very successful at being male fantasies, if that is their objective: they often inspire discomfort and anxiety among men who wish to read her as a genuine "Boy Toy."[7] And I am rather amused when men who are otherwise not conspicuously concerned with feminist issues attack Madonna for setting the cause of women back twenty years—especially because so many girls and women (some of them feminist theorists, including even Betty Friedan)[8] perceive her music and videos as articulating a whole new set of possible feminine subject positions. Furthermore, her spirited, self-confident statements in interviews (several of which are sprinkled liberally throughout this essay) tend to lend support to the interpretations of female fans.

Yet Madonna's agency is not hers alone: even if she wrote everything she performs all by herself, it would still be important to remember that her music and personae are produced within a variety of social discursive practices. Her style is assembled from the musics of many different genres, and her visual images draw upon the conventions of female representation that circulate in film, advertisements, and stage shows. Indeed, in order to be as effective as she unquestionably is, she has to speak intelligibly to the cultural experiences and perceptions of her audience. Her voices are credible precisely because they engage so provocatively with ongoing cultural conversations about gender, power, and pleasure.

Moreover, as will be demonstrated throughout this essay, Madonna's art itself repeatedly deconstructs the traditional notion of the unified subject with finite ego boundaries. Her pieces explore—sometimes playfully, sometimes seriously—various ways of constituting identities that refuse stability, that remain fluid, that resist definition. This tendency in her work has become increasingly pronounced: for instance, in her recent, controversial video "Express Yourself" (which borrows its imagery from Fritz Lang's *Metropolis*), she slips in and out of every subject position offered within the video's narrative context—including those of the cat and the tyrannical master of industry—refusing more than ever to deliver the security of a clear, unambiguous message or an "authentic" self.

Thus I do not want to suggest that she (of all artists!) is a solitary creator who ultimately determines fixed meanings for her pieces. But I will focus on how a woman artist can make a difference within discourse. To strip Madonna of all conscious intention in her work is to reduce her once again to a voiceless, powerless bimbo. In a world in which many people assert that she (along with most other women artists) can't have meant what one sees and hears because she isn't smart enough, claims of intentionality, agency, and authorship become extremely important strategically.

1

Although there are some notable exceptions, women have traditionally been barred from participating in Western music. The barriers that have prevented them from participation have occasionally been formal: in the seventeenth century there were even papal edicts proscribing women's musical education.[9] More often, however, women are discouraged through more subtle means from considering themselves as potential musicians. As macho rock star David Lee Roth (rarely accused of being an ardent feminist) observes: "What if a little girl picked up a guitar and said 'I wanna be a rock star.' Nine times out of ten her parents would never allow her to do it. We don't have so many lead guitar women, not because women don't have the ability to play the instrument, but because they're kept locked up, taught to be something else. I don't appreciate that."[10]

Women have, of course, been discouraged from writing or painting as well, and feminist scholars in literary and art history have already made the barriers hindering women in those areas familiar. But there are additional factors that still make female participation in music riskier than in either literature or the visual arts. First, the charismatic performance of one's music is often crucial to its promotion and transmission. Whether Liszt in his matinee-idol piano recitals, Elvis on "The Ed Sullivan Show," or the aforementioned David Lee Roth, the composer-performer often relies heavily on manipulating audience response through his enactments of sexual power and desire.[11]

However, for a man to enact his sexuality is not the same as for a woman: throughout Western history, women musicians have usually been assumed to be publicly available, have had to fight hard against pressures to yield, or have accepted the granting of sexual favors as one of the prices of having a career. The seventeenth-century composer Barbara Strozzi—one of the very few women to compete successfully in elite music composition—may have been forced by her agent-pimp of a father to pose for a bare-breasted publicity portrait as part of his plan for launching her career.[12] Women on the stage are viewed as sexual commodities regardless of their appearance or seriousness. Brahms pleaded with the aging Clara Schumann (provocatively dressed, to be sure, in widow's weeds) to leave off her immodest composition and concertizing.[13] One of Madonna's principal accomplishments is that she brings this hypocrisy to the surface and problematizes it.

Second, musical discourse has been carefully guarded from female participation in part because of its ability to articulate patterns of desire. Music is an extremely powerful medium, all the more so because most listeners have little rational control over the way it influences them. The mind/body split that has plagued Western culture for centuries shows up most paradoxically in attitudes toward music: the most cerebral, nonmaterial of media is at the same time the medium most capable of engaging the body. This confusion over whether music belongs with mind or with body is intensified when the fundamental binary opposition of masculine/feminine is mapped onto it.[14] To the very large extent that mind is defined as masculine and body as feminine in Western culture, music is always in danger of being perceived as a feminine (or effeminate) enterprise altogether.[15] And one of the means of asserting masculine control over the medium is by denying the very possibility of participation by women. For how can an enterprise be feminine if actual women are excluded?

Women are not, of course, entirely absent from traditional music spectacle: women characters may even be highlighted as stars in operas. But opera, like the other genres of Western music, is an almost exclusively male domain in that men write both libretti and music, direct the stage action, and interpret the scores. Thus it is not surprising that operas tend to articulate and reinforce precisely the sexual politics just described. The proceedings are controlled by a discourse organized in accordance with masculine interests—a discourse that offers up the female as spectacle while guaranteeing that she will not step out of line. Sometimes desire is articulated by the male character while the passive, domesticated female simply acquiesces. In such instances, the potential violence of male domination is not necessarily in evidence: the piece seems to unfold in accordance with the "natural" (read: patriarchal) sexual hierarchy.

But a kind of desire-dread-purge mechanism prevails in operas in which the tables are turned and a passive male encounters a strong, sexually aggressive female character. In operas such as *Carmen*, *Lulu*, and *Salome*, the "victimized male" who has been aroused by the temptress finally must kill her in order to reinstate social order.[16] Even in so-called absolute music (instrumental music in which there is no explicit extramusical or programmatic component), the themes conventionally designated as "feminine" must be domesticated or eradicated for the sake of narrative closure.[17]

The ways in which fear of female sexuality and anxiety over the body are inscribed in the Western music tradition are obviously very relevant for the would-be (wannabe?) woman musician. First, women are located within the discourse in a position of both desire and dread—as that which must reveal that it is controlled by the male or which must be purged as intolerable. Many male attacks on Madonna unself-consciously locate their terror in the fact that she is not under masculine control. Like Carmen or Lulu, she invokes the body and feminine sexuality; but unlike them, she refuses to be framed by a structure that will push her back into submission or annihilation. Madonna interprets the problem as follows:

> I think for the most part men have always been the aggressors sexually. Through time immemorial they've always been in control. So I think sex is equated with power in a way, and that's scary in a way. It's scary for men that women would have that power, and I think it's scary for women to have that power—or to have that power and be sexy at the same time.[18]

Second, the particular popular discourse within which Madonna works—that of dance—is the genre of music most closely associated with physical motion. The mind/body-masculine/feminine problem places dance decisively on the side of the "feminine" body rather than with the objective "masculine" intellect. It is for this reason that dance music in general usually is dismissed by music critics, even by "serious" rock critics. Recall the hysterical scorn heaped upon disco when it emerged, and recall also that disco was the music that underwrote the gay movement, black urban clubs, *Saturday Night Fever*'s images of working-class leisure, and other contexts that did not conform to the cherished ideal of (white, male, heterosexual, middle-class) rebel rock.[19] Similar dismissals of dance music can be found throughout the critical history of Western "serious" music. To the extent that the appeal is to physicality rather than abstracted listening, dance music is often trivialized at the same time that its power to distract and arouse is regarded with anxiety.[20]

Madonna works out of a discursive tradition that operates according to premises somewhat different from those of mainstream Western music. Her musical affiliations are with African-American music, with a culture that places great value on dance and physical engagement in music. It also is a culture that has always had prominent female participants: there are no white equivalents of Bessie Smith or Aretha Franklin—women who sing powerfully of both the spiritual and the erotic without the punitive, misogynist frame of European culture.[21] In critiquing Madonna's music, Dave Marsh (usually a defender of Madonna) once wrote, "A white Deniece Williams we don't need."[22] But perhaps that is precisely what we *do* need: a white woman musician who can create images of desire without the demand within the discourse itself that she be destroyed.

2

Madonna writes or co-writes most of her own material. Her first album was made up principally of her tunes. She surrendered some of the writing responsibility on *Like a Virgin* (interestingly, two of the songs that earned her so much notoriety—"Material Girl" and "Like a Virgin"—were written by men). But in her third album, *True Blue*, she is credited (along with her principal collaborators, Stephen Bray and Patrick Leonard) with co-production and with the co-writing of everything except "Papa Don't Preach." She co-wrote and co-produced (with Bray, Leonard, and Prince) all of the songs on her most recent album, *Like a Prayer*. It is quite rare for women singers to contribute so much to the composition of their materials, and it is almost unheard of for them to acquire the skills required for production. Indeed, very few performers of either sex attain sufficient prestige and power within the recording business to be able to demand that kind of artistic control.

Madonna's music is deceptively simple. On one level, it is very good dance music: inevitably compelling grooves, great energy. It is important to keep in mind that before she even presented her scandalous video images to the public, she had attracted a sizable following among the discerning participants of the black and gay disco scenes through her music alone. She remains one of the few white artists (along with George Michael) who regularly show up on the black charts.

Her music deliberately aims at a wide popular audience rather than at those who pride themselves on their elite aesthetic discrimination. Her enormous commercial success is often held against her, as evidence that she plays for the lowest common denominator—that she prostitutes her art (and, by extension, herself).[23] Moreover, the fact that her music appeals to masses of young girls is usually taken as proof that the music has absolutely no substance, for females in our culture are generally thought to be incapable of understanding music on even a rudimentary level. But surely Madonna's power as a figure in cultural politics is linked to her ability to galvanize that particular audience—among others.[24]

To create music within a male-defined domain is a treacherous task. As some women composers of so-called serious or experimental music are discovering, many of the forms and conventional procedures of presumably value-free music are saturated with hidden patriarchal narratives, images, agendas.[25] The options available to a woman musician in rock music are especially constrictive, for this musical discourse is typically characterized by its phallic backbeat. It is possible to try to downplay that beat, to attempt to defuse its energy—but this strategy often results in music that sounds enervated or stereotypically "feminine." It is also possible to appropriate the phallic energy of rock and to demonstrate (as Chrissie Hynde, Joan Jett, and Lita Ford do so very well) that boys don't have any corner on that market. But that beat can always threaten to overwhelm: witness Janet Jackson's containment by producers Jimmy Jam and Terry Lewis in (ironically) her song "Control."[26]

Madonna's means of negotiating for a voice in rock resemble very much the strategies of her visual constructions; that is, she evokes a whole range of conventional signifiers and then causes them to rub up against each other in ways that are open to a variety of divergent readings, many of them potentially empowering to girls and women. She offers musical structures that promise narrative closure, and at the same time she resists or subverts them. A traditional energy flow is managed—which is why to many ears the whole complex seems always already absorbed—but that flow is subtly re-directed.

The most obvious of her strategies is irony: the irony of the little-girl voice in "Like a Virgin" or of fifties girl-group sentiment in "True Blue." Like her play with the signs of famous temptresses, bustiers, and pouts, her engagement with traditional musical signs of childish vulnerability projects her knowledge that this is what the patriarchy expects of her and also her awareness that this fantasy is ludicrous. Her unsupervised parody destroys a much-treasured male illusion: even as she sings "True blue, baby, I love you," she becomes a disconcerting figure—the woman who knows too much, who is not at all the blank virginal slate she pretends to present. But to her female audience, her impersonation of these musical types is often received with delight as a knowing wink, a gesture of empowerment.[27]

Madonna's engagement with images of the past is not always to be understood as parody, however. Some of the historical figures she impersonates are victims of traditions in opera and popular culture that demand death as the price for sexuality.[28] Principal among the victims she invokes are Carmen and Marilyn Monroe, both highly desired, sexual women who were simultaneously idolized and castigated, and finally sacrificed to patriarchal standards of behavior. It is in her explicit acknowledgment of the traditional fate of artistic women who dare be erotic and yet in her refusal to fall likewise a victim that Madonna becomes far more serious about what have been referred to as "sign crimes."[29] If the strategy of appropriating and redefining conventional codes is the same in these more serious pieces as in the "True Blue" parody, the stakes are much, much higher.

3

In order to account for the radical quality of the music in "Live to Tell" (and later, "Like a Prayer"), I must once again return to the assumptions that guarantee the tonal narratives of the masculine canon since the seventeenth century. Since these assumptions have been discussed at length in previous chapters, I will only reiterate those that seem necessary for the purposes at hand. Tonal music is narratively conceived at least to the extent that the original key area—the tonic—also serves as the final goal. Tonal structures are organized teleologically, with the illusion of unitary identity promised at the end of each piece. But in order for pieces to have any narrative content, they must depart from the tonic and enact an adventure in which other key areas are visited (theorists sometimes say "conquered") and in which the certainty of tonal identity is at least temporarily suspended. Otherwise there is no plot. Yet with the exception of a few pieces in the nineteenth century and early twentieth that deliberately call into question the premises of this narrative schema, the outcome—the inevitable return to tonic—is always known in advance. To the extent that "Other" keys stand in the way of unitary identity, they must finally be subdued for the sake of narrative closure.[30] They serve as moments both of desire (because without the apparent longing to approach these other keys, there is only stagnation) and of dread (because they threaten identity).

As we have already seen, such narratives can easily be observed in nineteenth-century symphonies, in which lyrical "feminine" themes are encountered and then annexed (for the sake of closure and generic convention) to the key of the "masculine" theme. The more seductive or traumatic the encounter with the Other, the more violent the "necessary" heroic reaction. Beethoven's symphonies are especially telling in this regard: in the *Eroica*, an unprecedented level of dissonant bashing seems "required" to maintain thematic, rhythmic, and tonal identity. The struggle appears justified in the end, however, when we get to hear the uninterrupted transcendence of the theme in its tonic homeland.[31] In the Ninth Symphony, in which identity is marked as far more tentative, the violence levels are even higher. The arcadian third movement (a rare moment in which Beethoven permits dialogue and freedom of movement without the suggestion of overt anxiety) is self-consciously obliterated by the crashing dissonance introducing the finale's so-called "Ode to Joy."[32]

Most popular music avoids this schema, for songs typically are content with the sustaining of harmonic identity. There is usually no implied Other within these musical procedures, no structural obstacle or threat to overcome. However, all that is required to transform these stable procedures into narratives is for a detail to be problematized—to be construed as Other and as an obstacle to the configuration defined as Self or identity. In such songs, time becomes organized around the expectation of intensified conflict, climax, and eventual resolution. They adopt, in other words, the same desire-dread-purge sequence that characterizes the narratives of so much classical music and literature.

Rock songs that work on the basis of this sequence can be found from Led Zeppelin to The Cult's "Fire Woman [you're to blame]" or Dokken's "Kiss of Death." I will discuss as examples a couple of songs by the heavy metal band Whitesnake. Several of Whitesnake's songs quite clearly enact within the music the excitement of interacting with the area of the Other (personified in their videos by Tawny Kitaen as temptress) and yet the horror of being sucked in by that area, which precipitates and justifies outbreaks of violence for the sake of identity consolidation.

"Here I Go Again" defines the sixth degree of the scale as the moment of desire and also of potential entrapment. The choice of that scale degree is not accidental: there is a strong gravitational tendency in tonal music for six (a relatively weak position, sometimes referred to as "feminine") to resolve down to five, which belongs to the ("masculine") tonic triad. In pop as in classical music procedures, the tonic is rather boring by itself, and lingering on the sixth degree can create a delicious tension. However, if six threatens to take over, then identity may be destroyed. In "Here I Go Again," so-called deceptive cadences on the sixth degree repeatedly rob the piece of certainty, yet create precisely the sense of nostalgic longing that characterizes the song. Its spectacularly enacted "climax" occurs only after a prolonged episode in which the harmony seems paralyzed on the "feminine" modal degrees, and the violence of the climax permits the return to the progressions that define quintessential masculine cadential control. The piece concludes, however, not with certainty but with a fade; and in the video, the fade is accompanied by images of a devouring Kitaen hauling lead singer David Coverdale over into the back seat of the car he is driving. This is what happens, apparently, when the purge is unsuccessful.

In "Still of the Night," the threat is far more intense, both musically and theatrically. At the end of the first verse (on the words "in the still of the night"), Coverdale strains upward—both vocally and physically, as though in orgasm—to hold onto the sixth degree, before returning decisively to tonic control. The second time through, however, both the heroic Coverdale and the harmony get trapped for what seems an interminable duration in that position which has been so carefully defined as that of desire. The energy drains away, the musical and physical gestures mime impotence, and Kitaen struts about striking menacing poses. For a long time, there seems to be no possibility of escape or return. When the musical energy finally manages to extricate itself from the abyss, the rest of the piece is concerned with attempting violently to purge the contaminating element. In the video, this eradication sequence is dramatized visually as Kitaen is dragged off and tossed into a paddy wagon marked "Sex Police."

What we have here once again—in the abstract symphony as well as these particular metal fantasies—is the playing out in music of the same classic schema of Western masculine subjectivity we have been tracing throughout all of these essays. Of course, music is not the only cultural artifact that operates in this manner. John Fiske has written about how it informs the narrative conventions of popular episodic television shows such as "Magnum P.I.":

> Like all ideological constructs, masculinity is constantly under threat—it can never rest on its laurels. The threats come

internally from its insecure bases in the rejection of the mother
(and the guilt that this inspires) and the suppression of the
feminine, and externally from social forces, which may vary
from the rise of the women's movement to the way that the
organization of work denies many men the independence and
power that their masculinity requires. Thus masculinity has to be
constantly reachieved, rewon. This constant need to reachieve
masculinity is one of the underlying reasons for the popularity of
the frequent televisual display of male performance.[33]

Likewise, critics such as Teresa de Lauretis, Susan Bordo, and Mieke Bal
have written about how the schema is inscribed and transmitted in literature, film, philosophy, theology, science.[34] But our topic here is music, and,
as we have seen, a great deal of music too is organized in accordance with
this pattern. Indeed, music without words (so-called absolute music) is especially prone to relying on it, to treating it as though it were a design dictated by natural or metaphysical law.

But it is one thing to be aware of this schema and its implications as an
analyst and theorist. It is quite another to take the formal procedures conventionally inscribed within these discourses and cause them to tell another
story. Especially if one finds oneself always already cast by society in the
position of the Other rather than that of the "universal" (i.e., masculine)
Self.

4

In the stage performance of "Live to Tell," the backdrop of the stage is filled
with a huge projection of Madonna as Monroe, the quintessential female
victim of commercial culture. The instrumental introduction sets up a bass
pedal on D, performed by an inert synthesizer sonority utterly lacking in
warmth. Over the pedal, a series of bleak open fifths mechanically marks
the pulses of the metric order as though they are inevitable. This stark image
alternates with an energetic pattern that emerges suddenly in the area of the
relative major, F. The second sound-image differs from the opening sonority in part because the major key is semiotically associated with hope. Moreover, the bass is active rather than static, and it resists the apparent inevitability of the opening meter by anticipating slightly each of its changes: it
seems to possess freedom of motion. However, just as this passage seems on
the brink of establishing F major as the principal point of reference, it is recontained by the clanging fifths and the empty pedal on D. A traditional
reading would understand D (with its pedal and fifths) as fundamental (as
that which defines identity) and F major as the "feminine" region, which—

even if it offers the illusion of hope, escape, and freedom — must be contained and finally purged for the sake of satisfactory closure.[35]

When she begins singing the verse, Madonna steps temporarily outside of this dichotomy of D-versus-F to sing over a new pedal on C. As she sings, her voice repeatedly falls lethargically back to the void of the C-pedal, as though she cannot overcome the gravitational pull it and the meter exert. Her text suggests that she has a weighty, long-buried "tale to tell," and her language ("I was not ready for the fall," "the writing on the wall") resonates with biblical references. If she as a woman is necessarily identified as the Other, as she who is held responsible for "the Fall," how is she to enter into narrative? How to step into a musical procedure in which the choices are already so loaded?

With the chorus ("a man can tell a thousand lies"), she opts for the warmer major key of F, her momentum picks up, and she begins to sound as though she will establish this more affirmative region as her tonic or point of reference. However, to close in this second region — conventionally the "feminine" position — is to accept as identity the patriarchal definition of femininity. Moreover, to the extent that F major is not the opening key, to cadence here is to choose fantasy; for while this key is reassuring and nurturing, it is not "reality" as the piece defines it initially. And formal convention would dictate that this second key area must eventually be absorbed and purged. Thus closure here is revealed as perilous. At the last moment before the implied cadence ("it will burn inside of *me* "), she holds to a pitch incompatible with harmonic closure. The age-old contrapuntal norm would dictate that her melodic pitch (once again the sixth degree, the image of desire in the Whitesnake piece) must resolve down to conform with the bass. Instead, her melodic pitch and the harmonic backdrop hold in a standoff until the bass — not the melody — moves to conform to the melody's (that is, to *her*) will.

The pitch cadenced on, however, is D; and while it defies immediate closure, it also strikes the common tone that permits the pitiless pedal of the beginning to return. As before, Madonna steps outside the dilemma to C for a verse in which she wearily comments on her subjective knowledge of beauty, warmth, truth, light even in the face of this apparent no-win situation. But eventually she must rejoin the world in which she has to engage with the choice between F and D, and once again she works to avoid closure in either.

Finally, after this escape-recontainment process has occurred a couple of times, the bottom suddenly drops out. It sounds as though the piece has ended in the foreordained defeat of the victim — she who is offered only the second-position slot in the narrative schema. In her live performance, at this point Madonna sinks to the floor and lies motionless for what seems an interminable length of time. There is silence except for the low, lifeless synthesizer drone on D. For someone like myself who is used to this scenario as the inevitable end of my heroines, witnessing this moment from a performer who has been so brash, so bursting with erotic energy and animation, is bitter indeed. But then she rises from the floor, bearing with her the ghosts of all those victims—Marilyn most explicitly, but also Carmen, barebreasted Barbara Strozzi, and all the others who were purged for the sake of social order and narrative closure—and begins singing again.

In order to take charge of the narrative procedure, Madonna begins to oscillate strategically between the two tonal poles on D and F. As she sings "If I ran away, I'd never have the strength," she sings over a bass that moves up and down indecisively between D and A (mediant of F, but dominant of D), suggesting a blurred region in which both keys cohabit. When the opening dilemma returns, she prevents the recontainment gesture of the fifths by anticipating their rhythmic moment of reentry and jumping in to interpose the F-major refrain instead. So long as she manages thus to switch back and forth, she can determine the musical discourse. To settle for an option—either option—is to accept a lie, for it is flexibility in identity rather than unitary definition that permits her to "live to tell." The piece ends not with definitive closure but with a fade. As long as we can hear her, she continues to fluctuate.

This extraordinary song finally is not about unambiguous triumph: triumph would be easy to simulate, since this is what tonal pieces conventionally do. Yet given the premises of this song, triumphant closure would be impossible to believe. Moreover, it would merely reproduce the structure of oppression that informs narrative convention. Rather it is about staying in motion for the sake of survival, resisting closure wherever it lies in wait.[36]

By thus creating songs that refuse to choose between identity and Other—that invoke and then reject the very terms of this schema of narrative organization—Madonna is engaged in rewriting some very fundamental levels of Western thought. In "Live to Tell," the two clear regions of the traditional narrative schema seem to be implied. Semiotically, the unyielding fifths are "masculine," the lyrical, energetic refrain, "feminine," and the early part of the piece reveals that the fifths are formally designed to contain the excess and relative freedom of the refrain. But to the extent that identification with the feminine moment in the narrative spells death, the piece cannot embrace this space as reality without losing strategic control. Thus the singer risks resisting identification with "her own" area, even if it means repeated encounters with that which would contain her. In a sense, she sets up residence on the moments of the harmonic context that fluctuate between desire and dread on the one hand and resolution on the other. Rather than deciding for the sake of secure identity (a move that would lapse back into the narrative of masculine subjectivity), she inhabits both and thus refuses closure.

Formulations such as this are all the more remarkable because the ideological implications of musical narratives are only now beginning to be analyzed by cultural critics. The fact that some of Madonna's music enacts models of organization that correspond to formulations of critics such as Teresa de Lauretis need not suggest that Madonna is a connoisseur of critical theory. Yet to the extent that de Lauretis and Madonna inhabit the same historical world and grapple with the same kinds of problems with respect to feminine identity, their similarities are not entirely coincidental either. And Madonna is as much an expert in the arena of musical signification as de Lauretis is in theoretical discourse. It seems clear that she has grasped the assumptions embedded within these basic musical mechanisms and is audaciously redirecting them.

It must be conceded that male musicians could construct forms along these lines if they wanted to do so—there is nothing essentially feminine about what Madonna is doing in this piece. But most men would not perceive that there was a problem in the standard narrative, would not enact struggles that involve resistance to purging the alien element.[37] The strategies of Madonna's songs are those of one who has radically conflicting subject positions—one who has been taught to cheer for resolutions in cultural narratives, but who also realizes that she is of the sort that typically gets purged for the sake of that resolution. Madonna's refusal of definition (which infuriates many a critic) goes beyond the paradox of her name, her persona, her visual imagery. It also produces brave new musical procedures.

5

Having thus been converted to Madonna as a musician who dares to create liberatory visions, I find the necessity of reading her music videos all the more urgent. Visual images seem to speak much louder than music—at least critics of Madonna's videos have found it difficult to notice the music, given the provocative nature of the pictures. Yet it is generally accepted that music in film covertly directs the affective responses of viewers far more than they know. I would suggest that the *music* in music videos is largely responsible for the narrative continuity and the affective quality in the resultant work, even if it is the visual images we remember concretely.[38]

I was acquainted with the song "Open Your Heart" long before I saw the video attached to it. While affectively much more upbeat than "Live to

Tell," the musical imagery of "Open Your Heart" shares many of its resistant qualities: up against the shimmering, pulsating energy of the backup, Madonna avoids conforming to the beat; and, at cadences, she subverts expected points of arrival. But unlike in "Live to Tell," in which resistance indicates sheer survival, the play with closure in "Open Your Heart" creates the image of open-ended jouissance—an erotic energy that continually escapes containment.

By contrast, the video of "Open Your Heart" begins not in a visual field of open erotic joy but rather in the confined environment of a peep show. Madonna sings the song from the center of a carousel that revolves to display her to the gazes of customers peering safely from their cubicles. Here she becomes Marlene Dietrich in *The Blue Angel*, her usually exuberant motion restrained to what she is able to accomplish with her only prop: a stationary chair. At one point in the first segment of the video, she is filmed dancing; but the camera is almost still, and her motions are confined to the small range the static camera can take in.

This confinement is especially noteworthy given the extraordinary exhilaration of the music: the tension between the visual and musical dimensions of the video is extremely unsettling. Only when she disappears from the carousel and reappears to run away from her patriarchal boss with the young boy do the music and visuals begin to be compatible. In other words, two very different narrative strata are present in the video: that of the relatively consistent rhythmic energy in the music versus that of the transformation from patriarchal puppet to androgynous kid in the visuals.

Like many of Madonna's strategies, the one she attempts in this video is quite audacious. For instance, the peep show situation is shot in such a way that the leering patrons are rendered pathetic and grotesque, while she alone lays claim to subjectivity: thus, the usual power relationship between the voyeuristic male gaze and object is here destabilized. Likewise, the young boy's game of impersonating the femme fatale and Madonna's transvestism at the end both refuse essentialist gender categories and turn sexual identity into a kind of play. Still, the video is risky, because for all those who have reduced her to "a porn queen in heat," there she is: embodying that image to the max. Those features of the video that resist a reductive reading of this sort—the nonfit of the music, the power inversions, the narrative of escape to androgyny—can easily be overlooked. This is, of course, always the peril of attempting to deconstruct pornographic images: it becomes necessary to invoke the image in order to perform the deconstruction; but, once presented, the image is in fact there in all its glory.

In this video, Madonna confronts the most pernicious of her stereotypes and then attempts to channel it into a very different realm: a realm where the feminine erotic need not be the object of the patriarchal gaze, where its energy can motivate play and nonsexual pleasure. The end of this video is as tenuous as the transcendent pitch in "Live to Tell": it speaks not of certainty, but of horizons, of possibilities, of the hope of survival within available discursive practices.

6

These themes—survival, pleasure, resistance to closure—are reengaged most dramatically in Madonna's recent song and video, "Like a Prayer." In contrast to the relationship between sight and sound in "Open Your Heart," the tensions she is putting into play in this music video are virtually all audible within the music itself, prior to the visual images. Moreover, many of the tensions that have always surrounded her personae are here made explicit.

The central dichotomy she inevitably invokes is that of the virgin and the whore.[39] Her name (actually, fortuitously, her given name: Madonna Louise Veronica Ciccone), her apparently casual flaunting of crucifixes and rosaries as accessories, and her overtly erotic dress and behavior have consistently thrown into confusion the terms of that standard binary opposition; but what precisely she means by this play of signs has never been obvious. Indeed, many critics have taken her use of religious imagery to be a prime example of what Fredric Jameson calls "blank pastiche": the symbols are seen as detached from their traditional contexts and thus as ceasing to signify.[40] However, Madonna's insistence on the codes of Catholic iconography has always at least potentially engaged with the sedimented memory of that tradition, even if only negatively—as blasphemy. In "Like a Prayer," the religious connotations of her entire project are reactivated and reinterpreted. But although this set of issues is finally foregrounded, her treatment of these highly sensitive themes is quite unexpected and, as it turns out, highly controversial.

The song draws upon two very different semiotic codes associated with two very different forms of Christianity: Catholicism and the black Gospel church. These codes would seem at first glance to be incompatible. But Madonna is tapping into a tradition of Catholicism that has long been suppressed: that of the female mystics such as Saint Teresa who claimed to have experienced mystical union with Christ.[41] In Saint Teresa's writings, religious ecstasy is described through images of sexual ecstasy, for the intensity of her relationship with the deity could only be expressed verbally to other human beings through metaphors of submission, penetration, even orgasm. In the seventeenth century, composers of sacred music freely borrowed images of desire and eroticism from the steamy operatic stage for purposes of their devotionals and worship services, for these experiences were thought to be relevant to the new forms of personalized faith encouraged by both the Reformation and the Counter-Reformation.[42]

After the seventeenth century, this strain of religious erotic imagery was purged from most mainstream Christian denominations, only to reemerge occasionally during moments of intense emotional revivalism. Certain forms of charismatic fundamentalism since the eighteenth century have employed erotic imagery for purposes of inducing personalized meditation or even trance states and speaking in tongues. Both Bach's pietistic bride-and-groom duets (see Cantata 140) and Jerry Lee Lewis's evangelical rock 'n' roll ("Whole Lot of Shakin' Goin' On") testify to this phenomenon. However, the semiotic connections between religious and sexual ecstasy are most consistently apparent in the black Gospel churches. Throughout its history (as preserved on recordings), Gospel has freely borrowed musical and poetic styles from the secular music of its day: witness, for instance, the mergers with jazz, blues, funk, and rap evident on present-day Gospel radio stations—or, for that matter, the entire career of Aretha Franklin. Moreover, the Gospel church continually produces new generations of black pop musicians whose music is fueled by the fervent energy of that spiritual context.

"Like a Prayer" opens with an invocation of stereotyped mystical Catholicism: with the halo of a wordless (heavenly) choir and the fundamental accompaniment of a "timeless" pipe organ as she sings of how "Life is a mystery." But with the words "When you call my name" (when, in other words, she is hailed as a new kind of subject), Madonna breaks into ecstatic, funky, Gospel-flavored dance music. These two moments are distinguished for narrative purposes through the same harmonic contrast between D minor and F major as in "Live to Tell." What seems to be a struggle between mystical timelessness on D minor and exuberant, physical celebration on F major ensues. This time, however, she is not afraid to embrace F as tonic, especially when halfway through, on the words "your voice can take me there," she lands decisively on that pitch.

But D minor does not disappear entirely—it reenters for a long, rather sinister return of the beginning material in the middle of the song. Eventually, however, the music is channeled back to F major for more celebration. Gradually D minor comes to serve only for "deceptive" cadences. Traditionally deceptive cadences spell disappointment, a jarring intervention at the promised moment of identity. But in "Like a Prayer," they provide the means of avoiding closure and maintaining the dance. Finally, in the long, ecstatic coda to the song, F major and D minor at cadences become in a sense interchangeable: no longer self and Other, they become two flickering moments in a flexible identity that embraces them both, that remains constant only insofar as both continue to be equally present.

This is similar to the strategy of "Live to Tell," except that here the music itself does not involve the suggestion of threatened annihilation. But the controversial video released with the album sets up something like the external threats of containment articulated in "Live to Tell." The video is organized in terms of an inside and an outside. Outside the church is the world of Ku Klux Klan cross-burnings, of rape and murder, of racist authority. One of the most striking moments in the video occurs when Madonna dances provocatively in front of the burning crosses, aggressively defying those who burn crosses to contain her and her sexuality as well. And, indeed, Madonna has testified to having planned originally to present an even more extreme scenario: "I had all these ideas about me running away with the black guy and both of us getting shot by the KKK."[43] Video director Mary Lambert says of the segment with the burning crosses: "That's an ecstatic vision. The cross is a cautionary symbol and Madonna's performance throughout has been tortured and emotional. The inference of Ku Klux Klan racism is there, but the burning cross is an older symbol than the Klan. Saints had it. It symbolizes the wrath of God."[44]

But inside the church is the possibility of community, love, faith, and interracial bonding. The references to Catholic mysticism and the black Gospel church are made explicit in the visuals, with a heady mixture of a miraculously weeping statue, the stigmata, the Saint Teresa-like union between the saint and the believer, and the highly physical musical performance by the Andraé Crouch choir. Within the security of the church, difference can be overcome and the boundless joy of the music can become reality.[45] As in "Live to Tell," this song is about survival rather than simple triumph. And it is about the possibility of creating musical and visual narratives that celebrate multiple rather than unitary identities, that are concerned with ecstatic continuation rather than with purging and containment.[46]

In a world in which the safe options for women musicians seem to be either denying gender difference or else restricting the expression of feminine pleasure to all-women contexts, Madonna's counternarratives of female heterosexual desire are remarkable. The intelligence with which she zeroes in on the fundamental gender tensions in culture and the courage with which she takes them on deserve much greater credit than she usually is given. That she manages both to outrage those who would have her conform and to delight those who are still trying to puzzle out their own future options within this society indicates that her strategies are by and large successful. If

Madonna does, in fact, "live to tell"—that is, survive as a viable cultural force—an extraordinarily powerful reflex action of patriarchy will have been successfully challenged.

Notes

Notes

Chapter 1. Introduction: A Material Girl in Bluebeard's Castle

1. Bruno Bettelheim, *The Uses of Enchantment: The Meaning and Importance of Fairy Tales* (New York: Vintage Books, 1977), 299-303.

2. See, for instance, Carol Neuls-Bates, ed., *Women in Music: An Anthology of Source Readings from the Middle Ages to the Present* (New York: Harper & Row, 1982); Jane Bowers and Judith Tick, eds., *Women Making Music: The Western Art Tradition, 1150-1950* (Urbana: University of Illinois Press, 1986); James R. Briscoe, ed., *Historical Anthology of Music by Women* (Bloomington: Indiana University Press, 1987); and Nancy B. Reich, *Clara Schumann: The Artist and the Woman* (Ithaca: Cornell University Press, 1985).

3. See, for instance, Bowers and Tick, *Women Making Music*; Eva Rieger, *Frau, Musik und Männerherrschaft* (Frankfurt: Ullstein, 1981); Ellen Koskoff, ed., *Women and Music in Cross-Cultural Perspective* (Westport, Conn.: Greenwood Press, 1987); and Judith Lang Zaimont, ed., *The Musical Woman: An International Perspective, 1983* (Westport, Conn.: Greenwood Press, 1984).

4. Stanley Sadie, ed., *The New Grove Dictionary of Music and Musicians* (New York: W. W. Norton, 1980).

5. The *Man and Music* videos were produced and shown by Granada Television International in 1986, and the books are now beginning to be released by Macmillan Press, with Prentice-Hall as the American publisher. Stanley Sadie serves as series editor and adviser for the videos, which are available through Films for the Humanities, Inc. (Princeton, N.J.). *The Music of Man* series is designed to accompany a textbook by K. Marie Stolba, *The Development of Western Music: A History* (Dubuque, Iowa: Wm. C. Brown, 1990). Ironically, Stolba is the first to incorporate some of what we now know about women composers and musicians into a general music history textbook.

6. The Ottawa conference "Alternative Musicologies" was organized by John Shepherd, and its proceedings are being published by the *Canadian University Music Review* and in a collection, *New Musicology*, edited by Shepherd for Routledge. The conference at Dartmouth, "Music and Literature," sparked many kinds of lively critical discussions. The principal feminist contribution was Ruth Solie's superb

"Whose Life? The Gendered Self in Schumann's *Frauenliebe* Songs." I wish to thank Prof. Solie for permitting me to read a copy of this paper.

7. There were two sessions devoted specifically to feminist issues at the meeting: "Feminist Scholarship and the Field of Musicology," organized by Jane Bowers, and panel, "The Implications of Feminist Scholarship for Teaching," organized by Susan Cook. In addition, there were several explicitly feminist talks scattered throughout many other sessions, including papers by Suzanne Cusick, Linda Austern, Jenny Kallick, and Marcia Citron. I list them here because the public surfacing of these women was such an extraordinary event.

8. The two anthologies are Ruth Solie, ed., *Music and Difference* (Berkeley: University of California Press, forthcoming); and Susan Cook and Judy Tsou, eds., *Cecilia: Feminist Perspectives on Women and Music*.

9. There are a few studies of musical semiotics available, though most of them prove not to be especially useful for my purposes. Jean-Jacques Nattiez, *Fondements d'une sémiologie de la musique* (Paris: Union Générale d'Éditions, 1975), is probably the most elaborate work to address these issues, though his theory operates entirely within a self-contained, formalistic context with scrupulous disregard for social signification. At the other extreme, Deryck Cooke, *The Language of Music* (London: Oxford University Press, 1974), presents a semantics of Western music, the usefulness of which is limited by his failure to ground his observations socially or historically. For astute analyses of the politics of "apolitical" semiotics, see Teresa de Lauretis, "Semiotics and Experience," *Alice Doesn't* (Bloomington: Indiana University Press, 1984), 158–86; and Edward W. Said, *The World, the Text, and the Critic* (Cambridge, Mass.: Harvard University Press, 1983).

10. Stephen Heath, *The Sexual Fix* (New York: Schocken Books, 1982), 3. I wish to thank Gary Thomas for bringing this formulation to my attention. See Chapters 2, 3, and 5 for more detailed expositions of gender and sexuality in music.

11. Willi Apel, *Harvard Dictionary of Music*, 2nd ed., rev. and enlarged (Cambridge, Mass.: Harvard University Press, 1970), 506. The entry "Feminine cadence," reads: "See Masculine, feminine cadence."

12. Edward T. Cone, *Musical Form and Musical Performance* (New York: W. W. Norton, 1968), 45. I should add that I find this to be the most insightful book available on the practical relationship between analysis and performance, and it is required reading for some of my courses.

13. Georg Andreas Sorge, *Vorgemach der musicalischen Composition* (1745-47), trans. Allyn Dixon Reilly (Ph.D. dissertation, Northwestern University, 1980), 179-80. I wish to thank Lawrence Zbikowski for bringing this passage to my attention.

14. Arnold Schoenberg, *Theory of Harmony* (1911), trans. Roy E. Carter (Berkeley: University of California Press, 1983), 96. My thanks to Andrew Jones for this citation.

15. See Chapter 4 for a more extensive discussion of the politics of Schoenberg's *Theory of Harmony* and of his musical compositions. Because it would have been problematic for Schoenberg to have put himself on the side of the "feminine" along with chromaticism and dissonance, he carefully remapped the conventional binarisms in terms of the struggle against class oppression. He then could valorize and even identify with what had traditionally been relegated to the "feminine" side of the equations. The passage cited above is one of the few that slip back into gendered terms.

16. Heinrich Schenker, *Harmony*, ed. Oswald Jonas, trans. Elisabeth Mann Borgese (Cambridge, Mass.: MIT Press, 1973), 28. See also xxv, 6, 28, 30. My thanks again to Larry Zbikowski. Schenker likewise subscribes to the nineteenth-

century concept of the "unconscious genius" who appropriates the passivity and breeding qualities from the female. See *Harmony*, 60 and 69, and *Der freie Satz*, trans. and ed. Ernst Oster (New York: Longman, 1979), xxv.

17. For an examination of "organicism" in musical thought, see Ruth Solie, "The Living Work: Organicism and Musical Analysis," *19th-Century Music* 4, no. 2 (Fall 1980): 147-56. For an analysis of the nineteenth-century identification of "genius" and organicism with male sexuality, see Christine Battersby, *Gender and Genius: Towards a Feminist Aesthetics* (London: Women's Press, 1989).

18. See Mark Johnson, *The Body in the Mind: The Bodily Basis of Meaning, Imagination, and Reason* (Chicago: University of Chicago Press, 1987), for a superb epistemological theory that posits metaphor as the principal means by which humans orient themselves to the world. Johnson analyzes verbal tropes not as decorative language but as evidence of the basic analogues that structure thought. Cultural discourses such as music are likewise meaningful because they draw upon the organizing metaphors shared by a particular social group. For a demonstration of how central cultural tropes organize ostensibly objective writing about music, see Janet M. Levy, "Covert and Casual Values in Recent Writings about Music," *Journal of Musicology* 5 (1987): 3-27.

19. As cited and translated in the communication from Peter Bloom in *Journal of the American Musicological Society* 27 (1974): 161-62. This communication presents a succinct account of the origins of the verbal convention of "masculine" and "feminine" themes.

See also the analysis of the description of sonata procedure from *Musik in Geschichte und Gegenwart* in Eva Rieger, " 'Dolce Semplice'? On the Changing Role of Women in Music," *Feminist Aesthetics*, ed. Gisela Ecker, trans. Harriet Anderson (Boston: Beacon Press, 1985), 139-40.

20. Teresa de Lauretis, "Desire in Narrative," *Alice Doesn't*, 118-19.

21. De Lauretis, "Desire in Narrative," 103-57, and "The Violence of Rhetoric: Considerations on Representation and Gender," *Technologies of Gender* (Bloomington: Indiana University Press, 1987), 31-50. See also Vladimir Propp, *Morphology of the Folktale*, 2nd ed., rev. and ed. Louis A. Wagner (Austin: University of Texas Press, 1968); and especially Jurij Lotman, "The Origin of Plot in the Light of Typology," trans. Julian Graffy, *Poetics Today* 1, no. 1-2 (Autumn 1979): 161-84. These narratological models have the drawback, however, of being relatively ahistorical. See the critique in Jay Clayton, "Narrative and Theories of Desire," *Critical Inquiry* 16 (Autumn 1989): 33-53. The essays in this volume are concerned with problematizing the historicity of narrative processes in music, even though they draw on the formulations of de Lauretis for purposes of explicating the musical repertories most devoted to the schemata she describes.

22. For an analysis of the ways the narrative structures of the principal operas of the standard repertory demand the subjugation of women, see Catherine Clément, *Opera, or the Undoing of Women*, trans. Betsy Wing (Minneapolis: University of Minnesota Press, 1988). If her litany is depressingly redundant, so are the schemata of dominant narratives. See also Chapters 3 and 4.

23. Schoenberg, *Theory of Harmony*, 129. For a more extensive discussion of Schoenberg's agenda, see Chapter 4.

24. James Webster, "Sonata Form," *New Grove* 17, 498.

25. Fredric Jameson, "Reification and Utopia in Mass Culture," *Social Text* 1 (1980): "Now none of these readings can be said to be wrong or aberrant, but their very multiplicity suggests that the vocation of the symbol—the killer shark—lies less in any single message or meaning than in its very capacity to absorb and orga-

nize all of these quite distinct anxieties together. As a symbolic vehicle, then, the shark must be understood in terms of its essentially polysemous function rather than any particular content attributable to it by this or that spectator. Yet it is precisely this polysemousness which is profoundly ideological, insofar as it allows essentially social and historical anxieties to be folded back into apparently 'natural' ones, to be both expressed and recontained in what looks like a conflict with other forms of biological existence" (142).

26. See Chapters 3 and 4 for more extensive discussions of chromaticism as gendered.

27. See Rieger, *Frau, Musik und Männerherrschaft*, and Battersby, *Gender and Genius*.

28. Linda Austern, " ' Alluring the Auditorie to Effeminacie': Music and the English Renaissance Idea of the Feminine," paper presented to the American Musicological Society, Baltimore (November 1988); Richard Leppert, *Music and Image: Domesticity, Ideology and Socio-cultural Formation in Eighteenth-Century England* (Cambridge: Cambridge University Press, 1989). Jeffrey Kallberg's "Genre and Gender: The Nocturne and Women's History" (CUNY Graduate Center, April 1989) also addresses the anxiety over the perceived effeminacy of certain genres. I wish to thank Prof. Kallberg for permitting me to read a copy of this paper.

Debussy reception has likewise been waged in terms of the "masculinity" or "effeminacy" of his musical style. See Daniel Gregory Mason, *Contemporary Composers* (London: Macmillan, 1929): "Sybaritism, too, has its own vulgarity; the question of aim is fundamental in art; and in judging the distinction of Debussy's aims we cannot evade the question whether physical pleasure, however refined, is the highest good an artist can seek. His charm, beyond doubt, is great enough to justify his popularity. Yet it would be regrettable if the student of modern French music, satisfied with this charm, were to neglect the less popular but more virile, more profound, and more spiritual music of Cesar Franck, Ernest Chausson, and Vincent d'Indy" (151). See also Robin Holloway, *Debussy and Wagner* (London: Eulenburg Books, 1979); and Robert Schmitz, *The Piano Works of Claude Debussy* (London: Duell, Sloan, and Pearce, 1950). I am indebted to Karen Schoenrock for these citations.

29. Solomon, "Charles Ives: Some Questions of Veracity," *Journal of the American Musicological Society* 40 (Fall 1987): 467.

30. For other discussions of the genderings of these style periods, see Jochen Schulte-Sasse, "Imagination and Modernity: Or the Taming of the Human Mind," *Cultural Critique* 5 (Winter 1986-87): 23-48; Alan Richardson, "Romanticism and the Colonization of the Feminine," in *Romanticism and Feminism*, ed. Anne Mellor (Bloomington: Indiana University Press, 1988), 13-25; Marlon B. Ross, "Troping Masculine Power in the Crisis of Poetic Identity," also in Mellor, *Romanticism*, 26-51; Andreas Huyssen, "Mass Culture as Woman: Modernism's Other," *Studies in Entertainment: Critical Approaches to Mass Culture*, ed. Tania Modleski (Bloomington: Indiana University Press, 1986), 188-207; Sandra M. Gilbert and Susan Gubar, *No Man's Land: The Place of the Woman Writer in the Twentieth Century* (New Haven, Conn.: Yale University Press, 1988); and Christine Buci-Glucksmann, *La raison baroque de Baudelaire à Benjamin* (Paris: Éditions Galilée, 1984). See also Chapter 4.

31. Robert Schumann, "Schubert's Symphony in C," *Neue Zeitschrift für Musik*, 10 March 1840. The translation of these concluding lines is by Sanna Pederson. A translation of the complete essay is available in *Schumann on Music*, trans., ed., and annotated Henry Pleasants (New York: Dover, 1988), 163-68. I wish to thank Ms. Pederson for bringing this essay to my attention.

32. For critiques of the crippling effect of this masculinist epistemology, see Carol Gilligan, *In a Different Voice: Psychological Theory and Women's Development* (Cambridge, Mass.: Harvard University Press, 1982); Mary Field Belenky et al., *Women's Ways of Knowing: The Development of Self, Voice, and Mind* (New York: Basic Books, 1986); Evelyn Fox Keller, *Reflections on Gender and Science* (New Haven, Conn.: Yale University Press, 1985); and Sandra Harding, *The Science Question in Feminism* (Ithaca: Cornell University Press, 1986).

33. See the documents included under the heading of "The 'Woman Composer Question'" and "The 'Woman Composer Question' Revisited" in Neuls-Bates, ed., *Women in Music*, 206-27 and 278-302. For classic accounts of the exclusion and denigration of women artists and writers, see Linda Nochlin, "Why Have There Been No Great Women Artists?" *Art and Sexual Politics*, ed. Thomas B. Hess and Elizabeth C. Baker (New York: Collier Books, 1973), 1-43; and Sandra M. Gilbert and Susan Gubar, *The Madwoman in the Attic: The Woman Writer and the Nineteenth-Century Literary Imagination* (New Haven, Conn.: Yale University Press, 1979), 3-104.

34. See the responses by women composers to Elaine Barkin's questionnaire published in *Perspectives in New Music* 19 (1980-81): 460-62; and 20 (1981-82): 288-330. See also Nicola LeFanu, "Master Musician: An Impregnable Taboo?" *Contact: A Journal of Contemporary Music* 31 (Autumn 1987): 4-8, for an argument similar to mine by a woman composer.

35. Joseph Kerman has explained the historical conditions that led to this state of affairs in American musicology. See his *Contemplating Music: Challenges to Musicology* (Cambridge, Mass.: Harvard University Press, 1985), 31-59.

There is, to be fair, a tiny cadre of American musicologists that has persistently advocated and practiced music criticism for the last thirty years. They include most prominently Edward T. Cone, Joseph Kerman, Leonard B. Meyer, Charles Rosen, Maynard Solomon, and Leo Treitler. Over the years, these critics have been a salutary presence in an otherwise arid discipline, for their work focuses on the music itself and attempts to deal with meaning as it is produced in various moments of music history. Their detailed, insightful interpretations of musical compositions have demonstrated over and over again how to write about music with tremendous lucidity and integrity—in a field otherwise noteworthy for its absence and suspicion of intellectual activity.

36. See, for instance, David Epstein's methodological statement in *Beyond Orpheus: Studies in Musical Structure* (Cambridge, Mass.: MIT Press, 1979), 11. While acknowledging that the question of expression is important, he concludes that "it is first of all essential clearly to perceive, to recognize, and to comprehend what it is we hear, *free of external or misconstrued meanings*" (my emphasis). I am dubious that one can ever get from such formalistic explanations to anything having to do with social signification. Moreover, I would argue that hearing Beethoven's *Eroica* through a complex theoretical grid derived from Schenker and Babbitt is a far greater imposition of "external" meanings (available only to a few highly trained professionals) than listening by means of inherited semiotic codes, which informed the composer as well as his various audiences.

37. A great deal of work has been done on how the reader—and not simply the author—produces meaning for literary texts. See, for instance, Stanley Fish, *Is There a Text in This Class: The Authority of Interpretive Communities* (Cambridge, Mass.: Harvard University Press, 1980); Susan R. Suleiman and Inge Crosman, *The Reader in the Text: Essays on Audience and Interpretation* (Princeton: Princeton University Press, 1980); and Judith Fetterly, *The Resisting Reader: A Feminist Approach to American Fiction* (Bloomington: Indiana University Press, 1978). Similarly, feminist film

theory has concentrated heavily on how meaning is construed variously by male and female spectators. See, for instance, Laura Mulvey, "Visual Pleasure and Narrative Cinema," *Screen* 16, no. 3 (Fall 1975): 6-18; Mary Ann Doane, *The Desire to Desire: The Woman's Film of the 1940s* (Bloomington: Indiana University Press, 1987); and Tania Modleski, *The Women Who Knew Too Much: Hitchcock and Feminist Theory* (New York: Methuen, 1988).

The only book dealing with a woman's reception of opera—Clément's *Opera, or the Undoing of Women*—has been heavily criticized since its publication in English precisely because it draws upon Clément's own experiences with opera. What she is doing is in line with much of the intellectual work being done in other areas of the humanities. She is not trying to present an "objective" account of opera (what would that be?), but rather is relating how opera has moved her to tears, how it has helped shape her own identity, and how she has tried to become a resisting listener: how, in other words, opera participates in social formation.

38. Raymond Williams, *The Long Revolution* (London: Cox & Wyman, 1961), 66-69.

39. Johnson, *The Body in the Mind*, all emphases in the original. These passages are excerpted from Johnson's preface, xiii-xvi. See also George Lakoff and Mark Johnson, *Metaphors We Live By* (Chicago: University of Chicago Press, 1980).

40. Schenker—our father of formalist analysis—comes surprisingly close to this position: "As the image of our life-motion, music can approach a state of objectivity, never, of course, to the extent that it need abandon its own specific nature as an art. Thus, it may almost evoke pictures or seem to be endowed with speech; it may pursue its course by means of associations, references, and connectives; it may use repetitions of the same tonal succession to express different meanings; it may simulate expectation, preparation, surprise, disappointment, patience, impatience, and humor. Because these comparisons are of a biological nature, and are generated organically, music is never comparable to mathematics or to architecture, but only to language, a kind of tonal language." *Der freie Satz*, 5. See also the biological metaphors cited in note 16.

41. Jay Clayton likewise has argued for regarding such phenomena as desire as mutable and socially constituted rather than as a biological universal. See his "Narrative and Theories of Desire."

42. For excellent discussions of the political nature of humanities scholarship that pretends to neutrality as well as criticism that announces its agenda, see Said, *The World, the Text, and the Critic*, especially 1-53; Terry Eagleton, *Literary Theory* (Minneapolis: University of Minnesota Press, 1983), especially 194-217; and *The Function of Criticism* (London: Verso, 1984). For music, see Rose Rosengard Subotnik, "The Role of Ideology in the Study of Western Music," *Journal of Musicology* 2 (1983): 1-12.

43. See, for instance, Bruno Nettl, *The Study of Ethnomusicology* (Urbana: University of Illinois Press, 1983); and Koskoff, *Women and Music in Cross-Cultural Perspective*. For a study that reveals especially well the specificity of the cultural metaphors that can inform music, see Stephen Feld, *Sound and Sentiment: Birds, Weeping, Poetics, and Song in Kaluli Expression* (Philadelphia: University of Pennsylvania Press, 1982).

44. A few musicologists are beginning to make use of anthropological methodologies. For instance, Gary Tomlinson, "The Web of Culture: A Context for Musicology," *19th-Century Music* 7 (Spring 1984): 350-62, draws upon the models developed by Clifford Geertz. Henry Kingsbury recently carried out anthropological

fieldwork in an American conservatory. See his *Music, Talent, and Performance: A Conservatory Cultural System* (Philadelphia: Temple University Press, 1988).

For discussions of ethnography that seem especially relevant to musicological work, see Geertz, *The Interpretation of Cultures* (New York: Basic Books, 1973); and, more recently, George E. Marcus and Michael Fischer, *Anthropology as Cultural Critique: An Experimental Moment in the Human Sciences* (Chicago: University of Chicago Press, 1980); James Clifford and George E. Marcus, eds., *Writing Culture: The Poetics and Politics of Ethnography* (Berkeley: University of California Press, 1986); Clifford, *The Predicament of Culture: Twentieth-Century Ethnography, Literature, and Art* (Cambridge, Mass.: Harvard University Press, 1988).

45. "A Musical Dialectic from the Enlightenment: Mozart's *Piano Concerto in G Major, K. 453*, Movement 2," *Cultural Critique* 4 (Fall 1986): 129-70; and "The Blasphemy of Talking Politics during Bach Year," *Music and Society: The Politics of Composition, Performance and Reception*, ed. Richard Leppert and Susan McClary (Cambridge: Cambridge University Press, 1987), 13-62.

46. "Pitches, Expression, Ideology: An Exercise in Mediation," *Enclitic* 7, no. 1 (Spring 1983): 76-86. See Chapter 4 for a discussion of the flat-six excursion in *Lucia di Lammermoor*. This effective rhetorical move is still very much in use in popular music—see Chapter 7.

47. Jacques Attali, *Noise*, trans. Brian Massumi (Minneapolis: University of Minnesota Press, 1985). See my afterword, "The Politics of Silence and Sound," 149-58.

48. See, for instance, Adorno's *Prisms*, trans. Samuel Weber and Shierry Weber (Cambridge, Mass.: MIT Press, 1981); *Philosophy of Modern Music*, trans. Anne G. Mitchell and Wesley V. Blomster (New York: Seabury Press, 1973); and *In Search of Wagner*, trans. Rodney Livingstone (London: New Left Books, 1981).

Rose Rosengard Subotnik has been largely responsible for bringing Adorno's work to the attention of American musicology. See especially her "Adorno's Diagnosis of Beethoven's Late Style: Early Symptom of a Fatal Condition," *Journal of the American Musicological Society* 29 (1976): 242-75; "The Historical Structure: Adorno's 'French' Model for the Criticism of Nineteenth-Century Music," *19th-Century Music* 2 (1978): 36-60. Because Subotnik has been severely chastised for having thus brought Continental criticism into the discipline, I want to go on record expressing my gratitude to her. Hers is the richest critical work to have emerged in musicology in the last fifteen years. See the collection that includes the preceding and other of her essays, *Developing Variations: Style and Ideology in Western Music* (Minneapolis: University of Minnesota Press, forthcoming).

49. See, for instance, Foucault's *The Order of Things: An Archaeology of the Human Sciences* (New York: Random House, 1970); *Madness and Civilization: A History of Insanity in the Age of Reason*, trans. Richard Howard (New York: Random House, 1965); and *The History of Sexuality, Vol. I: An Introduction*, trans. Robert Hurley (New York: Random House, 1978).

50. For perceptive critiques of Foucault, see Irene Diamond and Lee Quinby, eds., *Feminism & Foucault: Reflections on Resistance* (Boston: Northeastern University Press, 1988); and Said, "Criticism between Culture and System," *The World, the Text, and the Critic*, 178-225.

51. Antonio Gramsci, *Selections from the Prison Notebooks*, ed. and trans. Quintin Hoare and Geoffrey Nowell-Smith (New York: International Publishers, 1971); and *Selections from Cultural Writings*, ed. David Forgacs and Geoffrey Nowell-Smith; trans. William Boelhower (Cambridge, Mass.: Harvard University Press, 1985); Mikhail Bakhtin, *The Dialogic Imagination*, ed. Michael Holquist; trans. Caryl Em-

erson and Michael Holquist (Austin: University of Texas Press, 1981); and *Rabelais and His World*, trans. Hélène Iswolsky (Bloomington: Indiana University Press, 1984).

See also Stuart Hall, "Cultural Studies: Two Paradigms," *Media, Culture & Society*, ed. Richard Collins et al. (London: Sage, 1986). For especially fine examples of music criticism utilizing Gramsci, Bakhtin, and Hall, see George Lipsitz, "Cruising Around the Historical Bloc: Postmodernism and Popular Music in East Los Angeles," *Cultural Critique* 5 (Winter 1986-87): 157-78; and "Mardi Gras Indians: Carnival and Counter-Narrative in Black New Orleans," *Cultural Critique* 10 (Fall 1988): 99-122. These essays are included in the collection titled *Time Passages: Collective Memory and American Popular Culture* (Minneapolis: University of Minnesota Press, 1990).

52. See, for instance, Fernand Braudel, *The Structures of Everyday Life: Civilization & Capitalism, 15th-18th Century*, vol. 1, trans. Siân Reynolds (New York: Harper & Row, 1981); Stephen Greenblatt, *Shakespearean Negotiations* (Berkeley: University of California Press, 1988); Joan Kelly, *Women, History, and Theory* (Chicago: University of Chicago Press, 1984); and Nancy Armstrong, *Desire and Domestic Fiction* (Oxford: Oxford University Press, 1987). For an impressive attempt at rereading European literary history in anthropological and sociological terms, see Denis Hollier, ed., *A New History of French Literature* (Cambridge, Mass.: Harvard University Press, 1989).

53. There are no terms for this repertory that are not deeply dissatisfying. It is not accidental that the music produced by the "mainstream" has no convenient adjective: the labels for other repertories (popular, folk, commercial, experimental, and so forth) were invented to hold them apart from this, "the real stuff." In semiotic terms, this repertory is the unmarked member of many loaded binary oppositions, and the inadequacy of labels such as "classical," "concert," "serious," or "art" only emphasizes the problem. I have no solution to offer here—only an indication that I am aware of the dilemma.

54. Roland Barthes, *The Pleasure of the Text*, trans. Richard Miller (New York: Noonday Press, 1989), 53.

Chapter 2. Constructions of Gender in Monteverdi's Dramatic Music

1. For passages concerning *Licori*, see Claudio Monteverdi, *The Letters of Claudio Monteverdi*, trans. Denis Stevens (Cambridge: Cambridge University Press, 1980), 315, 318, 320, 335-36; concerning *Combattimento*, see the foreword to his eighth book of madrigals, *Madrigali guerrieri ed amorosi* (Venice, 1638), trans. Oliver Strunk, *Source Readings in Music History* (New York: W. W. Norton, 1950), 413-15.

2. José Antonio Maravall, *Culture of the Baroque: Analysis of a Historical Structure*, trans. Terry Cochran (Minneapolis: University of Minnesota Press, 1986); Jacques Attali, *Noise*, trans. Brian Massumi (Minneapolis: University of Minnesota Press, 1985), especially 46-86; and Lorenzo Bianconi, *Music in the Seventeenth Century*, trans. David Bryant (Cambridge: Cambridge University Press, 1987). Bianconi states: "Attribute of authority, pedagogical requisite of the ruling classes, instrument of propaganda and persuasion: these are the three central features of seventeenth-century music as an agent of 'publicity'" (65). See also Leonard Tennenhouse, *Power on Display: The Politics of Shakespeare's Genres* (New York: Methuen, 1986).

For information directly concerned with Monteverdi's patronage at the Gonzaga court and its political dimensions, see Iain Fenlon, "The Mantuan Stage Works," in *The New Monteverdi Companion*, ed. Denis Arnold and Nigel Fortune (London: Faber & Faber, 1985), 251-87. For a perceptive theoretical model through which to address these concerns, see Pierre Bourdieu, "The Production of Belief: Contributions to an Economy of Symbolic Goods," trans. Richard Nice, in *Media, Culture and Society: A Critical Reader*, ed. Richard Collins et al. (London: Sage, 1986), 131-63.

    3. Michel Foucault, *The History of Sexuality, Vol. I: An Introduction*, trans. Robert Hurley (New York: Vintage Books, 1980), 12. For a discussion of the "putting into discourse of sex" for political purposes in Elizabethan England, see Tennenhouse, *Power on Display*, 17-71.

    4. For discussions of tonality in these terms, see my "The Transition from Modal to Tonal Organization in the Works of Monteverdi" (Ph.D. dissertation, Harvard University, 1976); and "The Blasphemy of Talking Politics during Bach Year," *Music and Society: The Politics of Composition, Performance and Reception*, ed. Richard Leppert and Susan McClary (Cambridge: Cambridge University Press, 1987), especially 21-23.

    5. See, for instance, Sherry B. Ortner and Harriet Whitehead, eds., *Sexual Meanings: The Cultural Construction of Gender and Sexuality* (Cambridge: Cambridge University Press, 1981); Ian Maclean, *The Renaissance Notion of Woman* (Cambridge: Cambridge University Press, 1980); and Denise Riley, *"Am I That Name?": Feminism and the Category of "Women" in History* (Minneapolis: University of Minnesota Press, 1988).

    6. See, for instance, Monteverdi's "Vattene pur crudel" (Book III), with its fierce depiction of feminine rage; "Io mi son giovinetta" (Book IV), with its cute, mincing beginning (sung only by the women); or "O Mirtillo" (Book V), with its shy, hesitant opening and subsequent emotional outburst. Very little work has been done on the musical articulation of sexual desire in Renaissance repertories, perhaps because studies of that music tend to concentrate on theoretical issues such as modal identity, *musica ficta*, or signs of emerging tonal awareness, rather than on the ways modes were used to create particular kinds of images. See, however, my "The Transition." I am at present writing a book, *Power and Desire in Seventeenth-Century Music* (Princeton: Princeton University Press, forthcoming), that includes an examination of musical constructions of the erotic in the madrigal.

    Eric Chafe is completing a book titled *Monteverdi's Tonal Language*, which contains extraordinarily insightful analyses of Monteverdi's music. Chafe's theoretical model is somewhat different from mine, but he is concerned with images of the erotic and especially the allegorical dimensions of Monteverdi's structures. I am grateful for having been permitted to examine a manuscript of this book.

    7. For a provocative discussion of how the standard opera repertory organizes gender and sexuality, see Catherine Clément, *Opera, or the Undoing of Women*, trans. Betsy Wing (Minneapolis: University of Minnesota Press, 1988).

    It appears that madrigal composers too began interrogating the gender connotations of various conventions after opera's *stile rappresentativo* had sensitized these issues. In his collection *Primo Mazzetto di fiori musicalmente colti dal giardino Bellerofonteo* (Venice: Vincenti, 1623), Bellerofonte Castaldi remarks: "E perchè [questi madrigali] trattano o d'amore, o di sdegno che tiene l'Amante con la cosa amata, si rappresentano sotto chiave di Tenore i cui intervalli sono propri, e naturali del parlar mascolino, parendo pure al Autor sudetto cosa da ridere che un huomo con voce Feminina si metta a dir le sue ragioni, e dimandar pietà in Falsetto a la sua innamorata" (62). [And because (these madrigals) concern either love or the disdain that obtains between the lover and his beloved, they represent in the tenor clef the intervals that are proper and natural to masculine speech, because it seems to the aforementioned Author ridiculous that a man with a feminine voice should deliver his arguments and demand pity of his beloved in falsetto.] I wish to thank Andrew Dell'Antonio for sending me this reference. My translation.

8. Stephen Greenblatt, *Shakespearean Negotiations* (Berkeley: University of California Press, 1988), 66-93. See also Thomas Laqueur, "Orgasm, Generation, and the Politics of Reproductive Biology," *Representations* 14 (1986): 1-41; and Mary Beth Rose, *The Expense of Spirit: Love and Sexuality in English Renaissance Drama* (Ithaca: Cornell University Press, 1988).

9. Gary Tomlinson, *Monteverdi and the End of the Renaissance* (Berkeley: University of California Press, 1987), 7.

10. For extensive documentation concerning women's rhetorical training and their access to cultural production, see Joan Kelly-Gadol, "Did Women Have a Renaissance?" in *Becoming Visible: Women in European History*, ed. Renate Bridenthal and Claudia Koonz (Boston: Houghton Mifflin, 1977), 137-64; Patricia H. Labalme, ed., *Beyond Their Sex: Learned Women of the European Past* (New York: New York University Press, 1980). For information directly concerning music, see also the following essays in Jane Bowers and Judith Tick, eds., *Women Making Music: The Western Art Tradition, 1150-1950* (Urbana: University of Illinois Press, 1986); Howard M. Brown, "Women Singers and Women's Songs in Fifteenth-Century Italy," 62-89; Anthony Newcomb, "Courtesans, Muses, or Musicians? Professional Women Musicians in Sixteenth-Century Italy," 90-115; and Jane Bowers, "The Emergence of Women Composers in Italy, 1566-1700," 116-61.

For more on the "woman question" in the Renaissance and seventeenth century, see Joan Kelly, "Early Feminist Theory and the *Querelle des femmes*, 1400-1789," in *Women, History and Theory: The Essays of Joan Kelly* (Chicago: University of Chicago Press, 1984), 65-109; and Riley, "*Am I That Name?*" 25-35.

11. See Brown, "Women Singers," 62-67; and Ann Rosalind Jones, "City Women and Their Audiences: Louise Labé and Veronica Franco," in *Rewriting the Renaissance: The Discourses of Sexual Difference in Early Modern Europe*, ed. Margaret W. Ferguson et al. (Chicago: University of Chicago Press, 1986), 299-316.

12. See, for instance, Linda Phyllis Austern, " 'Sing Againe Syren': The Female Musician and Sexual Enchantment in Elizabethan Life and Literature," *Renaissance Quarterly* 42, no. 3 (Autumn 1989): 420-48. For a discussion of how this attitude informed the phenomenon of the female writer of the Renaissance, see Jones, "City Women," 299-316. See also the discussion of Poppea below. This attitude has persisted in Western culture. See Sandra M. Gilbert and Susan Gubar, *The Madwoman in the Attic: The Woman Writer and the Nineteenth-Century Literary Imagination* (New Haven: Yale University Press, 1979), especially Part I, 3-104.

13. For an examination of Catherine's imagery, see Sheila ffolliott, "Catherine de' Medici as Artemisia: Figuring the Powerful Widow," in *Rewriting the Renaissance*, 227-41. For Elizabeth's imagery, see Louis A. Montrose, "*A Midsummer Night's Dream* and the Shaping Fantasies of Elizabethan Culture: Gender, Power, Form," in *Rewriting the Renaissance*, 65-87. However, the fact that England's monarch during the reign of Elizabeth was female strongly influenced the constructions of femininity and sexuality in the arts developed under her patronage. See Tennenhouse, *Power on Display*, 17-71.

14. The theoretical discussions that follow are based on my "The Transition." Orfeo's headstrong impetuousness and Euridice's reticence do not exist in the notes

per se, but rather in the qualities of motion indicated by the designated pitches up against particular norms. Thus understanding the syntactical norms and expectations of this music affects critically the ways in which one perceives compositional strategies and, consequently, performance choices.

The reductions in the examples may resemble Schenkerian graphs, but they represent the linear modal processes that guarantee the coherence of the passages in question. These pieces are not tonally conceived (except for a few moments prolonged by cadential harmonies, such as the conclusion of Ex. 1); yet the strategy of implying long-term goals, persuading the listener to desire those promised goals, and manipulating expectations in the process of attaining the goals is crucial to the emergence of common-practice-period tonality.

15. Many of Monteverdi's and Striggio's rhetorical strategies are indebted to a venerable legacy of devices and tropes developed in literature. For a discussion of this literary tradition, see Ernst Robert Curtius, *European Literature and Latin Middle Ages*, trans. Willard R. Trask (Princeton: Princeton University Press, 1967). For two seventeenth-century attempts at borrowing rhetorical terminology for the purposes of music theory, see Joachim Burmeister, *Musica poetica* (1606; Kassel, 1955); and Christoph Bernhard, "The Treatises of Christoph Bernhard," trans. Walter Hilse, *Music Forum* 3 (1973): 31-196. Claude Palisca discusses Burmeister's rhetorical theory and offers an analytic demonstration in "*Ut oratoria musica:* The Rhetorical Basis of Musical Mannerism," *The Meaning of Mannerism*, ed. F. W. Robinson and Stephen Nichols (Hanover, N.H.: Dartmouth University Press, 1972), 37-65.

Because I am concerned with indicating how the music itself creates its rhetorical effects, I will not burden the discussion with Latin literary designations or correspondences. However, Orfeo's opening here might be fruitfully compared with the rhetorically dazzling opening of Milton's *Paradise Lost* (discussed briefly in Curtius, 243-44). Just as Monteverdi launches an extraordinarily prolonged "upbeat" that is released finally on the word "Dimmi" (tell me), so Milton too directs all the energy of this passage—a synopsis of the entire Christian history of humankind—toward "Sing." In both instances the listener is swept up in an onrushing flow toward the suspended outcome.

The sexual connotations of such musical devices seems at least implicitly recognized by Joseph Kerman, "Orpheus: The Neoclassic Vision," *Claudio Monteverdi: "Orfeo,"* ed. John Whenham (Cambridge: Cambridge University Press, 1986): "Monteverdi met this ideal with a perfect genius for declamation. . . . And to whip the recitative line into passion, he harrowed every available musical means for tension. Declamation guided him to sudden halts and spurting cascades in rhythm, and to precipitous, intense rises and falls in melodic line"(129).

16. This figure of the exchange of hearts between lovers is a convention of lyric verse and romance narratives since medieval times. It is significant here that Euridice alone testifies to this condition. A similar kind of speaking void can be found in Mimì's self-deprecating "Mi chiamano Mimì" in Puccini's *La bohème*. See the discussion in Arthur Groos and Roger Parker, *La bohème* (Cambridge: Cambridge University Press, 1986), 71-73.

17. For another reading of this passage, see Robert Donington's treatment of Euridice's vow in "Monteverdi's First Opera," *The Monteverdi Companion*, ed. Denis Arnold and Nigel Fortune (New York: W. W. Norton, 1972), 263-64. Donington rightly argues that the pitch-center A is associated in the opera with death, and he thus sees in Euridice's own utterances the foreshadowing of her doom. I accept this argument concerning long-term symbolism, but would also interpret the details of Euridice's speech on the more local and immediate level in which her gendered iden-

tity is delineated. For Monteverdi here creates a perfect musical instance of the "enclosed" woman. See Peter Stallybrass, "Patriarchal Territories: The Body Enclosed," *Rewriting the Renaissance*, 123-42.

18. Compare, for instance, Orfeo's madness with that of Monteverdi's sexually obsessed woman in "Lamento della ninfa" (Book VIII). "Lamento" is discussed along with questions of the historicity of madness in Chapter 4.

19. This reading of Orfeo's undoing in his moments of rhetorical excess is informed by Kaja Silverman, *The Acoustic Mirror: The Female Voice in Psychoanalysis and Cinema* (Bloomington: Indiana University Press, 1988), especially 51-54. See also Kerman, "Orpheus: The Neoclassic Vision," 132-37, for a discussion of the dramatic problems created by Orfeo's unconstrained passion.

Of course Orfeo's mourning of Euridice owes much rhetorically to Petrarch's reactions to Laura's death. But the two media—carefully constructed sonnets versus staged, enacted representation—produce very different effects, especially with respect to implied authority.

20. Clément, *Opera*, 118. In "Orpheus," Kerman (136-37) explains how Gluck's eighteenth-century Orfeo avoids this dilemma.

21. Iain Fenlon, "The Mantuan 'Orfeo'," *Claudio Monteverdi: "Orfeo,"* 1-19. See also Tomlinson's discussion of the differences between monodic style in *L'Orfeo* and *L'Arianna* in *Monteverdi*, 136-41.

22. Robert Walser's work demonstrates that it is precisely these taboos—the taboos traditionally circumscribing representations of masculinity in opera—that are seized and deliberately violated in heavy metal, today's answer to baroque spectacle. Metal bands regularly flaunt rhetorical and sexual excess, simulations of madness, and androgynous dress as antipatriarchal signs of hypermasculinity. See his "Running with the Devil: Power, Gender, and Madness in Heavy Metal Music" (Ph.D. dissertation, University of Minnesota, forthcoming).

23. Quoted in Jones, "City Women." As Jones comments: "Coryat reverses the gender roles on which love poetry was conventionally based. Constancy was assumed as a feminine trait, to be admired or overcome by men's uses of rhetoric; for Coryat, men's chastity is endangered by women's manipulations of language, and to encounter a 'public woman' is to risk the casuistries of a previously masculine discourse. Practically speaking, he was wrong; a man who had sought out a courtesan could hardly claim to be seduced by her rhetoric" (303-4). See also Arturo Graf, "Una cortigiana fra mille," *Attraverso il cinquecento* (Turin: Chiantore, 1926), 174-284; and Georgina Masson, *Courtesans of the Italian Renaissance* (London: St. Martin's Press, 1975).

24. For a different reading of Seneca's musical characterization, see Ellen Rosand, "Seneca and the Interpretation of *L'incoronazione di Poppea*," *Journal of the American Musicological Society* 38 (1985): 34-71.

25. There was, in fact, a notable feminist presence in the seventeenth century. See Kelly, "Early Feminist Theory"; and Riley, "*Am I That Name?*" 25-35. There seems even to have been an occasional feminist voice in opera, made feasible by the extraordinary coincidence of a female patron and a female composer. See Suzanne Cusick, "Francesca Caccini's *La Liberazione di Ruggiero dall'isola d'Alcina* (1625): A Feminist Misreading of *Orlando furioso*?" Paper presented to the American Musicological Society, Baltimore (November 1988), and Ellen Rosand, "The Voice of Barbara Strozzi," *Women Making Music*, 168-90.

26. For studies of the differences in social and emotional development between males and females in Western culture, see Nancy Chodorow, *The Reproduction of Mothering: Psychoanalysis and the Sociology of Gender* (Berkeley: University of Califor-

nia Press, 1978), 180-90; and Carol Gilligan, *In a Different Voice: Psychological Theory and Women's Development* (Cambridge, Mass.: Harvard University Press, 1982).

27. The Orpheus legend often makes it explicit that Orpheus turns to homosexuality after his loss of Euridice. See Charles Segal, *Orpheus: The Myth of the Poet* (Baltimore: Johns Hopkins University Press, 1989). Linda Austern has compiled extensive documentation demonstrating that music itself, often personified as Orpheus, was regarded by the Elizabethans as effeminate because of its tendency to rhetorical excess. See her " 'Alluring the Auditorie to Effeminacie': Music and the English Renaissance Idea of the Feminine," paper presented to the American Musicological Society, Baltimore (November 1988). See also John Guillory, "Dalila's House: *Samson Agonistes* and the Sexual Division of Labor," *Rewriting the Renaissance*, 106-22, for a discussion of how male sexual pleasure (even the heterosexual variety) comes to be regarded as effeminate during the seventeenth century.

28. See Clément, *Opera*. Film theory has dealt extensively with the organization of masculine desire and constructions of femininity. See, for instance, Laura Mulvey, "Visual Pleasure and Narrative Cinema," *Screen* 16, no. 3 (1975): 8-18; Silverman, *The Acoustic Mirror*; and Carol Flinn, "The 'Problem' of Femininity in Theories of Film Music," *Screen* 27, no. 6 (1986): 56-72.

29. See Stevens, *Letters of Monteverdi*, 56. Stevens protests this situation by lumping women professionals together with other fads he finds deplorable when he condemns "the Dukes with their lavish and uncontrolled devotion to dwarfs, alchemists and lady singers" (187). See also Bowers, "The Emergence of Women Composers." Bowers documents some of the ways in which women's activity as professionals begins to be curtailed during the seventeenth century (141-46).

30. Representations of feminine erotic pleasure abound in seventeenth-century music and then disappear with the eighteenth-century insistence on patriarchal values. See, for instance, the settings of texts from the *Song of Songs* by Schütz or Grandi, Frescobaldi's "Maddalena alla Croce," or Stradella's malignant *San Giovanni Battista*. This obsession with charting female sexuality is again something that needs much more research. It has fascinated me, however, to note that my women students immediately pick up on the erotic imagery of seventeenth-century music, while most of the men fail to recognize it as having anything to do with the erotic. They claim to associate sexuality rather with the forceful "thrusting" of Beethoven. See Chapter 5 for further discussion of the constructions of sexuality in both seventeenth- and nineteenth-century repertories.

31. In fact, the female characters in the premiere of *L'Orfeo* were all played by castrati (some of whom were scarcely able to learn their parts), despite the availability of virtuoso women singers. See Fenlon, "The Mantuan 'Orfeo,'" 9-16. As late as the 1780s, Goethe could still write that by observing female impersonators on the Roman stage, "we come to understand the female sex so much the better because some one has observed and meditated on their ways." See "Women's Parts Played by Men in the Roman Theatre," *Goethe's Travels in Italy*, trans. Charles Nisbet (London: G. Bell and Sons, 1883), 567-71.

The phenomenon of the castrato needs rethinking in terms of social gender construction. It stands as an extreme example of gender *re*-construction: the social "need" for adult males who could sound like women was literally and violently inscribed on the body itself. While the motivation was not quite as simple as the desire to usurp jobs that otherwise would have been held by women, the practice did emerge at the same time as women virtuoso singers were rising to fame and creating a new demand. If it is not easy to puzzle out quite what this practice meant, it most certainly is tangled up with notions of gender organization. For an imaginative reconstruction of the world of the castrati, see Anne Rice's novel, *Cry to Heaven* (New York: Pinnacle Books, 1982).

32. Nino Pirrotta, "Scelte poetiche di Monteverdi," *Nuova rivista musicale italiana* 2 (1968): 254. An extraordinary misogynist backlash followed the reign of Elizabeth and can be traced chillingly in Shakespeare's Jacobean plays. See Tennenhouse, *Power on Display*, 102-46. For discussions of similar periods of masculine paranoia and attendant antifeminist portrayals of "powerful" women, see Sander L. Gilman, *Difference and Pathology: Sexuality, Race, and Madness* (Ithaca: Cornell University Press, 1985), 15-33; my own discussion of Bizet's *Carmen* and Strauss's *Salome* in Chapters 3 and 4; and Sandra M. Gilbert and Susan Gubar, "Tradition and the Female Talent," *The Poetics of Gender*, ed. Nancy K. Miller (New York: Columbia University Press, 1986), 183-207. Although they have been heavily criticized for presenting somewhat prurient accounts of their subjects, see also Bram Dijkstra, *Idols of Perversity: Fantasies of Feminine Evil in Fin-de-Siècle Culture* (Oxford: Oxford University Press, 1986); and Klaus Theweleit, *Male Fantasies, I: Women, Floods, Bodies, History*, trans. Stephen Conway (Minneapolis: University of Minnesota Press, 1987). The recent film *Fatal Attraction* is an instance from our own time.

33. In addition to Bianconi, *Music in the Seventeenth Century*, 28-33, and Tomlinson, *Monteverdi*, 243-60, see Trevor Aston, ed., *Crisis in Europe 1560-1660* (London: Routledge & Kegan Paul, 1965), and Geoffrey Parker and Lesley M. Smith, eds., *The General Crisis of the Seventeenth Century* (London: Routledge & Kegan Paul, 1985).

34. See Mikhail Bakhtin, *Rabelais and His World*, trans. Hélène Iswolsky (Bloomington: Indiana University Press, 1984), for an explanation of how celebrations of the "grotesque body," taken from popular carnival festivities, can be used to challenge authority and official order. See Tennenhouse, *Power on Display*, 17-71, for an effective reading of Shakespeare in terms of Bakhtin's model. Tennenhouse argues that Shakespeare's inclusion of the carnivalesque in his Elizabethan plays served not to subvert authority but rather to create the image of a more inclusive society in a way that flattered the queen, his patron. See also Attali, *Noise*, 21-24, for a discussion of *Carnival's Quarrel with Lent* by Pieter Bruegel the Elder. Attali uses this painting as a preliminary way of illustrating the opposition between collective and official musical cultures. This model would seem to offer valuable insight into the use of comic and female characters in seventeenth-century opera.

35. Bianconi, *Music*, 183-84, explains the presence of these comic figures as the result of the merger in Venice between imported court opera and the network of professional *commedia dell'arte* theaters already established. He also argues (208-9) that they disappeared from opera at the turn of the century because of increasing specialization: comic episodes became autonomous and were eventually detached from the *dramma per musica*. That there are formal and practical considerations involved in the elimination of comic characters from serious opera is unquestionable. Yet even the increasing segregation of serious and comic figures in the later seventeenth century (a necessary step if the comic scenes were finally to be detachable) is part of a cleaning-up process that gradually rectifies their promiscuous intermingling in midcentury. The impudent interventions by comic characters in some of the most serious scenes in *L'incoronazione di Poppea* could not be excised without destroying the piece.

36. Bianconi, *Music*, 188.

37. Ellen Rosand has done extensive research concerning the Incogniti, some of which is contained in her "Seneca and the Interpretation of *L'incoronazione di Poppea*."

Her forthcoming book from the University of California Press on seventeenth-century music elucidates these issues more thoroughly.

Chapter 3. Sexual Politics in Classical Music

1. For studies on the social construction of sexuality, see Michel Foucault, *The History of Sexuality, Vol. 1: An Introduction*, trans. Robert Hurley (New York: Vintage Books, 1980); Sherry B. Ortner and Harriet Whitehead, eds., *Sexual Meanings: The Cultural Construction of Gender and Sexuality* (Cambridge: Cambridge University Press, 1981); and Nancy Armstrong, *Desire and Domestic Fiction: A Political History of the Novel* (Oxford: Oxford University Press, 1987).

2. For a formal presentation of this attitude, see Arthur Schopenhauer, *The World as Will and Representation*, vol. 2, trans. E. F. J. Payne (New York: Dover, 1966): "Because music does not, like all the other arts, exhibit the *Ideas* or grades of the will's objectification, but directly the *will itself*, we can also explain that it acts directly on the will, i.e., the feelings, passions, and emotions of the hearer, so that it quickly raises these or even alters them" (448, emphasis in the original). I would concur that music can give these impressions, but I would insist that music is a socially constructed discourse rather than a manifestation of metaphysics. See Chapter 1.

3. These figures have all been discussed extensively—and often quite perceptively—in the popular press. For more scholarly treatments of these issues, see Nancy J. Holland, "Purple Passion: Images of Female Desire in 'When Doves Cry,' " *Cultural Critique* 10 (Fall 1989): 89-98; Jon Savage, "The Enemy Within: Sex, Rock, and Identity," *Facing the Music*, ed. Simon Frith (New York: Pantheon Books, 1988), 131-72; Robert Walser, "Bon Jovi's Alloy: Discursive Fusion in Top 40 Pop Music," *OneTwoThreeFour* 7 (Winter 1989): 7-20, and "Forging Masculinity: Heavy Metal Sounds and Images of Gender," *Sound and Vision*, ed. Simon Frith, Andrew Goodwin, and Lawrence Grossberg (forthcoming); Susan McClary and Robert Walser, "Start Making Sense: Musicology Wrestles with Rock," *On Record: Rock, Pop, and the Written Word*, ed. Simon Frith and Andrew Goodwin (New York: Pantheon Books, 1990), 277-92.

4. I owe this model of cultural contestation to critics Stuart Hall and George Lipsitz. See, for instance, Hall, "Notes on Deconstructing 'The Popular,'" *People's History and Socialist Theory*, ed. Raphael Samuel (London: Routledge & Kegan Paul, 1981), 227-39; Lipsitz, "Cruising Around the Historical Bloc: Postmodernism and Popular Music in East Los Angeles," *Cultural Critique* 5 (Winter 1986-1987): 157-78; and "Mardi Gras Indians: Carnival and Counter-Narrative in Black New Orleans," *Cultural Critique* 10 (Fall 1988): 99-122. Both reprinted in *Time Passages: Collective Memory and American Popular Culture* (Minneapolis: University of Minnesota Press, 1990).

5. See, for example, Dorothy Dinnerstein, *The Mermaid and the Minotaur: Sexual Arrangements and Human Malaise* (New York: Harper Colophon Books, 1976); Genevieve Lloyd, *The Man of Reason: "Male" and "Female" in Western Philosophy* (Minneapolis: University of Minnesota Press, 1984); Susan Bordo, "The Cartesian Masculinization of Thought," *Signs* 11, no. 3 (1986): 439-56; Susan Griffin, *Pornography and Silence: Culture's Revenge Against Nature* (New York: Harper Colophon Books, 1981); and Evelyn Fox Keller, *Reflections on Gender and Science* (New Haven: Yale University Press, 1985).

6. See John Shepherd, "Music and Male Hegemony," *Music and Society: The Politics of Composition, Performance and Reception*, ed. Richard Leppert and Susan McClary (Cambridge: Cambridge University Press, 1987), 151-72; and Geraldine Finn, "Music, Masculinity and the Silencing of Women," *New Musicology*, ed. John Shepherd (New York: Routledge, forthcoming).

7. See, for instance, David Epstein, *Beyond Orpheus* (Cambridge, Mass.: MIT Press, 1979): "Our understanding of structure is still sufficiently unclear that it seems advisable to avoid the further complications of words and/or dramatic action — implicit or explicit — and their relations to structure, or their effects upon it" (11).

8. See, for instance, Armstrong, *Desire and Domestic Fiction*; Denise Riley, *"Am I That Name?" Feminism and the Category of "Women" in History* (Minneapolis: University of Minnesota Press, 1988), 40-55; Sander L. Gilman, "Male Stereotypes of Female Sexuality in Fin-de-Siècle Vienna," in *Difference and Pathology: Stereotypes of Sexuality, Race, and Madness* (Ithaca: Cornell University Press, 1985), 39-58; Gilman, "Strauss and the Pervert," *Reading Opera*, ed. Arthur Groos and Roger Parker (Princeton: Princeton University Press, 1988), 306-27; and Anne K. Mellor, ed., *Romanticism and Feminism* (Bloomington: Indiana University Press, 1988). The materials collected in Bram Dijkstra, *Idols of Perversity: Fantasies of Feminine Evil in Fin-de-Siècle Culture* (New York: Oxford University Press, 1986), are also extremely illuminating, though his discussions of them occasionally seem to indulge in the very attitudes he is critiquing.

9. In 1983 and 1984 alone, for instance, there was a spate of films based on *Carmen* by artists such as Jean-Luc Godard, Peter Brook, and Carlos Saura, as well as a film of the opera itself by Francesco Rosi. See the discussions of this phenomenon by Jeremy Tambling, "Ideology in the Cinema: Rewriting *Carmen*," *Opera, Ideology and Film* (New York: St. Martin's Press, 1987), 13-40; and David Wills, "Carmen: Sound/Effect," *Cinema Journal* 25, no. 4 (1986): 33-43. I am grateful to Carol Flinn for bringing the Wills article to my attention. See also Nelly Furman, "The Languages of Love in *Carmen*," *Reading Opera*, 168-83, for insightful readings of various versions of *Carmen*.

10. For more on the production and reception history of *Carmen*, see Mina Curtiss, *Bizet and His World* (New York: Alfred A. Knopf, 1958), 342-437. All of the issues presented in this essay will appear with more extensive treatment in my *Georges Bizet's* Carmen, which is in preparation for the Cambridge Opera Handbook series.

11. If Micaëla was added to "sweeten" the project for the Opéra-Comique, she principally serves to provide a foil for Carmen. As Winton Dean writes, she is "(a) a standard by which to measure Carmen, and (b) a symbol of José's character and psychological environment before he met Carmen. So far from being a sin against Mérimée, she is an ally." *Bizet* (London: J. M. Dent & Sons, 1975), 213. I quite agree that the addition of Micaëla enhances (rather than softens) the misogyny already amply present in Mérimée's text, though this is probably not quite what Dean means to suggest.

12. The expression is from Coventry Patmore's *The Angel in the House* (1854). For extensive discussions of both this nineteenth-century ideal of submissive femininity and its counterimage of the sexual woman as devourer (of which Carmen is a celebrated instance), see Sandra M. Gilbert and Susan Gubar, *The Madwoman in the Attic* (New Haven: Yale University Press, 1979), especially 3-104; Armstrong, *Desire and Domestic Fiction*; Mellor, *Romanticism and Feminism*; Gilman, *Difference and Pathology*; and Peter Gay, *Education of the Senses: The Bourgeois Experience, Victoria to Freud* (New York: Oxford University Press, 1984). For evidence of the extreme fetishizing of the domestic female in the nineteenth century, see also the celebrated photographs

of mothers and infants—posed according to madonna-and-child iconography—by Julia Margaret Cameron. Reproduced in Mike Weaver, *Julia Margaret Cameron 1815-1879* (Boston: Little, Brown, 1984).

13. For a discussion of the origins of Bizet's pseudogypsy material, see Dean, *Bizet*, 228-32. The "Habañera," for instance, is adapted from a song by Spanish-American composer Sebastían Yradier. Tambling points out that the fact that Carmen chiefly sings dance tunes means that she is denied interiority: she is principally an object for public display. *Opera, Film and Ideology*, 37. For a different reading of Carmen's use of pop tunes, see below.

14. Of course the physicality of this music depends upon the performers who enact it, and my interpretation of the opera is as much prescriptive (of *possible* performances) as descriptive. It is, nonetheless, instructive to compare available recorded performances. The rather formalistic recording of the "Habañera" by Troyanas/Solti, for instance, inspires very little hip action, while the Price/von Karajan virtually "rocks the house." Although the radically different vocal inflections of the two singers contribute heavily to their respective results, the effect also depends to a great extent upon the relative rhythmic rigidity or flexibility ("swing") in the accompaniments. My preference is clearly for Price/von Karajan, both because I find it more compelling musically (i.e., it makes greater sense of the musical details) and because it sets up more satisfactorily what I take to be the principal tension in the opera.

15. See Finn, "Music, Masculinity and the Silencing of Women"; Shepherd, "Music and Male Hegemony"; and Catherine Clément, *Opera, or the Undoing of Women*, trans. Betsy Wing (Minneapolis: University of Minnesota Press, 1988).

One does not need to have Carmen's body appear in order for this anxiety to occur. See Edward T. Cone, *Musical Form and Musical Performance* (New York: W. W. Norton, 1968): "Of course one often does hear exciting interpretations [of music in general] that build up so much energy that the overflow is imparted to the audience, which has to respond by immediate clapping; but I wonder whether these performances are not, for that very reason, a bit meretricious. Leo Stein has suggested that music requiring bodily motion on the part of the listener for its complete enjoyment, like much popular dance music, is by that token artistically imperfect; perhaps the same principle can be applied to performance" (16-17).

16. Once again, Leontine Price's performance is exemplary in its highly nuanced exploration of each moment of the chromatic descent. In her discussion of Wagner's Isolde, Clément characterizes chromaticism as a "feminine stink" (*Opera*, 55-58). Note that even Micaëla's first entrance is marked with what Mozart's Don Giovanni calls the "odor di femmina." Before we come to know who she is, the orchestra caricatures her with the same chromatic slippage as all other women, and the soldiers treat her accordingly.

17. Carl Dahlhaus, *Nineteenth-Century Music*, trans. J. Bradford Robinson (Berkeley: University of California Press, 1989), 280. For more extensive discussions of "lyric urgency" and its ejaculatory properties, see Chapters 1 and 5.

18. See Tambling, *Opera, Film and Ideology*, 27, for an interesting account of closure in *Carmen*, and 35 for other readings of the symbol of the bull in this scene. Of course it is not just *Carmen* that works according to this desire-dread-purge paradigm. See Teresa de Lauretis, "Desire in Narrative," *Alice Doesn't* (Bloomington: Indiana University Press, 1984), 103-57. Because of the prevalence of this narrative schema and its ubiquity in traditional music, virtually all of the essays in this volume deal with it. See Chapters 1 and 5 in particular.

19. See D. A. Miller, *Narrative and Its Discontents: Problems of Closure in the Traditional Novel* (Princeton: Princeton University Press, 1981). Chapters 4 and 5 in this volume deal more extensively with questions of adequate or arbitrary closure.

20. For more on the nonwhite as feminine and thus both alluring and threatening, see Edward Said, *Orientalism* (New York: Vintage Books, 1978), especially 167, 184, 207, and 309. For an examination of these issues in nineteenth-century French literature, see Christopher L. Miller, "Orientalism, Colonialism," in *A New History of French Literature*, ed. Denis Hollier (Cambridge, Mass.: Harvard University Press, 1989), 698-705.

21. See Winton Dean's account of Bizet's career in *New Grove Dictionary*. See also the chapter "Le Japonisme et l'Orientalisme," in Elaine Brody, *Paris: The Musical Kaleidoscope, 1870-1925* (New York: George Braziller, 1987), 60-76: "Bizet never visited the Orient, but had a natural instinct [*sic*] for the character, particularly the rhythms, of Arabic music. . . . Bizet's love of the Orient moved him to write *L'Arlésienne Suite* and *Carmen*. (As Hugo stated so definitively: Spain is still the Orient.)" (72). Arles would seem to count as the Orient even less than Spain.

22. Friedrich Nietzsche, *The Case of Wagner*, trans. Walter Kaufmann (New York: Vintage Books, 1967), 158. I wish to thank Barbara Engh for bringing this to my attention. See Gilman, *Difference and Pathology*, for both a theoretical explanation of how sexual and racial anxieties become interchangeable and also several fascinating case studies. See also n. 26 below.

23. This phrase is borrowed from Gayatri Chakravorty Spivak, "Can the Subaltern Speak?" *Marxism and the Interpretation of Culture*, ed. Cary Nelson and Lawrence Grossberg (Urbana: University of Illinois Press, 1988), 271-313, which addresses the dilemma faced by genuine colonials who have already been "spoken for" by imperialist discourses.

24. Dahlhaus, *Nineteenth-Century Music*, 282.

25. Mérimée's Carmen likewise is dangerous because of her ability to operate in a variety of languages. I am grateful to Peter Robinson and Kitty Millet for their insights on these issues.

26. Theodor W. Adorno, "Perennial Fashion—Jazz," *Prisms*, trans. Samuel Weber and Shierry Weber (Cambridge, Mass.: MIT Press, 1981), 129. To find "transcendental" classical music so explicitly linked to the defensive preservation of the male genitals is quite extraordinary.

For extensive discussions of the cultural slippage among the threats of feminine sexuality, the racial Other, and the working class in the late nineteenth and early twentieth centuries, see Gilman, *Difference and Pathology*, and Klaus Theweleit, *Male Fantasies, Vol. I: Women, Floods, Bodies, History*, trans. Stephen Conway (Minneapolis: University of Minnesota Press, 1987), and *Vol. II: Male Bodies: Psychoanalyzing the White Terror*, trans. Erica Carter and Chris Turner (Minneapolis: University of Minnesota Press, 1989). See also Andreas Huyssen, "Mass Culture as Woman: Modernism's Other," in *Studies in Entertainment: Critical Approaches to Mass Culture*, ed. Tania Modleski (Bloomington: Indiana University Press, 1986), 189-207.

27. See Clément, *Opera*, 48-53, and Furman, "The Languages of Love," for feminist readings that celebrate Carmen. Indeed, Carmen's principal crime is that she demands freedom and independence, and in several of her scenes (especially in Act III as well as in the final sequence) she demonstrates extraordinary strength of character and patriarchal resistance. I am not sure that noting this is truly reading "against the grain," however, for if the Carmen figure were not compelling, then the contradictions upon which the opera plays would not be so forcefully engaged. She could be domesticated, rather than seeming to demand murder.

28. See Chapter 4 for a more extensive discussion of the crisis over closure at the beginning of the twentieth century. See also Huyssen, "Mass Culture as Woman," for further discussion of Modernism as a radical masculine reaction against both popular culture and what was understood as the excess of Romanticism.

29. Allan Bloom, *The Closing of the American Mind* (New York: Simon & Schuster, 1987). For more on the backlash against the encroachment of feminism and area studies on the university, see Jon Wiener, "Campus Voices Right and Left," *The Nation*, December 12, 1988, 644-45, which reports on the conference "Reclaiming the Academy: Responses to the Radicalization of the University," held in New York, November 1988.

30. The classic argument is Eduard Hanslick, *The Beautiful in Music* (1854), trans. Gustav Cohen, ed. Morris Weitz (Indianapolis: Bobbs-Merrill, 1957). See also Carl Dahlhaus, *The Idea of Absolute Music*, trans. Roger Lustig (Chicago: University of Chicago Press, 1989). Tchaikovsky (for one) did not concur with this Absolutist position. In response to a criticism that the Fourth Symphony might be programmatic, he wrote: "As for your observation that my symphony is programmatic, I completely agree. The only thing I don't understand is why you consider this a defect. I fear the very opposite situation—i.e. I should not wish symphonic works to come from my pen which express nothing, and which consist of empty playing with chords, rhythms, and modulations." As quoted in David Brown, *Tchaikovsky: The Crisis Years, 1874-1878* (New York: W. W. Norton, 1983), 162-63.

31. For a discussion of the invention of these codes in the context of seventeenth-century opera, see Chapter 2. Eighteenth-century theorists such as Johann Mattheson were concerned with codifying the elements of musical semiotics in what we now call the *Affektenlehre*, for music was at the time recognized as a social discourse. In the nineteenth century, however, with the rise of the composer-prophet and the celebration of subjectivity, these publicly shared signs were no longer acknowledged, since to do so would damage the illusion of "authenticity." For more on the transformation of art as social practice to art as religion, see Jacques Barzun, *The Use and Abuse of Art* (Princeton: Princeton University Press, 1974).

32. See Clément, *Opera*; Gilman, *Difference and Pathology*; Dijkstra, *Idols of Perversity*; Theweleit, *Male Fantasies*; and de Lauretis, "Desire in Narrative."

33. There is, however, some popular music that plays off the same fear-of-women paradigm, especially in heavy metal. See the discussion in Chapter 7 and Walser, "Forging Masculinity." Metal is, perhaps not coincidentally, the pop music genre most self-consciously influenced by the rhetoric of classical music, especially the Baroque repertories of Bach and Vivaldi and nineteenth-century symphonies.

34. See Chapter 1 for a discussion of theories of narrative in literature and in music. See also the discussion of sonata procedure in Eva Rieger, " '*Dolce semplice*'? On the Changing Role of Women in Music," *Feminist Aesthetics*, ed. Gisela Ecker, trans. Harriet Anderson (Boston: Beacon Press, 1985), 139.

35. These particular pieces will be taken up for discussion again in Chapters 5 through 7.

36. Brown, *Tchaikovsky*, 59. What I find interesting about this fatalistic reading is Tchaikovsky's refusal to take sides against Carmen. (Compare Nietzsche's rather more cynical description of this passage in *The Case of Wagner*: "That love which is war in its means, and at bottom the deadly hatred of the sexes!—I know no case where the tragic joke that constitutes the essence of love is expressed so strictly, translated with equal terror into a formula, as in Don José's last cry, which concludes the work: 'Yes, *I* have killed her, *I*—my adored Carmen!'" [158-59; emphasis in the original].)

37. For Tchaikovsky's program to the symphony, see Brown, *Tchaikovsky*, 163-66. Brown also notes (168) the similarity of the brutal descending scales in the introductory theme to the fate-related Leitmotivs in Wagner's *Ring*, which Tchaikovsky had recently seen at Bayreuth and detested.

38. Compare this theme, for instance, with the "Arabian Dance" from *The Nutcracker*, for instance, to see how Tchaikovsky constructs the feminized exotic. And although its "other-worldly" instrumentation masks this somewhat, the "Dance of the Sugar Plum Fairy" shares the slinky chromaticism of the "Habañera" and this second theme. Later the Sugar Plum Fairy performs an extraordinarily passionate *pas de deux* with her consort, providing a respite of adult sexuality in what is otherwise an unrelieved fantasy for children. In point of fact, Tchaikovsky was criticized for including these themes, which sounded like ballet tunes to his first listeners. See Brown, *Tchaikovsky*, 161.

39. Tchaikovsky himself described this section as pasted together: "There is not a note in this symphony . . . which I did not feel deeply, and which did not serve as an echo of sincere impulses within my soul. The exception is perhaps the middle of the first movement, in which there are contrivances, seams, glueings together—in a word, *artificiality*." Brown, *Tchaikovsky*, 163.

40. Brown, *Tchaikovsky*, 166. Brown has noted the similarity between this and Tolstoy's descriptions celebrating the Russian people (167-68).

41. Dahlhaus, *Nineteenth-Century Music*, 266.

42. Stephen Houtz, who has been working at developing methods for gay music criticism, has suggested that this second theme might best be understood not as an actual woman, but rather as a feminized male—even a drag queen. The protagonist would thus seem to be trapped between two impossible models of behavior: if he cannot be a "real man" in line with the introduction, he must desire—or even become—a parody of a woman in line with the second theme. For many moments in the history of homosexuality, these were the only options available, and men who would not conform to the patriarchal mold often felt pressured to adopt effeminate behavior patterns.

Throughout most of this discussion, I will be using the word "homosexual" rather than "gay" because to be openly self-identified as "gay" was not necessarily an option in Tchaikovsky's day. To use the term "gay" for Tchaikovsky is both to misread his own moment and also to erase the political significance of the emergence of that term with the post-Stonewall liberation movement. The cultural environment for homosexuals is anything but universal. See the extensive discussion of homosexuality in Russia during Tchaikovsky's lifetime in Alexander Poznansky, "Tchaikovsky's Suicide: Myth and Reality," *19th-Century Music* 11, no. 3 (Spring 1988): 199-220.

43. For more information on the circumstances of Tchaikovsky's life at this time, see Brown, *Tchaikovsky*, 132-58. His father, who had wanted him to get married, was dying, and he was being pursued by Vera Davïdova. He had made the abstract decision to get married (to the horror of his siblings, especially his openly homosexual brother, Modest), but had actually drafted the symphony before his disastrous marriage to Antonina Milyukova later in the year: thus the piece was not influenced by their marriage per se.

For the last ten years, many scholars have accepted a theory that Tchaikovsky ultimately committed suicide at the insistence of former law school colleagues who were afraid of being implicated by the threatened public revelation of Tchaikovsky's homosexuality. This theory was first advanced in Alexandra Orlova, "Tchaikovsky: The Last Chapter," trans. David Brown, *Music and Letters* 62 (1981): 125-45, and

David Brown presented this theory uncritically in his *New Grove Dictionary* article on Tchaikovsky. Recently, however, Poznansky ("Tchaikovsky's Suicide") has argued that by the 1890s Tchaikovsky was no longer troubled by his homosexuality and that Orlova's arguments are riddled with errors and false assumptions. He reendorses, with much detailed evidence, the original story that Tchaikovsky died of cholera. Regardless of Tchaikovsky's attitudes at the end of his life, however, there is no question but that he was deeply troubled at the time he was composing his Fourth Symphony.

44. In "Franz Schubert and the Peacocks of Benvenuto Cellini," *19th-Century Music* 12, no. 3 (Spring 1989): 193-206, Maynard Solomon presents persuasive evidence of Schubert's homosexual orientation. He concludes: "It even seems possible that, through a reconsideration of Schubert's sexual unorthodoxy and his resistance to compulsion, we have touched on a heroic region of Schubert's personality" (206). But Solomon has also expressed grave concerns (following his presentation of this paper at the American Musicological Society meeting in Baltimore, 1988) that this new information about Schubert's sexuality might be applied to Schubert's music in a sensationalist fashion. And in conversation he has suggested that it would be difficult to distinguish between the narratives of resistance that show up in some of Schubert's music and the oedipal narratives of, say, Mozart. I would agree that similar musical strategies (such as resistance to the authority of convention) can be motivated from very different situations. I would not wish to reduce the richness of musical imagination back to biography or to comb music for evidence of hidden sexual proclivities. Yet we can sometimes find in biography partial explanations as to why a given composer favors one set of narrative moves over others.

45. Brown, "Tchaikovsky," *The New Grove Russian Masters: 1* (New York: W. W. Norton, 1986), 180-87.

46. See Poznansky's readings in "Tchaikovsky's Suicide" of Tchaikovsky's letters and his reconstruction of attitudes toward homosexuality in Russia at this time. See also Simon Karlinsky, "Should We Retire Tchaikovsky?" *Christopher Street* 123 (May 1988): 16-21, for a discussion of these issues and an explicitly homosexual reading of the Sixth Symphony.

47. Tchaikovsky complains bitterly of having to hide his sexuality. In a letter to his brother Modest, he writes: "There are people who cannot despise me for my vices simply because they began to love me when they still didn't suspect that I was, in fact, a man with a lost reputation. For instance, this applies to *Sasha* [his sister]. I know that she guesses *everything* and *forgives* everything. Many other people whom I love or respect regard me in the same way. Do you really believe that the consciousness *that they pity and forgive me* is not painful to me when, at bottom, I am guilty of nothing! And is it not a terrible thought that people who love me can sometimes *be ashamed* of me!" (Brown, *Tchaikovsky*, 105; emphasis in the original). I do not read this ("I am guilty of nothing") as self-loathing, but rather as a protest against a society that cannot accept him as he is.

48. Anthony Newcomb has likewise criticized the use of abstract standards for interpreting nineteenth-century symphonies that seem to be telling other stories. See his "Once More 'Between Absolute and Program Music': Schumann's Second Symphony," *19th-Century Music* 7, no. 3 (1984): 233-50.

49. For an insightful study demonstrating the mutual dependence of misogyny and homophobia in Western culture, see Eve Kosofsky Sedgwick, *Between Men: English Literature and Male Homosocial Desire* (New York: Columbia University Press, 1985). Sedgwick demonstrates that while compulsory heterosexuality is usually perpetrated by men, the anger, hatred, and horror it provokes tend to be focused on the

unsuspecting women upon whose bodies the patriarchal pact is concluded. Unfortunately, a very large number of culture producers and scholars find themselves in social binds similar to Tchaikovsky's, in that many of them are inclined to homosexuality in a culture that punishes such behavior and demands unwanted marriages as evidence of their being "okay." Narratives and caricatures such as his are carefully concealed in institutional contexts in which homosexuality still dares not speak its name.

Chapter 4. Excess and Frame: The Musical Representation of Madwomen

1. Ethan Mordden, *Demented: The World of the Opera Diva* (New York: Franklin Watts, 1984), 11-12. I am not criticizing Mordden for this model of opera criticism; on the contrary, it seems to me that musicology ought to pay closer attention to such accounts of how music is actually received by its fans, for those fans determine to a large extent the compositions that make up the standard repertory.

2. When I presented this essay as a talk, I found that some music professionals in my audiences wanted to argue that neither of these characters was mad at all. They proposed formal counterreadings as evidence: Salome as pitch-class sets, Lucia as sophomore-level chromatic harmony.

3. Michel Foucault, *Madness and Civilization: A History of Insanity in the Age of Reason*, trans. Richard Howard (New York: Vintage Books, 1988); Klaus Doerner, *Madmen and the Bourgeoisie: A Social History of Insanity and Psychiatry*, trans. Joachim Neugroschel and Jean Steinberg (Oxford: Basil Blackwell, 1981).

4. Elaine Showalter, *The Female Malady: Women, Madness, and English Culture, 1830-1980* (New York: Pantheon Books, 1985).

5. Foucault, *Madness and Civilization*, 64.

6. Doerner, *Madmen and the Bourgeoisie*, 16-17. This book compares the definitions and treatments of madness in modern England, France, and Germany.

7. Showalter, *The Female Malady*. See also George Frederick Drinka, *The Birth of Neurosis: Myth, Malady and the Victorians* (New York: Simon & Schuster, 1984).

8. See Showalter's discussion of attitudes toward and treatments of shell-shocked soldiers suffering from "hysteria" in World War I in *The Female Malady*, 167-94.

9. Showalter, *The Female Malady*. For more on attitudes contributed by Darwin and Freud, see also Nancy Armstrong, *Desire and Domestic Fiction* (New York: Oxford University Press, 1987), 221-50.

10. Showalter, *The Female Malady*, 4 and passim. I discuss the beginnings of this gender association in Chapter 2 of this volume. There are, of course, examples of male opera characters who go mad, but they are almost always of two sorts: their madness is either a manifestation of guilt (Boris Godunov) or of wounded or insufficient masculinity; i.e., they have become "like women" and thus participate in feminine excess (Orfeo, Tristan, Tom Rakewell). This phenomenon is discussed in Catherine Clément, *Opera, or the Undoing of Women*, trans. Betsy Wing (Minneapolis: University of Minnesota Press, 1988), 118-20. However, the link between madness and femininity is not to be understood as universal. Indeed, images of hypermasculine madness are extremely prevalent today in the genre of heavy metal. See Robert Walser, "Running with the Devil: Power, Gender, and Madness in Heavy Metal Music" (Ph.D. dissertation: University of Minnesota, forthcoming).

11. These paintings are reproduced in Showalter, *The Female Malady*, 2 and 149, and in Drinka, *The Birth of Neurosis*, 41 and 77. Charcot had extensive photographic studies made of his most famous patients. No male frame is visible in these, but there is considerable evidence that these patients were coached and posed to conform with the expected stereotypes—stereotypes that were borrowed from contemporary art. His "scientific" documentation is thus heavily mediated by conventions of cultural representation. See Showalter, 150-54, and Drinka, 92-101.

12. Even Freud's writing is interesting in this regard: when dealing with his male paranoid Schreber, Freud quotes extravagantly from Schreber's text and even praises it for its self-reflexivity; but when the patient is a woman of far more banal delusions—if, indeed, delusions they be at all—Freud continually intervenes in her report, alternatively silencing her and putting words into her mouth, as when, significantly, he transforms her perception of the sound of a camera shutter to that of her own (Freud hastens to assure us) clitoral shudder. See Freud, *Three Case Histories* (New York: Collier Books, 1963), and "A Case of Paranoia Running Counter to the Psychoanalytical Theory of the Disease," in *Sexuality and the Psychology of Love* (New York: Collier Books, 1963). I am indebted to Judith Halberstam's "Reading Counter-Clockwise: Paranoia and Feminism" (unpublished paper) for these examples. I owe the pun on shutter/shudder to John Mowitt.

13. See Foucault, *Madness and Civilization*, xi-xii; Showalter, *The Female Malady*, passim; and Sander L. Gilman, *Difference and Pathology: Stereotypes of Sexuality, Race, and Madness* (Ithaca: Cornell University Press, 1985), 217. Occasionally voice is very cautiously given to madwomen in the medium of film, though usually only as a way of gaining public access to her interior. See Mary Ann Doane, "Clinical Eyes: The Medical Discourse," *The Desire to Desire* (Bloomington: Indiana University Press, 1987), 38-69.

14. Film theorists have worked extensively with the psychological effects of music and sound in cinema. See especially Doane, *The Desire to Desire*, 96-103, and "The Voice in the Cinema: The Articulation of Body and Space," *Yale French Studies* 60 (1980): 33-51; and Kaja Silverman, *The Acoustic Mirror: The Female Voice in Psychoanalysis and Cinema* (Bloomington: Indiana University Press,1988). See also Chapter 2.

15. For instance, in the final act of *L'Orfeo*, Orfeo has lost his reason after his loss of Euridice, and his madness is manifested through the erratic quality of his singing—he is affectively decentered, he flips irrationally among unrelated modal areas, his declamation is rhythmically disjointed. The consummate orator has lost control of his rhetoric, his musical utterances are no longer sustained by their formerly compelling syntactical logic. I have argued in Chapter 2 that the musical depiction of madness in the character of Orfeo so threatens masculine authority that in operatic representations after this, it is almost invariably women who are the objects of the spectacle of madness. Other examples of male lamenters and madmen in early music drama include Giasone and Orlando, and their portrayals would make for an interesting study.

Monteverdi's most intensive experimentation with the construction of madness, *La finta pazza Licori*, does not survive in score, but we have considerable documentation in his letters concerning his construction of this character. Indeed, the correspondence about *Licori* is a treasure in that it traces the development of a new semiotic code from the composer's point of view. The central quality informing Licori's feigned madness is her distractedness: she was to respond flamboyantly to the images of individual words rather than the sense of the sentences she uttered—she was given, in other words, to excessive and inappropriate madrigalisms. See Claudio

Monteverdi, *The Letters of Claudio Monteverdi*, trans. Denis Stevens (Cambridge: Cambridge University Press, 1980), 315, 318, 320, 335-36.

16. Monteverdi, Book VIII (1638). See also the discussions by Lorenzo Bianconi, *Music in the Seventeenth Century*, trans. David Bryant (Cambridge: Cambridge University Press, 1987), 209-15; and Gary Tomlinson, *Monteverdi and the End of the Renaissance* (Berkeley: University of California Press, 1987), 213.

17. Not all seventeenth-century ostinati represent madness: they also may depict grief (as in Dido's lament in Purcell's *Dido and Aeneas*) or erotic transport (as in the duet closing Monteverdi's *L'incoronazione di Poppea*). But whether in the semiotic service of grief, erotic transport, or madness, the ostinato is always associated with some obsessive condition. Indeed, virtually all of these conditions are invoked in the present case. See Chapter 5 for more on distinctions between ostinato procedures and other devices of seventeenth-century musical rhetoric.

18. There are a few other instances in Monteverdi of "performed frames." The most comparable is the testo in the *Combattimento di Tancredi e Clorinda*. The testo serves to narrate and musically mime the dramatic action between the verbal exchanges of the two characters, but he does not interject comments into their statements. There are also some concerted madrigals (e.g., "Misero Alceo" or "Presso un fiume tranquillo" in Book VI), in which a full group sets up a situation, then permits a character or pair of lovers to speak, and finally wraps the piece up. But the group does not run interference throughout the composition.

19. Much work has been done in feminist film theory on the structuring of the male gaze in spectacle. See, for instance, Laura Mulvey, "Visual Pleasure and Narrative Cinema," *Screen* 16, no. 3 (1975): 8-18; Teresa de Lauretis, *Alice Doesn't: Feminism, Semiotics, Cinema* (Bloomington: Indiana University Press, 1984); and Doane, *The Desire to Desire*.

20. Sir Walter Scott, *The Bride of Lammermoor* (1819). The libretto was written by Salvadore Cammerano, but he was not the only one to set this popular novel. See William Ashbrook, *Donizetti and His Operas* (Cambridge: Cambridge University Press, 1982), 631 n. 9, for more concerning the construction of the libretto. See also John Black, "Cammarano's Libretti for Donizetti," *Studi donizettiani* 3 (1978): 115-29.

21. William Ashbrook and Julian Budden, "Gaetano Donizetti," *The New Grove Masters of Italian Opera* (New York: W. W. Norton, 1983), 114. However, see Ashbrook, *Donizetti and His Operas*, 376-79, for a perceptive discussion of some other manifestations of Lucia's madness.

22. For a sustained discussion of the formal and affective properties of flat-six pivots and envelopes, see my "Pitches, Expression, Ideology: An Exercise in Mediation," *Enclitic* 7, no. 1 (Spring 1983): 76-86.

23. In the recorded performance by Anna Moffo, for instance, one actually hears the singer strain erotically. Moffo dramatizes the move from high $b^\flat$ to $c^\flat$ with a slow, teasing turn figure. Most other performances seem to understand Lucia as the pure virgin who has snapped as the result of her forced marriage (making her madness a refuge, an escape from sexuality) and thus do not read "Spargi" in erotic terms. Such performances lead to the kind of criticism—i.e., that the ornamentation in "Spargi" is incongruous with the situation—leveled by Ashbrook and Budden above.

24. Ashbrook, *Donizetti and His Operas*, 193-96.

25. For an examination of the political situation within which Donizetti was writing and its influence on his compositional choices see Gary Tomlinson, "Italian

Romanticism and Italian Opera: An Essay in Their Affinities," *19th-Century Music* 10, no. 1 (Summer 1986): 43-60.

26. Showalter, *The Female Malady*, 17.

27. Gustave Flaubert, *Madame Bovary*, trans. Eleanor Marx Aveling (New York: Holt, Rinehart & Winston, 1962), 233. See also Donal Henehan, "Why They Were Crazy about Mad Scenes," *New York Times* September 21, 1980, Arts and Leisure, 21 and 24.

28. See Peter Gay, *Education of the Senses: The Bourgeois Experience, Victoria to Freud* (New York: Oxford University Press, 1984), 169-225; Armstrong, *Desire and Domestic Fiction*, 221-50; and Showalter, *The Female Malady*. For incorrigible women who resisted domesticity or desired active participation in the public sphere, rest cures were often imposed or even, in stubborn cases, clitoridectomies and later lobotomies or electroshock.

29. See Gay, *Education of the Senses*, 197-213; Christine Buci-Glucksmann, *La raison baroque* (Paris: Éditions Galilée, 1984), 162-224; Gilman, *Difference and Pathology*, 39-58; and Bram Dijkstra, *Idols of Perversity: Fantasies of Feminine Evil in Fin-de-Siècle Culture* (New York: Oxford University Press, 1986).

30. Sander L. Gilman, "Strauss and the Pervert," *Reading Opera*, ed. Arthur Groos and Roger Parker (Princeton: Princeton University Press, 1988), 306-27. See, however, Jane Marcus, "Salomé: The Jewish Princess Was a New Woman," in her *Art and Anger* (Columbus: Ohio State University Press, 1988), 3-19, for an attempt at salvaging both Wilde and Strauss.

31. Quoted in Gilman, "Strauss and the Pervert," 316. A production in Vienna in the 1960s had a set designed to resemble a huge diseased womb.

32. See my "The Undoing of Opera: Toward a Feminist Criticism of Music," foreword to Clément, *Opera*, xiii-xiv, and Chapter 3 in this volume.

33. The inimitable late Virgil Thomson characterized the opera thus: "*Tristan and Isolde* is the most sustained tract ever mounted on the stage in favor of the right to female ejaculation. It isn't enough that they come together seven times in the second act. No. She depletes the poor guy, then hangs around to demand one last orgasm of her own. Women are like that." Private conversation, July 1980.

34. See the interpretations of Schoenberg's stylistic move in Carl E. Schorske, *Fin-de-Siècle Vienna* (New York: Vintage Books, 1981), 344-62, especially 354; and in Buci-Glucksmann, *La raison baroque*, 205-6.

35. Quite a bit has been written linking early twentieth-century Modernism in various ways with femininity and/or madness. See Buci-Glucksmann, "La scène du moderne et le regard de la Méduse," *La raison baroque*, 225-44, and "Catastrophic Utopia: The Feminine as Allegory of the Modern," trans. Katharine Streip, in *The Making of the Modern Body: Sexuality and Society in the Nineteenth Century*, ed. Catherine Gallagher and Thomas Laqueur (Berkeley: University of California Press, 1987), 220-29; Schorske, *Fin-de-Siècle Vienna*; Gilman, *Difference and Pathology*, especially 229-30; Andreas Huyssen, "Mass Culture as Woman: Modernism's Other," in *Studies in Entertainment: Critical Approaches to Mass Culture*, ed. Tania Modleski (Bloomington: Indiana University Press, 1986), 188-207; Sandra M. Gilbert and Susan Gubar, "Tradition and the Female Talent," *The Poetics of Gender*, ed. Nancy K. Miller (New York: Columbia University Press, 1986), 183-207, and *No Man's Land: The Place of the Woman Writer in the Twentieth Century, Vol. 1: The War of the Words* (New Haven: Yale University Press, 1988); and my "Terminal Prestige: The Case of Avant-Garde Music Composition," *Cultural Critique* 12 (Spring 1989): 57-81.

36. For an extensive reading of the Brandenburg in these terms, see my "The Blasphemy of Talking Politics during Bach Year," *Music and Society: The Politics of*

Composition, Performance and Reception, ed. Richard Leppert and Susan McClary (Cambridge: Cambridge University Press, 1987), 20-41.

37. Henehan, "Why They Were Crazy for Mad Scenes," 24.

38. Roland Barthes, *"Rasch," The Responsibility of Forms*, trans. Richard Howard (New York: Hill & Wang, 1985), 308. The association of artistic creation and madness can be traced back to Greek antiquity. For instance, Plato writes: "But if any man come to the gates of poetry without the madness of the Muses, persuaded that skill alone will make him a good poet, then shall he and his works of sanity with him be brought to naught by the poetry of madness." *Phaedrus*, trans. R. Hackforth, 245A, from *The Collected Dialogues*, ed. Edith Hamilton and Huntington Cairns (Princeton: Princeton University Press, 1982), 492.

39. Jacques Attali, *Noise*, trans. Brian Massumi (Minneapolis: University of Minnesota Press, 1985).

40. Christine Battersby, *Gender and Genius* (London: Women's Press, 1989). Klaus Doerner, in *Madmen and the Bourgeoisie*, 175-245, discusses at length the peculiar attraction of madness for German culture from the *Sturm und Drang* period on. He argues that the particular social conditions of the German eighteenth and nineteenth centuries led to the cult of the genius and a fascination with morbid subjectivity: "Liberal capitalism and its economic crises were accompanied by waves of Romanticism, a testimony to the fact Romanticism was no match for rational social reality. The antirational realities were as much an expression of social refusal as of escapist movements, as much a realistic protest against all rational constriction of bourgeois existence as an irrational cul-de-sac. That held true for the evolutionary development of history, for the myth of the *Volk*, and for emanational logic, as well as for the romanticization of the sinister-mysterious, the imaginary and unconscious, the dreams and utopian wish-fulfillments, of wandering, solitude, and homelessness, of childhood and fairytales, of strangeness and estrangement, of moods and drives, of physical and mental disease" (195). For more on the nineteenth-century associations among genius, femininity, and madness, see also Jochen Schulte-Sasse, "Imagination and Modernity: or the Taming of the Human Mind," *Cultural Critique* 5 (Winter 1986-87): 23-48; and Anne Mellor, ed., *Romanticism and Feminism* (Bloomington: Indiana University Press, 1988), especially Alan Richardson, "Romanticism and the Colonization of the Feminine," 13-25, and Marlon B. Ross, "Troping Masculine Power in the Crisis of Poetic Identity," 26-51.

41. Otto Weininger, *Sex and Character* (New York: Putnam, 1906). Shortly after this work was published in 1903, Weininger went to Beethoven's deathplace and there committed suicide. His work is not only misogynist but also shockingly anti-Semitic—all the more horrible because Weininger was himself Jewish. Despite his public displays of imbalance, however, the book was internationally hailed as finally solving the problem of women. It would be nice to be able to dismiss Weininger's work as the product of a mere lunatic. But the positions he presents are very similar to those articulated by Schopenhauer, Nietzsche, and many others. See the discussions in Battersby, *Gender and Genius*, 113-23, and in David Abrahamsen, *The Mind and Death of a Genius* (New York: Columbia University Press, 1946).

42. Heinrich Schenker, *Der freie Satz*, trans. and ed. Ernst Oster (New York: Longman, 1979): "'And the Spirit of God moved upon the face of the waters.' But the Creative Will has not yet been extinguished. Its fire continues in the ideas which men of genius bring to fruition for the inspiration and elevation of mankind. In the hour when an idea is born, mankind is graced with delight. That rapturous first hour in which the idea came to bless the world shall be hailed as ever young!" (xxiv). Compare Schenker's language here with that of the Magnificat. See also *Harmony*,

ed. Oswald Jonas, trans. Elisabeth Mann Borgese (Cambridge, Mass.: MIT Press, 1973), 60 and 69, for the composer as passive vessel.

43. James Huneker, *Chopin: The Man and His Music* (1900; reprint, New York: Dover, 1966), 142. As cited in Jeffrey Kallberg, "Genre and Gender: The Nocturne and Women's History," unpublished paper delivered at the Graduate Center, CUNY (April 1989). I wish to thank Professor Kallberg for permitting me to read a draft of this paper.

44. For extensive documentation in literature and visual art of this dread and its link to the rise of fascism, see Klaus Theweleit, *Male Fantasies, Vol. I: Women, Floods, Bodies, History*, trans. Stephen Conway (Minneapolis: University of Minnesota Press, 1987); and *Vol. II: Male Bodies: Psychoanalyzing the White Terror*, trans. Erica Carter and Chris Turner (Minneapolis: University of Minnesota Press, 1989). See also Gilman, *Difference and Pathology*, and Huyssen, "Mass Culture as Woman."

45. Joseph Kerman, "How We Got into Analysis and How to Get Out," *Critical Inquiry* 7 (1980): 311-31.

46. In "Genre and Gender," after he has carefully demonstrated how nineteenth-century critics had categorized Chopin's nocturnes as "feminine," Kallberg observes: "The very fact that the likes of Heinrich Schenker and Hugo Leichtentritt would devote serious analytical attention to the nocturnes of Chopin served to 'validate' the genre by negating its gendered past. That is, analyses like Schenker's glossed over the same sense of detail that helped link the nocturne with the feminine in the first place. Analytical detail remained, of course, but of a 'deep,' not 'surface' variety, and of a sort that commentators like Kahlert already in the nineteenth century would have found appropriate to 'great, German' art" (22).

47. Schoenberg, *Theory of Harmony*, trans. Roy E. Carter (Berkeley: University of California Press, 1983), 128-29. I am grateful to Michael Cherlin for bringing this very rich source to my attention for purposes of this essay.

48. See Theodor W. Adorno, "Arnold Schoenberg, 1874-1951," *Prisms*, trans. Samuel Weber and Shierry Weber (Cambridge, Mass.: MIT Press, 1981), 147-72, concerning Schoenberg's move to serialism. Adorno, of course, does not construct his argument in terms of gender.

49. Schoenberg, "Composition with Twelve Tones," in *Style and Idea*, ed. Leonard Stein; trans. Leo Black (Berkeley: University of California Press, 1975), 218, emphasis in the original. This essay begins with Schoenberg's customary modesty as follows: "To understand the very nature of creation one must acknowledge that there was no light before the Lord said: 'Let there be Light.' And since there was not yet light, the Lord's omniscience embraced a vision of it which only His omnipotence could call forth" (214).

50. Schoenberg's own psychological condition during the period in question was none too stable. See Jane Kallir, *Arnold Schoenberg's Vienna* (New York: Galerie St. Etienne and Rizzoli, 1984). When his atonal compositions are held up against his painted self-portraits from that same time, it is much more difficult to hear them as just another brand of order. Yet if Schoenberg's personal neuroses are relevant to his artistic choices of this period, they are not sufficient explanation: the culture of the moment was participating in and encouraging precisely these kinds of expressions and excesses. See Schorske, *Fin-de-Siècle Vienna*, and the sources cited in n. 35.

51. See, for instance, George Perle, *Serial Composition and Atonality* (Berkeley: University of California Press, 1962); and Allen Forte, *The Structure of Atonal Music* (New Haven: Yale University Press, 1973).

52. Concerning the process of psychoanalysis, Foucault has written: "When the role of the doctor consists of lending an ear to this finally liberated speech [of the

lunatic], this procedure still takes place in the context of a hiatus between listener and speaker. For he is listening to speech invested with desire, crediting itself—for its greater exultation or for its greater anguish—with terrible powers. If we truly require silence to cure monsters, then it must be an attentive silence, and it is in this that the division [between reason and madness] lingers." "The Discourse on Language," trans. Rupert Swyer, appendix to *The Archaeology of Knowledge* (New York: Pantheon, 1972), 217.

53. Sandra M. Gilbert and Susan Gubar, *The Madwoman in the Attic* (New Haven: Yale University Press, 1979).

54. See RoseLee Goldberg, *Performance Art: From Futurism to the Present*, rev. ed. (New York: Harry N. Abrams, 1988); Moira Roth, ed., *The Amazing Decade: Women and Performance Art in America, 1970-1980* (Los Angeles: Astro Artz, 1983); and the examination of Laurie Anderson's performance art in Chapter 6 of this volume.

55. Her recordings include *Diamanda Galas* (Metalanguage 119, 1984: contains "Panoptikon" and "Tragouthia"); and the trilogy: *The Divine Punishment* (Stumm 27, 1986); *Saint of the Pit* (Stumm 33, 1986); and *You Must Be Certain of the Devil* (Restless/Mute 7 71403-1, 1988).

56. Diamanda Galas, "Intravenal Song," *Perspectives of New Music* 20 (1981-82): 59-62.

57. For more on the politics of self-representation, see Gayatri Chakravorty Spivak, "Can the Subaltern Speak?" *Marxism and the Interpretation of Culture*, ed. Cary Nelson and Lawrence Grossberg (Urbana: University of Illinois Press, 1988), 271-313, and *In Other Worlds: Essays in Cultural Politics* (New York: Routledge, 1988); Henry Louis Gates, Jr., ed., *"Race," Writing, and Difference* (Chicago: University of Chicago Press, 1986); and Rita Felski, *Beyond Feminist Aesthetics: Feminist Literature and Social Change* (Cambridge, Mass.: Harvard University Press, 1989).

Chapter 5. Getting Down Off the Beanstalk

1. See the discussion of these compositions and also Dahlhaus's concept of "lyric urgency" in Chapter 3.

2. Patrick McCreless, "Drama, Agency, and New Music Performance Practice," paper read at the conference "Time, Space and Drama in Recent Music," SUNY—Stony Brook, April 1989. For more on the rejection of narrative in early Modernism, see the discussions of Schoenberg in Chapters 1 and 4.

3. John Adams describes the writing process of his *Harmonielehre* as well as its musical imagery, in terms of impotence (the "Amfortas Wound," which Adams defines as "testicular") and phallic explosions. See the interview printed on the cover of the Nonesuch recording. See also the "Climax of Climaxes" segment, complete with a battery of bullwhips and police sirens, in David Del Tredici's *In Memory of a Summer Day*, one of his series of meditations on *Alice in Wonderland*. In the album notes Del Tredici writes of this passage: "With the clanging of an anvil, marking the long withheld return of A Major, the listener may think he is at the sonic peak, but a succession of climaxes leading at length to a screaming siren (marked *Climax of Climaxes* in the score) will prove him wrong. . . . In its rapturous, impassioned, even tortured outpourings [it] is an imagined portrait of Carroll the man, stripped of his decorous Victorian inhibitions. It is a love song to Alice."

4. See Linda Williams, *Hard Core: Power, Pleasure, and the "Frenzy of the Visible"* (Berkeley: University of California Press, 1989).

5. "The Blasphemy of Talking Politics during Bach Year," in *Music and Society: The Politics of Composition, Performance and Reception*, ed. Richard Leppert and Susan McClary (Cambridge: Cambridge University Press, 1987), 13-62.

6. See, for instance, LeRoi Jones, *Blues People: Negro Music in White America* (New York: William Morrow, 1963); Ben Sidran, *Black Talk* (New York: Holt, Rinehart & Winston, 1971); and Henry Louis Gates, Jr., *The Signifying Monkey: A Theory of African-American Literary Criticism* (Oxford: Oxford University Press, 1988), for treatments of American black music and literature; and George Lipsitz, "Cruising Around the Historical Bloc: Postmodernism and Popular Music in East Los Angeles," *Cultural Critique* 5 (Winter 1986-87): 157-77, for a discussion of His-panic-American music. Reprinted in *Time Passages: Collective Memory and American Popular Culture* (Minneapolis: University of Minnesotas Press, 1990).

7. To be sure, since the beginnings of the women's movement in the late 1960s, there has been an explosion in women's music with the emergence of figures such as Holly Near, Chris Williamson, and Joan Armatrading, and groups such as Alive and Sweet Honey in the Rock. Special contexts for its performance (women's coffee-houses and music festivals) have been created, and certain communities shape their identities in part in terms of that music. This phenomenon is extremely important: it might potentially furnish "serious women musicians" with models, both musical and institutional.

8. See Catherine Clément, *Opera, or the Undoing of Women*, trans. Betsy Wing (Minneapolis: University of Minnesota Press, 1988); and my "Mozart's Women," *Hurricane Alice* 3 (1986): 1-4.

9. See the discussion of Galas in Chapter 4, and also the strategies by Laurie Anderson and Madonna in Chapters 6 and 7.

10. Both Nochlin's article and the solicited responses are contained in *Art and Sexual Politics*, ed. Thomas Hess and Elizabeth Baker (New York: Collier, 1973). For a similar set of statements by women composers, see the responses to Elaine Bar-kin's questionnaire in *Perspectives in New Music* 19 (1980-81): 460-62; and 20 (1981-82): 288-330. See also Nicola LeFanu, "Master Musician: An Impregnable Taboo?" *Contact: A Journal of Contemporary Music* 31 (Autumn 1987): 4-8.

For a perceptive review essay evaluating the contributions of women in the visual arts since 1970, see Arthur Danto, "The Breakthrough Decade: Women in the Arts," *The Nation* 249, no. 22 (December 25, 1989): 794-98. The headline on the cover of this issue reads, "Women did not so much enter the mainstream as redefine it," and Danto argues that it was precisely in reshaping aesthetics from a feminist point of view that women artists managed to alter the face of the art world.

11. "The Artist as Housewife," in *In Her Own Image*, ed. Elaine Hedges and In-grid Wendt (Old Westbury, N.Y.: Feminist Press, 1980), 115-20. Laura Mulvey has theorized this problem with respect to the female spectator of film in "Visual Plea-sure and Narrative Cinema," *Screen* 16, no. 3 (1975): 8-18. Her rather pessimistic interpretation of the options available to women viewers motivated responses from other feminists in film theory. See especially Teresa de Lauretis, *Alice Doesn't* (Bloomington: Indiana University Press, 1984), and *Technologies of Gender* (Bloom-ington: Indiana University Press, 1987); Tania Modleski, *The Women Who Knew Too Much* (New York: Methuen, 1988); and Mary Ann Doane, *The Desire to Desire* (Bloomington: Indiana University Press, 1987). See Clément, *Opera*, for a presen-tation of the comparable dilemmas facing a woman spectator of opera.

12. For further reading on these issues with respect to literature, see Sandra M. Gilbert and Susan Gubar, *The Madwoman in the Attic: The Woman Writer and the Nine-teenth-Century Literary Imagination* (New Haven: Yale University Press, 1979); with

respect to dance, see Judith Lynne Hanna, *Dance, Sex and Gender* (Chicago: University of Chicago Press, 1988); and with respect to the visual arts, see Rozsika Parker and Griselda Pollock, *Framing Feminism: Art and the Women's Movement 1970-1985* (London: Pandora, 1987).

13. The problem of "representation" is dealt with repeatedly in several different theoretical contexts in Janet Wolff, *The Social Production of Art* (New York: St. Martin's Press, 1981). See also Alice Jardine, *Gynesis: Configurations of Woman and Modernity* (Ithaca: Cornell University Press, 1985).

14. I have discussed the ideological agendas of musical-theoretical formalisms elsewhere. See my "The Politics of Silence and Sound," afterword to Jacques Attali, *Noise*, trans. Brian Massumi (Minneapolis: University of Minnesota Press, 1985), 149-53; and also Chapter 1 of this volume. See also Carl Dahlhaus, *The Idea of Absolute Music*, trans. Roger Lustig (Chicago: University of Chicago Press, 1989).

15. The composition was premiered in 1983 and revised in 1984. A performance by the Mirecourt Trio is available on *À la Carte* (1986), a recording in the Minnesota Composers Forum McKnight series. The complete cycle of "Genesis" pieces was completed with the composition of *Genesis VII* in 1989. All of them share with *Genesis II* the feature of the "clockwork," and all enclose their more narrative components within open-ended prologues, one at either end. This is the only one of the series, however, to enact a deconstruction of the traditional narrative schema.

16. Authorial intentions are especially important in feminist art and need to be taken into account when they are obtainable, so long as we keep in mind that intentions do not necessarily communicate and certainly do not comprise the only possible reading. For instance, in the recording of *Genesis II*, the Mirecourt Trio perform this opening section as a classical "beanstalk" gesture. An earlier, taped recording (not publicly available) conveys far more successfully a sonic metaphor of childbirth, in part because in refusing to accelerate to its conclusion it avoids the impression of excitement and desire.

17. In the visual arts, Judy Chicago's *The Birth Project* similarly seeks to develop images celebrating the experience of giving birth. The project is documented in Chicago's *The Birth Project* (Garden City, N.Y.: Doubleday, 1985).

18. See Marshall Berman, *All That Is Solid Melts into Air: The Experience of Modernity* (New York: Simon & Schuster, 1982), for a discussion of this dimension of modern culture.

19. Leonard B. Meyer introduced the idea of "teleological" music in "End of the Renaissance?" in his *Music, the Arts and Ideas* (Chicago: University of Chicago Press, 1967), 72. Christopher Small, in his *Music — Society — Education* (London: John Calder, 1980), argues compellingly that the assumptions underlying Western science and its desire to control nature also inform our concert music.

20. For recent work by historians on this period see *Crisis in Europe, 1560-1660*, ed. Trevor Aston (London: Routledge & Kegan Paul, 1965); and *The General Crisis of the Seventeenth Century*, ed. Geoffrey Parker and Lesley Smith (London: Routledge & Kegan Paul, 1985). For a discussion of the shifts in cultural production, see José Antonio Maravall, *Culture of the Baroque*, trans. Terry Cochran (Minneapolis: University of Minnesota Press, 1986).

21. See again Chapter 2. I am writing a book, *Power and Desire in Seventeenth-Century Music* (Princeton: Princeton University Press, forthcoming) that will deal with these phenomena in detail.

22. De Lauretis, "Desire in Narrative," 132-33. She is here paraphrasing Laura Mulvey, whose original statement differs only in that it begins: "Sadism demands a story." In "Visual Pleasure and Narrative Cinema," 14.

23. The "Resurrection" does end in the key of the relative major, but others of Mahler's pieces end in more distant keys, for instance the key a half-step above the original tonic: a move that is not rationally explicable within tonal convention. When I play the end of the "Resurrection" Symphony in high schools, the heavy metal fans respond most enthusiastically to what they recognize as the gestural vocabulary and narrative paradigm of their own chosen music. They do, however, note this difference: Mahler is much more violent. See Chapter 7 for a discussion of narratives of desire and violence in metal. The violent conclusions of *Carmen* and *Salome* likewise are on the "wrong" triads. See the discussions in Chapters 3 and 4.

24. See my "Music and Postmodernism," *Contemporary Music Review* (forthcoming). See also, however, the other side of postmodern music—the unabashed celebrations of phallic narrative discussed in n. 3.

25. See Julia Kristeva, "Women's Time," in *Critical Theory Since 1965*, ed. Hazard Adams and Leroy Searle (Tallahassee: Florida State University Press, 1986), 471-84; and Berman, *All That Is Solid*.

26. Linda Williams points out that cultural critic Andrew Ross has the same reaction to women's erotica—that it is too concerned with the "education of desire" and is insufficiently exciting. See her analysis and response in *Hard Core*, 263-64.

27. A woman character could, of course, be assigned this discourse as well, though usually to do so was to indicate that she had appropriated the prerogatives of masculine speech. See the discussion of *L'incoronazione di Poppea* in Chapter 2.

28. Robert Scholes, *Fabulation and Metafiction* (Urbana: University of Illinois Press, 1979), 26.

29. See the discussion by Teresa de Lauretis in "Desire in Narrative." For recent discussions of the constructions of gender and sexuality in the modern era see Nancy Chodorow, *The Reproduction of Mothering: Psychoanalysis and the Sociology of Gender* (Berkeley: University of California Press, 1978), especially 180-90; Michel Foucault, *The History of Sexuality, Vol. 1* (New York: Vintage, 1980); Eve Kosofsky Sedgwick, *Between Men: English Literature and Male Homosocial Desire* (New York: Columbia University Press, 1985); and much of the work by French feminists, including Luce Irigaray, *This Sex Which Is Not One*, trans. Catherine Porter (Ithaca: Cornell University Press, 1985).

30. John Donne, "Elegie: To His Mistress Going to Bed."

31. See D. A. Miller, *Narrative and Its Discontents: Problems of Closure in the Traditional Novel* (Princeton: Princeton University Press, 1981). See also Chapters 3 and 4.

32. From *Diving into the Wreck* (New York: W. W. Norton, 1973), 205-6.

33. See the critique of "essentialism" and women's art in Gisela Ecker's introduction to *Feminist Aesthetics*, 15-22. For more on the problem of defining "woman," see de Lauretis, *Technologies of Gender*, and Jardine, *Gynesis: Configurations of Woman and Modernity*.

Following the model of the feminist research that has investigated the historical constructions of "femininity," some work similarly investigating "masculinity" has begun to appear. See, for instance, Victor J. Seidler, *Rediscovering Masculinity: Rea-*

son, Language and Sexuality (London: Routledge, 1989); and Arthur Brittan, *Masculinity and Power* (Oxford: Basil Blackwell, 1989).

Chapter 6.   This Is Not a Story My People Tell

1. Laurie Anderson, "Langue d'amour," recorded on *United States* (Warner Bros. Records, 9 25192-1, 1984), and *Mister Heartbreak* (Warner Bros. Records, 9 25077-1, 1984). The two recordings are quite different: the first is performed in keeping with the austere performance-art style of the rest of *United States*, while the second is part of a collection designed specifically for distribution through recording. Like the other numbers on *Mister Heartbreak*, it is musically more complex. Peter Gabriel sings backup vocals, and electronic conches (played by Anderson) are added to the mix. The text is available in Laurie Anderson, *United States* (New York: Harper & Row, 1984), no pagination.

2. See also Anderson's piece "Hey Ah," also in *United States*, in which a Native American is asked to sing for a documentary and finds he no longer knows any of the traditional songs. In performance Anderson accompanies this piece with a video animation of a powerful buffalo trying to run, always to be looped back. For a collection of poststructuralist critiques of anthropology that resonate with some of Anderson's strategies, see James Clifford and George E. Marcus, eds., *Writing Culture: The Poetics and Politics of Ethnography* (Berkeley: University of California Press, 1986).

3. Robert Morgan, "Musical Time/Musical Space," *Critical Inquiry* 7 (1980): 527-38.

4. For more recent diatribes against the body in musical performance, see Theodor W. Adorno, "Perennial Fashion—Jazz," *Prisms*, trans. Samuel Weber and Shierry Weber (Cambridge, Mass.: MIT Press, 1981), 119-32 (quoted in Chapter 3). Robert Walser has written on Adorno's erasure of the body and the consequences in Adorno's criticism of both classical and popular music in "Retooling with Adorno: Bach's Ontology and the Critique of Jazz" (unpublished paper, Minneapolis, 1988). See also Edward T. Cone, *Musical Form and Musical Performance* (New York: W. W. Norton, 1968): "Leo Stein has suggested that music requiring bodily motion on the part of the listener for its complete enjoyment, like much popular dance music, is by that token artistically imperfect; perhaps the same principle can be applied to performance" (17).

This denial of the body in music is not, however, a constant, even in Western culture. For instance, C. P. E. Bach advocates physical motion on the part of performers. See his *Essay on the True Art of Playing Keyboard Instruments*, trans. and ed. William J. Mitchell (New York: W.W. Norton, 1949), 152-53. Caricatures of the great nineteenth-century virtuosi (Berlioz, Liszt, etc.) suggest both how scandalized and yet titillated audiences were by their outrageous histrionics.

5. See Richard Leppert, "Music, Representation, and Social Order in Early Modern Europe," *Cultural Critique* 12 (Spring 1989): 26.

6. See Milton Babbitt, "Who Cares If You Listen?" *High Fidelity Magazine* 8, no. 2 (February 1958): "I dare suggest that the composer would do himself and his music an immediate and eventual service by total, resolute, and voluntary withdrawal from this public world to one of private performance and electronic media, with its very real possibility of complete elimination of the public and social aspects of musical composition. By so doing, the separation between the domains would be defined beyond any possibility of confusion of categories, and the composer would

be free to pursue a private life of professional achievement, as opposed to a public life of unprofessional compromise and exhibitionism" (126). For an analysis of this attitude and its effect on academic music as well as music in the academy, see my "Terminal Prestige: The Case of Avant-Garde Music Composition," *Cultural Critique* 12 (Spring 1989): 57-81

7. For background reading in performance art, see Moira Roth, ed., *The Amazing Decade: Women and Performance Art in America, 1970-1980* (Los Angeles: Astro Artz, 1983); RoseLee Goldberg, *Performance Art: From Futurism to the Present*, rev. ed. (New York: Harry N. Abrams, 1988); and Greil Marcus, *Lipstick Traces: A Secret History of the Twentieth Century* (Cambridge, Mass.: Harvard University Press, 1989).

8. Walter Benjamin addressed this priority very early on in the history of the media. See his "The Work of Art in the Age of Mechanical Reproduction," *Illuminations*, trans. Harry Zohn (New York: Schocken, 1977), 217-51. Film theorists often demonstrate how the apparatuses of cinema manage to manipulate us while erasing themselves. Concerning the coordination of sound and visual image, see especially Mary Ann Doane, *The Desire to Desire: The Woman's Film of the 1940s* (Bloomington: Indiana University Press, 1987); and Kaja Silverman, *The Acoustic Mirror: The Female Voice in Psychoanalysis and Cinema* (Bloomington: Indiana University Press, 1988). And digitally processed music gives the impression of pure, unmediated, hyperreal sound by breaking sounds down into binary bits and then carefully reassembling them after the "noise" of actual reality has been removed. See also John Mowitt, "The Sound of Music in the Era of Its Electronic Reproducibility," *Music and Society: The Politics of Composition, Performance and Reception*, ed. Richard Leppert and Susan McClary (Cambridge: Cambridge University Press, 1987), 173-97.

9. The piece using a pillow speaker is "Small Voice," from *United States*. There is a diagram explaining how the mechanism works, as well as a photograph of Anderson with the speaker in her mouth, in the book *United States*, no pagination.

10. Mary Ann Doane, "The Voice in the Cinema: The Articulation of Body and Space," *Yale French Studies 60* (1980): 33-50.

11. For some balanced and perceptive discussions of Anderson and her technology, see Greil Marcus, "Speaker to Speaker," *Artforum* 25 (February 1987): 9-10; and Billy Bergman and Richard Horn, *Recombinant Do · Re · Mi: Frontiers of the Rock Era* (New York: Quill, 1985), 93-97.

12. Adam Block, "Laurie Anderson in Her Own Voice," *Mother Jones* 10 (August/September 1985): 44. She says this in response to Block's observation: "You seem very ambivalent about technology—fascinated, yet convinced that it may prove malignant and lethal."

13. See John Berger, *Ways of Seeing* (London: BBC and Penguin Books, 1972), 45-64; Laura Mulvey, "Visual Pleasure and Narrative Cinema," *Screen* 16, no. 3 (Autumn 1975): 6-18; Teresa de Lauretis, *Alice Doesn't: Feminism, Semiotics, Cinema* (Bloomington: Indiana University Press, 1984); Susan Rubin Suleiman, ed., *The Female Body in Western Culture* (Cambridge, Mass.: Harvard University Press, 1986). See also Chapter 3.

14. The "living doll" image in conjunction with Anderson is John Mowitt's. See his "Performance Theory as the Work of Laurie Anderson," *Discourse* 12, no. 2 (1990). I wish to thank John for permitting me to read the prepared typescript. See also Donna Haraway, "A Manifesto for Cyborgs: Science, Technology, and Socialist Feminism in the 1980s," *Socialist Review* 80 (1985): 65-107.

15. Craig Owens, "Amplifications: Laurie Anderson," *Art in America* (March 1981): "*United States II* marked Anderson's recent transformation from a radiant midwestern Madonna into an expressionless, neuter 'punk'—a transformation that corresponds to a shift in musical styles" (122).

16. See Chapter 7.

17. Block, "Laurie Anderson in Her Own Voice," 42.

18. See Bergman and Horn, *Recombinant*, 93 and 97. See also Patrick Goldstein, "An Overexposure of Home," *Los Angeles Times*, June 20, 1986, Section 6: "Anderson is so busy showing off her electronic wizardry that we never feel any sense of intimacy or identification with her performances" (1).

19. Block, "Laurie Anderson in Her Own Voice," 42. She appropriates yet another masculine prerogative when she constructs her own Other: a male counterpart produced when she speaks through the Vocoder. Later, in her video work for the PBS series "Live from Off Center," she created a body for this voice—a compressed image of herself dressed as a man, who is known as her "Clone." The "Clone" serves as a kind of oppressed wife/assistant/slave doing all the work while Anderson typically lounges in the background.

20. See the discussions of "serious" women composers in Chapters 1 and 5. For a wide range of attitudes of women composers toward gender issues, see the questionnaire by Elaine Barkin in *Perspectives of New Music* 19 (1980-81): 460-62, and the responses in *Perspectives* 20 (1981-82): 288-330.

21. Hélène Cixous, "The Laugh of the Medusa," trans. Keith Cohen and Paula Cohen, *New French Feminisms*, ed. Elaine Marks and Isabelle de Courtivron (New York: Schocken, 1981), 245-64; and Luce Irigaray, "This Sex Which Is Not One," trans. Claudia Reeder, *New French Feminisms*, 99-106. See also the following anthologies: Elaine Hedges and Ingrid Wendt, eds., *In Her Own Image: Women Working in the Arts* (Old Westbury, N.Y.: Feminist Press, 1980); and Rozsika Parker and Griselda Pollock, eds., *Framing Feminism: Art and the Women's Movement 1970-1985* (London: Pandora, 1987). The best-known works from this perspective are Judy Chicago, *The Dinner Party: A Symbol of Our Heritage* (New York: Anchor Press, 1979) and *The Birth Project* (Garden City, N.Y.: Doubleday, 1985).

22. For an excellent discussion of this debate, see Toril Moi, *Sexual/Textual Politics: Feminist Literary Theory* (London: Routledge, 1985).

23. Teresa de Lauretis, "The Technology of Gender," *Technologies of Gender: Essays on Theory, Film, and Fiction* (Bloomington: Indiana University Press, 1987), 26. See also Denise Riley, "*Am I That Name?*" *Feminism and the Category of "Women" in History* (Minneapolis: University of Minnesota Press, 1988); and the discussion of Janika Vandervelde's *Genesis II* in Chapter 5.

24. "O Superman" is available on *United States* and on *Big Science* (Warner Bros. Records, WB M5 3674, 1982). The two performances are quite different, especially with respect to pacing. The former is a recording of a live performance that incorporated visuals. The latter was recorded in a studio specifically for audio release, and it is much tighter musically since sound is its only available parameter. The piece lasts three minutes longer in the live recording.

25. See, for instance, Claude Lévi-Strauss, *The Raw and the Cooked*, trans. John Weightman and Doreen Weightman (New York: Harper & Row, 1975); and Ferdinand de Saussure, *Course in General Linguistics*, ed. Charles Bally and Albert Sechehaye, trans. Wade Baskin (New York: McGraw-Hill, 1966). For deconstruction, see Jacques Derrida, *Of Grammatology*, trans. Gayatri Chakravorty Spivak (Baltimore: Johns Hopkins University Press, 1976). A useful guide to this complex terrain is Christopher Norris, *Deconstruction: Theory and Practice* (London: Methuen, 1982).

26. See my "Pitches, Expression, Ideology: An Exercise in Mediation," *Enclitic* 7, no. 1 (Spring 1983): 76-86. For more on theories of narrative in tonality and sonata, see Chapters 1, 3, and 5.

27. This sense of narrative security is not universally desirable, however. In both his theories and music, Arnold Schoenberg resisted precisely these "givens" of tonality, though his solutions were very different from Anderson's. See the discussions in Chapters 1 and 4.

28. Morgan, "Musical Time/Musical Space," 530-34. See also Jean-François Lyotard, "Several Silences," trans. Joseph Maier, *Driftworks*, ed. Roger McKean (New York: Semiotext(e), 1984), 95-98, for a discussion of the depth-producing premises of tonal music and the implications of both serialism and Cage's experimentation.

29. This is what has been called "the postmodern condition." See Jean-François Lyotard, *The Postmodern Condition: A Report on Knowledge*, trans. Geoff Bennington and Brian Massumi (Minneapolis: University of Minnesota Press, 1984), for a discussion of the breakdown in the great narratives of Western culture. For some extremely perceptive discussions of Anderson as the postmodern artist par excellence, see Craig Owens, "The Discourse of Others: Feminists and Postmodernism," *The Anti-Aesthetic: Essays on Postmodern Culture*, ed. Hal Foster (Port Townsend, Wash.: Bay Press, 1983), 57-82; Owens, "The Allegorical Impulse: Toward a Theory of Postmodernism," *Art after Modernism: Rethinking Representation*, ed. Brian Wallis, (Boston: David R. Godine, 1984); and Fred Pfeil, "Postmodernism as a 'Structure of Feeling,'" *Marxism and the Interpretation of Culture*, ed. Cary Nelson and Lawrence Grossberg (Urbana: University of Illinois Press, 1988), 381-403.

30. See the essays in Jean Baudrillard, *Selected Writings*, ed. Mark Poster (Stanford: Stanford University Press, 1988), especially "Simulacra and Simulations," 166-84.

31. Fredric Jameson, "Postmodernism and Consumer Society," in Foster, *The Anti-Aesthetic*, 111-25.

32. See, for instance, the reaction in Allan Bloom, *The Closing of the American Mind* (New York: Simon & Schuster, 1987). For a discussion of what is at stake in the intersection between modernism and postmodernism in music, see my "Music and Postmodernism," *Contemporary Music Review* (forthcoming).

33. See Anders Stephanson, "Interview with Cornel West," *Universal Abandon? The Politics of Postmodernism*, ed. Andrew Ross (Minneapolis: University of Minnesota Press, 1988), 269-86. See also Edward W. Said, "Opponents, Audiences, Constituencies and Community," *The Anti-Aesthetic*, 135-59.

34. John Rockwell, "Laurie Anderson: Women Composers, Performance Art and the Perils of Fashion," *All American Music* (New York: Alfred A. Knopf, 1983), 131.

35. For a discussion of the emergence of twentieth-century formalist music theory, see Chapter 4.

36. For discussions of how narrative closure operates in music, see Catherine Clément, *Opera, or the Undoing of Women*, trans. Betsy Wing (Minneapolis: University of Minnesota Press, 1988), and also Chapters 1, 3, 4, and 5. *Carmen* is dealt with extensively in Chapter 3, *Salome* in Chapter 4. For a discussion of how narrative in general works with respect to gender, see de Lauretis, "The Violence of Rhetoric," *Technologies of Gender*, 42-48.

Quite a bit of feminist work has been done on the Adam and Eve story as presented in Genesis. Donna Haraway, in "Manifesto for Cyborgs," 94, rereads this story of origin as a struggle for language. See also Elaine Pagals, *Adam, Eve, and the*

Serpent (New York: Random House, 1988), and Kim Chernin, *Reinventing Eve* (New York: Harper & Row, 1987).

37. See the discussion of Beethoven's Ninth Symphony in Chapter 5.

38. For a new epistemology that argues persuasively that all human knowledge is grounded metaphorically in bodily experience, see Mark Johnson, *The Body in the Mind: The Bodily Basis of Meaning, Imagination, and Reason* (Chicago: University of Chicago Press, 1987). Johnson's formulation is extremely useful for avoiding disembodied rationalism on the one hand and unmediated essentialism on the other. See the discussion of Johnson in Chapter 1.

39. See Julia Kristeva, "Women's Time," *Critical Theory Since 1965*, ed. Hazard Adams and Leroy Searle (Tallahassee: Florida State University Press, 1986), 471-84.

Chapter 7. Living to Tell: Madonna's Resurrection of the Fleshly

1. J. D. Considine, "That Girl: Madonna Rolls Across America," *BuZZ* 2, no. 11 (September 1987): "According to the PMRC's Susan Baker, in fact, Madonna taught little girls how to act 'like a porn queen in heat'" (17). E. Ann Kaplan describes her image as a combination of bordello queen and bag lady. See *Rocking Around the Clock: Music Television, Postmodernism, and Consumer Culture* (New York: Methuen, 1987), 126.

2. Milo Miles, music editor of *Boston Phoenix*, as quoted in Dave Marsh, "Girls Can't Do What the Guys Do: Madonna's Physical Attraction," *The First Rock & Roll Confidential Report* (New York: Pantheon, 1985), 161. Compare the imagery in Considine, "That Girl": "By some accounts—particularly a notorious *Rolling Stone* profile—Madonna slept her way to the top, sucking her boyfriends dry, then moving on to the next influential male" (16). Both Marsh and Considine refute this image, but it is a fascinating one that combines the predatory sexuality of the vampire and succubus with the servile masochism of the female character in *Deep Throat*. For a reasonably detailed (if positively slanted) account of Madonna's early career, see Debbi Voller, *Madonna: The Illustrated Biography* (London: Omnibus Press, 1988).

3. John Fiske, "British Cultural Studies and Television," *Channels of Discourse*, ed. Robert C. Allen (Chapel Hill: University of North Carolina Press, 1987), 297.

4. Ibid., 270.

5. See Kaplan, *Rocking Around the Clock*, especially 115-27; and "Feminist Criticism and Television," *Channels of Discourse*, 211-53.

6. Mikal Gilmore, "The Madonna Mystique," *Rolling Stone* 508 (September 10, 1987): 87. I wish to thank Ann Dunn for this citation.

7. In his interview with Madonna in *Rolling Stone* 548 (March 28, 1989), Bill Zehme says: "Maybe you noticed this already, but a number of songs on the new album [*Like a Prayer*] have sort of antimale themes." Her response: "[*Surprised*] Well, gee, I never thought of that. This album definitely does have a very strong feminine point of view. Hmmm. I've had some painful experiences with men in my life, just as I've had some incredible experiences. Maybe I'm representing more of the former than the latter. I certainly don't hate men. No, no, no! Couldn't live without them!" (180). Madonna is caught typically in a double bind in which she is chastised at the same time for being a passive doll and for being an aggressive man-hater. See again the citations in note 1.

8. On a special MTV broadcast called "Taboo Videos" (March 26, 1988), Betty Friedan states in an interview: "I tell you, Madonna—in contrast to the image of women that you saw on MTV—at least she had spirit, she had guts, she had vitality."

She was in control of her own sexuality and her life. She was a relatively good role model, compared with what else you saw."

9. Jane Bowers, "Women Composers in Italy, 1566-1700," *Women Making Music: The Western Art Tradition, 1150-1950,* ed. Jane Bowers and Judith Tick (Urbana: University of Illinois Press, 1986): "On 4 May 1686 Pope Innocent XI issued an edict which declared that 'music is completely injurious to the modesty that is proper for the [female] sex, because they become distracted from the matters and occupations most proper for them.' Therefore, 'no unmarried woman, married woman, or widow of any rank, status, condition, even those who for reasons of education or anything else are living in convents or conservatories, under any pretext, even to learn music in order to practice it in those convents, may learn to sing from men, either laymen or clerics or regular clergy, no matter if they are in any way related to them, and to play any sort of musical instrument'" (139-40).

An especially shocking report of the silencing of women performers is presented in Anthony Newcomb, *The Madrigal at Ferrara, 1579-1597* (Princeton: Princeton University Press, 1980). The court at Ferrara had an ensemble with three women virtuoso singers who became internationally famous. Duke Alfonso of Ferrara had the "three ladies" sing for Duke Guglielmo of Mantua and expected the latter to "praise them to the skies." "Instead, speaking loudly enough to be heard both by the ladies and by the Duchesses who were present [Duke Guglielmo] burst forth, 'ladies are very impressive indeed—in fact, I would rather be an ass than a lady.' And with this he rose and made everyone else do so as well, thus putting an end to the singing" (24).

See also the examinations of the restrictions placed on women as musicians and performers in Richard Leppert, *Music and Image: Domesticity, Ideology and Socio-cultural Formation in Eighteenth-Century England* (Cambridge: Cambridge University Press, 1988); and Julia Kosa, "Music and References to Music in *Godey's Lady's Book,* 1830-77" (Ph.D. dissertation, University of Minnesota, 1988).

10. David Lee Roth, cited in Marsh, "Girls Can't Do," 165. I might add that this is a far more liberal attitude than that of most academic musicians.

11. This is not always an option socially available to male performers, however. The staged enactment of masculine sensuality is problematic in Western culture in which patriarchal rules of propriety dictate that excess in spectacles be projected onto women. Thus Liszt, Elvis, and Roth can be understood as effective in part because of their transgressive behaviors. This distinction in permissible activities in music theater can be traced back to the beginnings of opera in the seventeenth century. See Chapter 2. See also Robert Walser, "Running with the Devil: Power, Gender, and Madness in Heavy Metal Music" (Ph.D. dissertation, University of Minnesota, forthcoming).

12. Ellen Rosand, "The Voice of Barbara Strozzi," *Women Making Music,* 185. See also Anthony Newcomb, "Courtesans, Muses, or Musicians? Professional Women Musicians in Sixteenth-Century Italy," *Women Making Music,* 90-115; and Linda Phyllis Austern, " 'Sing Againe Syren': The Female Musician and Sexual Enchantment in Elizabethan Life and Literature," *Renaissance Quarterly* 42, no. 3 (Autumn 1989): 420-48. For more on the role of Renaissance courtesans in cultural production, see Ann Rosalind Jones, "City Women and Their Audiences: Louise Labé and Veronica Franco," *Rewriting the Renaissance: The Discourses of Sexual Difference in Early Modern Europe,* ed. Margaret W. Ferguson, Maureen Quilligan, and Nancy J. Vickers (Chicago: University of Chicago Press, 1986), 299-316.

13. See the excerpts from Clara's diary entries and her correspondences with Robert Schumann and Brahms in Carol Neuls-Bates, ed., *Women in Music: An An-*

thology of Source Readings from the Middle Ages to the Present (New York: Harper & Row, 1982), 92-108; and Nancy B. Reich, *Clara Schumann: The Artist and the Woman* (Ithaca: Cornell University Press, 1985). *Women in Music* contains many other documents revealing how women have been discouraged from participating in music and how certain of them persisted to become productive composers nonetheless.

14. For examinations of how the mind/body split intersects with gender in Western culture see Genevieve Lloyd, *The Man of Reason: "Male" and "Female" in Western Philosophy* (Minneapolis: University of Minnesota Press, 1984); Susan Bordo, "The Cartesian Masculinization of Thought," *Signs* 11, no. 3 (1986): 439-56; and Evelyn Fox Keller, *Reflections on Gender and Science* (New Haven: Yale University Press, 1985).

For discussions of how these slipping binary oppositions inform music, see Geraldine Finn, "Music, Masculinity and the Silencing of Women," *New Musicology*, ed. John Shepherd (New York: Routledge, forthcoming); and my "Agenda for a Feminist Criticism of Music," *Canadian University Music Review*, forthcoming.

15. This binary opposition is not, of course, entirely stable. Imagination, for instance, is an attribute of the mind, though it was defined as "feminine" during the Enlightenment and consequently becomes a site of contestation in early Romanticism. See Jochen Schulte-Sasse, "Imagination and Modernity: Or the Taming of the Human Mind," *Cultural Critique* 5 (Winter 1986-87): 23-48. Likewise, the nineteenth-century concept of "genius" itself was understood as having a necessary "feminine" component, although actual women were explicitly barred from this category. See Christine Battersby, *Gender and Genius* (London: Women's Press, 1989).

The common association of music with effeminacy is only now being examined in musicology. See Leppert, *Music and Image*; Linda Austern, " 'Alluring the Auditorie to Effeminacie': Music and the English Renaissance Idea of the Feminine," paper presented to the America Musicological Society, Baltimore (November 1988); Jeffrey Kallberg, "Genre and Gender: The Nocturne and Women's History," unpublished paper; and Maynard Solomon, "Charles Ives: Some Questions of Veracity," *Journal of the American Musicological Society* 40 (1987): 466-69.

16. See Catherine Clément, *Opera, or the Undoing of Women*, trans. Betsy Wing (Minneapolis: University of Minnesota Press, 1988); and Chapters 3 and 4 .

17. See Chapter 3.

18. Quoted in Gilmore, "The Madonna Mystique," 87. Nevertheless, Madonna is often collapsed back into the stereotype of the *femme fatale* of traditional opera and literature. See the comparison between Madonna and Berg's Lulu in Leo Treitler, "The Lulu Character and the Character of *Lulu*," *Music and the Historical Imagination* (Cambridge, Mass.: Harvard University Press, 1989), 272-75.

19. See Richard Dyer, "In Defense of Disco," *On Record: Rock, Pop, and the Written Word*, ed. Simon Frith and Andrew Goodwin (New York: Pantheon Press, 1990), 410-18.

20. See, for instance, Theodor W. Adorno's hysterical denouncements of jazz in "Perennial Fashion—Jazz," *Prisms*, trans. Samuel Weber and Shierry Weber (Cambridge, Mass.: MIT Press, 1981), 121-32: "They [jazz fans] call themselves 'jitterbugs,' bugs which carry out reflex movements, performers of their own ecstasy" (128). See again the quotation from Adorno on jazz and castration in Chapter 3.

21. However, I have often encountered hostile reactions on the part of white middle-class listeners to Aretha Franklin's frank sensuality, even when (particularly when) it is manifested in her sacred recordings such as "Amazing Grace." The argument is that women performers ought not to exhibit signs of sexual pleasure, for

this invariably makes them displays for male consumption. See the discussion in John Shepherd, "Music and Male Hegemony," *Music and Society: The Politics of Composition, Performance and Reception*, ed. Richard Leppert and Susan McClary (Cambridge: Cambridge University Press, 1987), 170-72.

22. Marsh, "Girls Can't Do," 162.

23. See Mary Harron's harsh and cynical critique of rock's commercialism in general and Madonna in particular in "McRock: Pop as a Commodity," *Facing the Music*, ed. Simon Frith (New York: Pantheon Books, 1988), 173-220. At the conclusion of a reading of Madonna's "Open Your Heart" video, Harron writes: "The message is that our girl [Madonna] may sell sexuality, but she is free" (218). See also Leslie Savan, "Desperately Selling Soda," *Village Voice* (March 14, 1989): 47, which critiques Madonna's decision to make a commercial for Pepsi. Ironically, when her video to "Like a Prayer" (discussed later in this essay) was released the day after the first broadcast of the commercial, Pepsi was pressured to withdraw the advertisement, for which it had paid record-high fees. Madonna had thus maintained her artistic control, even in what had appeared to be a monumental sellout.

24. See the discussion of the responses to Madonna of young girls in Fiske, "British Cultural Studies," 269-83. See also the report of responses of young Japanese fans in Gilmore, "The Madonna Mystique," 38. Madonna's response: "But mainly I think they feel that most of my music is really, really positive, and I think they appreciate that, particularly the women. I think I stand for everything that they're really taught to *not* be, so maybe I provide them with a little bit of encouragement." Considine, "That Girl," quotes her as saying: "Children always understand. They have open minds. They have built-in shit detectors" (17).

25. See Chapter 5.

26. When Jackson first signed on with Jam and Lewis, the music for this song was already "in the can" awaiting an appropriate singer. The mix throughout highlights the powerful beats, such that Jackson constantly seems thrown off balance by them. At one point the sound of a car collision punctuates her words, "I never knew what hit me"; and the ironic conclusion depicts the crumbling of her much-vaunted control. Not only was Jackson in a more dependent position with respect to production than Madonna, but the power relations *within the song itself* are very diferent from those Madonna typically enacts.

27. "There is also a sense of pleasure, at least for me and perhaps a large number of other women, in Madonna's defiant look or gaze. In 'Lucky Star' at one point in the dance sequence Madonna dances side on to the camera, looking provocative. For an instant we glimpse her tongue: the expectation is that she is about to lick her lips in a sexual invitation. The expectation is denied and Madonna appears to tuck her tongue back into her cheek. This, it seems, is how most of her dancing and groveling in front of the camera is meant to be taken. She is setting up the sexual idolization of women. For a woman who has experienced this victimization, this setup is most enjoyable and pleasurable, while the male position of voyeur is displaced into uncertainty." Robyn Blair, quoted in Fiske, "British Cultural Studies," 283.

28. For the ways women performers have been seen as inviting tragic lives, see Robyn Archer and Diana Simmonds, *A Star Is Torn* (New York: E.P. Dutton, 1986); Gloria Steinem, *Marilyn* (New York: Henry Holt, 1986). For an analysis of Hitchcock's punishments of sexual women, see Tania Modleski, *The Women Who Knew Too Much: Hitchcock and Feminist Theory* (New York: Methuen, 1988). For treatments of these issues in classical music, see my "The Undoing of Opera: Toward a Feminist Criticism of Music," foreword to Clément, *Opera*, ix-xviii; and Chapter 3 in this volume.

29. In Gilmore, "Madonna Mystique," Madonna states: "I do feel something for Marilyn Monroe. A sympathy. Because in those days, you were really a slave to the whole Hollywood machinery, and unless you had the strength to pull yourself out of it, you were just trapped. I think she didn't know what she was getting herself into and simply made herself vulnerable, and I feel a bond with that. I've certainly felt that at times — I've felt an invasion of privacy and all that — but I'm determined never to let it get me down. Marilyn Monroe was a victim, and I'm not. That's why there's really no comparison"(87). The term "sign crimes" is from Arthur Kroker and David Cook, *The Postmodern Scene: Excremental Culture and Hyper-Aesthetics* (New York: St. Martin's Press, 1986), 21.

30. All previous chapters have dealt extensively with these mechanisms.

31. For an excellent narrative account of the *Eroica*, see Philip Downs, "Beethoven's 'New Way' and the Eroica," *The Creative World of Beethoven*, ed. Paul Henry Lang (New York: W.W. Norton, 1970), 83-102. Downs's interpretation is not inflected, however, by concerns of gender or "extramusical" notions of alterity.

32. See the discussion in Chapter 5. For other readings of the Ninth Symphony, see Leo Treitler, "History, Criticism, and Beethoven's Ninth Symphony" and " 'To Worship That Celestial Sound': Motives for Analysis," *Music and the Historical Imagination*, 19-66; and Maynard Solomon, "Beethoven's Ninth Symphony: A Search for Order," *19th-Century Music* 10 (Summer 1986): 3-23.

33. Fiske, "British Cultural Studies," 262. For more on constructions of masculine subjectivity, see Arthur Brittan, *Masculinity and Power* (London: Basil Blackwell, 1989), and Klaus Theweleit, *Male Fantasies*, Vols. I and II, trans. Stephen Conway, Erica Carter, and Chris Turner (Minneapolis: University of Minnesota Press, 1987 and 1989). I owe my knowledge of and interest in metal to Robert Walser. I wish to thank him for permitting me to see his "Forging Masculinity: Heavy Metal Sounds and Images of Gender," in *Sound and Vision*, ed. Simon Frith, Andrew Goodwin, and Lawrence Grossberg (forthcoming).

34. See again the citations in note 14; Teresa de Lauretis, "Desire in Narrative," *Alice Doesn't* (Bloomington: Indiana University Press, 1984), 103-57, and "The Violence of Rhetoric: Considerations on Representation and Gender," *Technologies of Gender* (Bloomington: Indiana University Press, 1987), 31-50; and Mieke Bal, *Lethal Love: Feminist Literary Readings of Biblical Love Stories* (Bloomington: Indiana University Press, 1987).

35. Compare, for example, the opening movement of Schubert's "Unfinished" Symphony, in which the tune we all know and love is in the second position and is accordingly quashed. George Michael's "Hand to Mouth" (on the *Faith* album) is a good example of the same imperatives at work in popular music. In both the Schubert and Michael, the pretty tune represents illusion up against harsh reality. My thanks to Robert Walser for bringing the Michael song to my attention.

36. This strategy of always staying in motion is advocated in Teresa de Lauretis, "The Technology of Gender," especially 25-26. See also Denise Riley, *"Am I That Name?": Feminism and the Category of "Women" in History* (Minneapolis: University of Minnesota Press, 1988); and Kaja Silverman, "Fragments of a Fashionable Discourse," in *Studies in Entertainment: Critical Approaches to Mass Culture*, ed. Tania Modleski (Bloomington: Indiana University Press, 1986), 150-51. I discuss Laurie Anderson's "O Superman" or "Langue d'amour" in terms of these strategies in Chapter 6.

37. Some of the so-called Minimalist composers such as Philip Glass and Steve Reich also have called the conventions of tonal closure into question, as did Debussy at an earlier moment. See my "Music and Postmodernism," *Contemporary Music Re-*

view, forthcoming. And see the discussions of Schoenberg's (very different) strategies for resisting the narrative schemata of tonality and sonata in Chapters 1 and 4.

38. Andrew Goodwin advances a similar argument in "Music Video in the (Post) Modern World," *Screen* 18 (Summer 1987): 39–42.

39. In the souvenir program book from her 1987 tour, Madonna is quoted as saying: "Madonna is my real name. It means a lot of things. It means virgin, mother, mother of earth. Someone who is very pure and innocent but someone who's very strong." Needless to say, this is not how the name has always been received.

40. For a cynical interpretation, see Steve Anderson, "Forgive Me, Father," *Village Voice*, April 4, 1989: "Madonna snags vanguard attention while pitching critics into fierce Barthesian discussions about her belt buckles. Certainly she's an empire of signs, but the trick behind the crucifixes, opera gloves, tulle, chains, and the recent rosary-bead girdle is that they lead only back to themselves, representing *nothing*" (68).

But see also the complex discussion in Fiske, "British Cultural Studies," 275–76, which quotes Madonna as saying: "I have always carried around a few rosaries with me. One day I decided to wear [one] as a necklace. Everything I do is sort of tongue in cheek. It's a strong blend—a beautiful sort of symbolism, the idea of someone suffering, which is what Jesus Christ on a crucifix stands for, and then not taking it seriously. Seeing it as an icon with no religiousness attached. It isn't sacrilegious for me." Fiske concludes that "her use of religious iconography is neither religious nor sacrilegious. She intends to free it from this ideological opposition and to enjoy it, use it, for the meanings and pleasure that it has for *her* and not for those of the dominant ideology and its simplistic binary thinking."

41. For excellent discussions of the Catholic tradition of female saints and erotic imagery, see Caroline Walker Bynum, "The Female Body and Religious Practice in the Later Middle Ages," *Zone: Fragments for a History of the Human Body*, ed. Michel Feher et al. (New York: Zone, 1989), 160–219; and Julia Kristeva, *Tales of Love*, trans. Leon S. Roudiez (New York: Columbia University Press, 1987), especially 83–100 and 297–317.

This association is in line with many of Madonna's statements concerning Catholicism, such as her claim that "nuns are sexy" (Fiske, "British Cultural Studies," 275). However, she need not be aware of Saint Teresa in order for these kinds of combinations of the sacred and erotic to occur to her. Once again, her experiences as a woman in this culture mesh in certain ways with the traditional symbolism of holy submission in Christianity, and thus her metaphors of spirituality are similar in many ways to Saint Teresa's. She also intends to create this collision in the song and video. In Armond White, "The Wrath of Madonna," *Millimeter*, June 1989, Mary Lambert (director of the "Like a Prayer" video) states: "Madonna and I always work together on a concept. We both felt the song was about sexual and religious ecstasy" (31). The black statue in the church is identified as Saint Martin de Porres. I wish to thank Vaughn Ormseth for bringing this article to my attention.

42. See the many settings of texts from the Song of Songs by composers such as Alessandro Grandi and Heinrich Schütz. The sacred erotic likewise influenced the literary and visual arts. See Bernini's sculpture of, or Richard Crashaw's poem concerning, Saint Teresa. I am at the moment writing a book, *Power and Desire in Seventeenth-Century Music* (Princeton: Princeton University Press, forthcoming), that examines this phenomenon.

43. Quoted in Liz Smith's column, *San Francisco Chronicle*, April 19, 1989, E1. I wish to thank Greil Marcus for bringing this to my attention. Lydia Hamessley first

pointed out to me the significance of inside and outside in the organization of the video.

44. White, "The Wrath of Madonna," 31.

45. For an excellent discussion of the political strength of the music, rhetoric, and community of the black church today, see the interview of Cornel West by Anders Stephanson in *Universal Abandon? The Politics of Postmodernism*, ed. Andrew Ross (Minneapolis: University of Minnesota Press, 1988), 277-86. Madonna speaks briefly about her identification with black culture in Zehme, "Madonna," 58.

46. For another sympathetic discussion of the politics of this video, see Dave Marsh, "Acts of Contrition," *Rock & Roll Confidential* 67 (May 1989): 1-2.

Index

Index

Susan McClary is professor of musicology at the University of Minnesota and is an adjunct faculty member in Comparative Studies in Discourse and Society, Women's Studies, and American Studies. She is also a member of the Center for Advanced Feminist Studies and served as acting director of the Center for Humanistic Studies in 1984–85. McClary received her Ph.D. in musicology from Harvard University in 1976. She was coeditor, with Richard Leppert, of *Music and Society: The Politics of Composition, Performance and Reception* (1987), and she has published articles on music ranging from the sixteenth century to the present. At present McClary is completing *Georges Bizet's Carmen* for Cambridge University Press and *Power and Desire in Seventeenth-Century Music* for Princeton University Press. She has also been active in the experimental arts scene in the Twin Cities and has written *Susanna Does the Elders* (1987) and co-written *Hildegard* (1989).